4, 258
25

D0629127

Sociological Observation

ISSUES AND TRENDS

IN SOCIOLOGY

a series of

The American Sociological Association

INTERGROUP RELATIONS
Edited by Pierre van den Berghe

THE FORMAL ORGANIZATION
Edited by Richard H. Hall

NEIGHBORHOOD AND GHETTO
Edited by Scott Greer and Ann Lennarson Greer

SOCIOLOGICAL OBSERVATION
Edited by Matilda White Riley and Edward E. Nelson

SOCIOLOGICAL OBSERVATION

A Strategy for New Social Knowledge

EDITED BY

Matilda White Riley
and Edward E. Nelson

Basic Books, Inc., Publishers

NEW YORK

Editors and Contributors

EDITORS

Matilda White Riley is Chairman, Department of Sociology and Anthropology, Bowdoin College, Brunswick, Maine. Her related works include *Sociological Research* (two volumes) and *Aging and Society* (three volumes). Dr. Riley is a continuing participant in the Study Group in Age Stratification, Rutgers University, New Brunswick, New Jersey.

Edward E. Nelson is Assistant Professor of Sociology, California State University, Fresno. He has written articles on status inconsistency, social change, and research methods. His current research, with Elizabeth Ness Nelson, is on work alienation.

CONTRIBUTORS

Kurt W. Back is Professor of Sociology and Psychiatry, Duke University. He is the author of *Beyond Words: The Story of Sensitivity Training and the Encounter Movement.*

Robert F. Bales is Professor of Social Relations, Harvard University. His most recent work is *Personality and Interpersonal Behavior.*

Gordon Bear (formerly Goldberg) is Assistant Professor of Psychology, University of Wisconsin, Madison. He is currently working on a theoretical paper on the equilibrium phenomenon.

Howard S. Becker is Professor of Sociology and Urban Affairs, Northwestern University. His most relevant book is *Sociological Work.*

Joseph Berger is Professor of Sociology, Stanford University. He is the co-author of *Expectation States Theory: A Theoretical Research Program.*

Donald Black is Associate Professor of Sociology and Lecturer in Law, Yale University. He is currently working on a variety of empirical and theoretical studies concerned with patterns of law and social control.

Arlene Brandon (now Arlene Brandon Marcus), Berkeley, California.

Francesca M. Cancian is Assistant Professor, Stanford University. She is the author of *What Are Norms?*

Bernard P. Cohen is Professor of Sociology, Stanford University. He is the co-author of *Conflict, Conformity and Social Status.*

Barry E. Collins is Professor of Psychology, University of California, Los Angeles. He is the editor of *Public and Private Conformity: Competing Explanations by Improvisation, Cognitive Dissonance, and Attribution Theories.*

Rose Laub Coser is Professor of Medical Social Science and Sociology, State University of New York, Stony Brook. Her most relevant work is *Life in the Ward.*

Roy G. D'Andrade is Professor of Anthropology, University of California, San Diego. He is currently doing research on beliefs about interpersonal behavior.

Melville Dalton is Professor and Research Sociologist Emeritus, Department of Sociology and Institute of Industrial Relations, University of California, Los Angeles. He is the author of *Men Who Manage.*

Vattell Elbert Daniel, formerly of Wiley College, is deceased.

Thomas E. Drabek is Associate Professor of Sociology, University of Denver. He is the co-author (with J. Eugene Haas) of *Complex Organizations: A Sociological Perspective.*

Richard M. Emerson is Professor of Sociology, University of Washington. His current research project is "Power and Position in Exchange Networks."

Linton C. Freeman is Lucy G. Moses Professor of Social Relations, Lehigh University, Bethlehem, Pennsylvania. He is currently working on social networks and social structure.

Herbert J. Gans is Professor of Sociology, Columbia University and Senior Research Associate, Center for Policy Research. His recent works are *More Equality* and *Popular Culture and High Culture* (in press).

Blanche Geer is Professor of Sociology, Northeastern University. She has written for various publications on occupations and professions.

Erving Goffman is Benjamin Franklin Professor of Anthropology and Sociology, University of Pennsylvania. A related work of his is *Asylums.*

Gordon N. Goldberg, *see* Gordon Bear.

J. Eugene Haas is Professor of Sociology and Head, Research Program on Technology, Environment and Man, University of Colorado. He is the co-author (with Thomas E. Drabek) of *Complex Organizations: A Sociological Perspective.*

Hugh Hartshorne is deceased. He co-authored (with Mark A. May) *Studies in Deceit.*

Kenneth I. Howard is Professor of Psychology, Northwestern University. His most current work is *Varieties of Psychotherapeutic Experience.*

Laud Humphreys is Associate Professor of Sociology, Pitzer College. He is the author of *Out of the Closets: The Sociology of Homosexual Liberation.*

Charles A. Kiesler is Professor and Chairman, Department of Psychology, University of Kansas. He is the author of *The Psychology of Commitment: Experiments Linking Behavior to Belief.*

Gladys Engel Lang is Professor of Sociology and Communication, State University of New York, Stony Brook. A related book of hers is *Collective Dynamics.*

Kurt Lang is Professor of Sociology, State University of New York, Stony Brook. He is the co-author (with Gladys Engel Lang) of *Television and Politics.*

Frédéric Le Play was a French sociologist, 1806-1882.

Eugene Litwak is Professor of Sociology and Social Work, Columbia University. He is the author of *School, Family, and Neighborhood*: *The Theory and Practice of School-Community Relations.*

Mark A. May is Professor of Educational Psychology Emeritus, and former Director of the Institute of Human Relations, Yale University. A related work of his is *Learning from Films.*

Walter B. Miller is a Research Fellow, Center for Criminal Justice, Law School of Harvard University. He is currently working in the area of gangs and delinquency.

Ralph C. Patrick is with the Department of Epidemiology, University of North Carolina.

Stuart A. Queen is Professor of Sociology Emeritus, Washington University. He is the author of many books and articles on problems of sociological inquiry.

Bernard C. Rosen is Professor of Sociology, Cornell University. He is co-editor of *Achievement in American Society.*

Julius A. Roth is Professor of Sociology, University of California, Davis. He is currently involved in research on the organizational and social-psychological aspects of medical emergency care.

Donald F. Roy is Professor of Sociology, Duke University. He is currently involved in research on labor union organizing campaigns in the South.

Editors and Contributors

Edward E. Sampson is Professor and Chairman, Department of Sociology and Adjunct Professor of Psychology, Clark University. His book, *Ego at the Threshold*, is currently in process.

James F. Short, Jr. is Director, Social Research Center, Washington State University. He is the co-author of *Group Process and Gang Delinquency*.

Howard R. Stanton is Chairman, Department of Psychology/Sociology, Staten Island Community College. He is currently involved in research on adult-community learning centers.

Fred L. Strodtbeck is Professor of Social Psychology in Sociology, University of Chicago. He is the co-author of "Latency of Verbal Response and Participation in Small Groups."

Mortimer A. Sullivan, Jr. is an Attorney at Law, Buffalo, New York. He was formerly a Research Psychologist with the U.S. Air Force.

Ray A. Tennyson is Associate Professor, Institute of Criminal Justice, University of Maryland.

William Foote Whyte is Professor of Industrial and Labor Relations and Professor of Sociology, Cornell University. He is currently working on studies of organizational change in Peru.

Robert F. Winch is Professor of Sociology, Northwestern University. He is the author of books and articles involving collection and interpretation of data on family relationships.

Morris Zelditch, Jr. is Professor of Sociology, Stanford University. He is co-editor of *Sociological Theories in Progress*. He is currently engaged in a wide variety of methodological inquiries.

Contents

PART III

Data Gathering

PART IV

Systematic Control over the Observed Action

Contents

PART V
Measurement and Analysis

PART VI
Sampling

Figures and Tables

new: John W. Riley, Jr., Marilyn Johnson, and Robert K. Merton, with whom the senior editor has explored methodological issues for many years, and W. Dale Dannefer, a promising entrant to the sociological community.

Other colleagues and students kind enough to read the manuscript and comment on it include Robert F. Bales, Anne Foner, Beth Hess, Everett C. Hughes, and Theodore Settle. For preparing the manuscript for publication, we are indebted to Ann Joan Bondira and Marion Erhart.

M.W.R., E.E.N.

New Brunswick, New Jersey, July, 1973

Sociological Observation

Introduction

This book provides a case approach to observation in sociological research. In an area in which there are many specific methodological formulations but few overarching principles, the reader is invited to assess for himself the methods actually used in a selection of concrete studies, and to consider their potential for innovation in the search for new sociological knowledge. These studies—a mere smattering from the literature—are chosen to suggest the largely unexploited relevance of the method for examining a wide range of sociological theories today. The studies demonstrate that observation, however defined, is not only a special method with its own problems and possibilities; it is also an integral but neglected part of the generic methodology of social research.

Trends

Drawn primarily from the publications of the American Sociological Association (according to the format for this series on "Issues and Trends in Sociology"), most of these studies derive from the era following the inception in 1936 of the *American Sociological Review*. This era is not only relatively brief; it is also atypical. Any perusal of the literature prior to 1936 reveals a longstanding concern of sociologists with observing what people do and say to one another (e.g., Sorokin, 1928; Lécuyer and Oberschall, 1968). The decades since that date, however, have witnessed a clear trend away from observation and toward exclusive use of other sources of data. In particular, many technical innovations, and a spate of textbooks, have been devoted to the cross-section survey,[1] with its panoply of associated procedures for sampling, measurement, and analysis (see, e.g., the comments of Stouffer, 1954, p. v; Lazarsfeld, 1968, p. vii). In an attempt to counterbalance the ahistoricism of the cross-sectional approach, heed has also been given to use of documents and other available data (see, e.g., Angell and Freedman, 1953; J. W. Riley, 1962; Webb et al., 1966, chaps. 2, 3, 4) and to development of trend data as social indicators (Bauer, 1966; Sheldon and Moore, 1968).

That sociological attention has been largely diverted in recent decades from use of observation is documented by Brown and Gilmartin (1969, pp. 287-288), who report that this method accounted for some 13 percent of the studies in the two leading sociological journals in 1940-1941, and only 4 percent by 1965-1966 (see also M. W. Riley, 1964, p. 1004).[2] This small and declining incidence of observation coincides with an increase in questionnaire and interview studies from 25 percent to 48 percent. Obviously, then, the veritable revolutions that have occurred in methods of survey research, and that are affecting uses of available data, have not yet occurred in observation.

Nevertheless, the potential for rapid methodological advances is clearly apparent here. Recent studies based on observation, though comparatively few, exhibit wide variability. Moreover, we have also drawn examples for this book from the long and distinguished early history of the use of sense data in the search for understanding social phenomena. The range and inventiveness of the studies assembled here, and the scope and depth of the insights they afford, suggest that the method may regain its traditional prominence, and perhaps even evolve along entirely new lines as well.

Issues

The fact that only a few contemporary sociologists have yet applied their methodological talents to observation seems to have arisen more from historical accident than from the nature of the issues involved. Indeed, at least three sets of issues fundamental to observation are shared by the discipline as a whole.

First, there is little peculiar to observation in the basic *epistemological* questions: What can we, as humankind, know about reality at large—especially about the social world in which we ourselves participate? Is there a social order that lends itself to rational inquiry? Is all observation identified with "an immediate, ineffable experience" (as, e.g., Cohen and Nagel, 1934, p. 216, strongly assert it is not)? Is all knowledge apprehended through a subjectivity that approaches the mystical (as discussed, e.g., by Greer, 1969; Erikson, 1970; Friedrichs, 1970)?

Apart from the epistemological quandary, there are, in the second place, *practical* issues in observation as in all research. If observation can lead to new understandings, can these understandings serve useful social purposes? (In nineteenth-century England, e.g., social research tended to increase as the problems of society, attributed to indigence or low education, were perceived as amenable to reform, but to decrease when these ills were later attributed to race, heredity, and other biological factors [Lécuyer and Oberschall, 1968, pp. 43-44]. This early trend is not without parellels today.)

Third, there are *ethical* issues: How can the researcher avoid harming the people under study or interfering with their lives? While ethical dilemmas pervade all social investigation, they can take special, often unrecognized, forms as the observer comes into direct contact with his subjects [as elucidated in Parts III and IV of this book]. These issues are perhaps most clearly manifested under conditions of deliberate control—where, for example, the researcher makes the explicit decision to stimulate hostility among groups of children (cf. Sherif, 1951, p. 246), or to withhold presumably efficacious treatment from the socially disabled.

Only after the sociologist is clearly aware of such fundamental and difficult issues is he prepared for the *methodological* issues[3] addressed in this book: How can methods of observation be used, adapted, even originated, to study distinctively sociological theories? What are the strengths and weaknesses of observation in various research designs and for various objectives? What problems must be solved, what aspects emphasized or strengthened, if observation is more nearly to fulfill its potential in sociological research? Before examining the studies for possible answers to such methodological questions, it will be useful to consider in some detail what is meant by the term "sociological observation."

The Nature of Observation

In the broadest sense, all science rests upon observation—upon data accessible to the researcher through his senses. But the sociologist typically uses the term in its more limited meaning, to refer to data obtained by watching the behavior of the group, listening to its members, and noting its physical characteristics. In effect, observation is a residual category that excludes: (1) sole reliance upon documentary and other data already available; or (2) sole reliance upon data obtained by questioning—marks made on paper by the respondent himself or his oral reports as recorded by an interviewer. As a residual category observation has many variants. Occasionally it is narrowly defined as just watching and listening. But often it is defined broadly, as diverse combinations of watching and listening— with questioning; with use of mechanical recording instruments, cameras, or other hardware; or with the artifacts of past interaction or any other pertinent data. There are no fixed boundaries.

One can scarcely be surprised, then, that there is no clearly formulated general methodology of sociological observation. Several strands of observational procedure, though not articulated with one another, include ethnography—adapted from anthropology (see, e.g., Conklin, 1968; Leach, 1968); small group studies—kin to much psychological research (cf. Weick, 1968; Medley and Mitzel, 1963); and various types of "community studies" and "participant observation," each a particular hybrid of observation, questioning, and documentary materials. Often without benefit of formal methodological guidance, researchers have put observation to practical use, defining their problems and trying to work out solutions, long before the time of Villermé or Parent-Duchâtelet, who respectively studied textile workers and prostitutes in early nineteenth-century France (Lécuyer and Oberschall, 1968, pp. 47-49).

Observation vs. questioning. Overlooking for the moment the great diversity of these research procedures and objectives, we can begin to clarify the primary *focus* of observation by counterposing two oversimplified ideal types: direct observation of group interaction and private questioning of discrete individual group members (M. W. Riley et al., 1954). This comparison suggests how observation focuses most directly on the network of overt interaction among group members—on objective properties of the system. In contrast, questioning in this context deals most directly with the subjective network of orientations and interpersonal relationships—the underlying ideas, feelings, and perceptions of the members, their hopes and fears, and their dispositions to act toward others and to define and evaluate them in various ways. The "structure of orientations" underlying the interaction can be pieced together for the group as a whole from the questionnaire responses of the several members combined (M. W. Riley, 1963, Unit 4). It should be noted, however, that the focus on individuals *as group members* is more inherent to observation than to questioning, a point that finds confirmation in the atomistic treatment of individuals in much survey research.

The differences highlighted by this ideal-typical comparison lie only in the direct foci of the two methods. *Indirectly*, the two are inextricably bound together, because actions and orientations, though distinguishable types of properties, are interdependent aspects of the same system. Each method provides indirect information about the properties not directly examined. Orientations, defined as dispositions to act, are at any given moment being partially acted out (within the constraints of the group situations, the relevant orientations may remain latent or concealed). Conversely, these orientations are themselves formed, confirmed, or modified by interaction; each actor's definitions and expectations of the other actors are constantly being tested and revised in the light of what these others actually do. Thus, orientations are indirectly reflected in data from observation, and interactions indirectly reflected in data from questioning.

Focused primarily on overt interaction, the observer often goes on to make indirect inferences about orientations. He assumes that such inferences will be correct most of the time. He may be able, as Shakespeare wrote in *Julius Caesar* (Act I, Scene 2), to "look quite through the deeds of men." In some instances, of course, the observer's inferences will be wrong, as individual actors successfully conceal from the group certain attitudes and feelings (which they might be willing to express in a private interview). Similarly, the questioner may elicit reports from respondents about their actions as well as their orientations. Useful as such reports may often be, they describe the interaction as the actor himself perceives and evaluates it and thus may be quite different from an outside observer's report of the same interaction.

This schematized example aims to demonstrate a general principle:

Each method of data gathering is especially valid for one set of system properties, but often misses information about the other set of properties which is directly available only through the other approach. The two methods parallel and supplement one another, and both are often necessary for a reasonably full understanding. (Among the many illustrations and discussions comparing questioning and observation, see, e.g., LaPiere, 1934; Vidich and Shapiro, 1955, with the rejoinder by Moore, 1955; Zelditch, 1962; Becker, 1970; Phillips, 1972.)

Observation vs. available data. Just as data from observation differ in direct focus from data gathered by questioning, they differ also from data that already exist in some form. No researcher can personally make observations for a period longer than his own lifetime. If inquiry into social process and change is to transcend the capabilities of the investigator who goes into the field himself to observe interaction directly or to talk with individuals at first hand, it must exploit the untapped resources of relevant data that already exist.

Letters, television transcripts, records of corporations or of police courts, historical documents, journalistic accounts, tribal artifacts, and pieces of sculpture—to list only a few—exemplify the impressive array of available materials. (Since many such materials constitute the products or records of social interaction, the line dividing them from observational data is often blurred.) Exploiting the advantages of available data thus promises macrocosmic and macrotemporal extensions of the scope of materials obtainable by the lone observer [as discussed in Part VI].

The need for multiple methods. These comparisons of observation with other sources of data emphasize the direct focus of observation on overt behavior, and lay the groundwork for assessing the methodological strengths and weaknesses evidenced throughout the studies in this book. In addition, the comparisons underscore the inadequacy of any single source of data unsupported by other sources. One advantage of combining sources is dramatized by Webb and his associates (1966, p. 3) in such passages as the following:

> The most persuasive evidence comes through a triangulation of measurement processes. If a proposition can survive the onslaught of a series of imperfect measures, with all their irrelevant error, confidence should be placed in it.

In addition to such "triangulation" for ruling out rival interpretations of the findings, multiple sources have the second advantage we have been discussing: Each source, having a special validity of its own, provides information about a different aspect of the system under study. Thus, wherever feasible, the researcher would do well to supplement observation with other methods.[4]

Synopsis of the book

The studies are chosen to illustrate for the reader the intricacy and variety of observational procedures—the forms they take, their relationship to other sources and other aspects of research design, and their degree of correspondence with particular sociological objectives and interpretations. Their arrangement in six parts is fairly arbitrary, since each study (though excerpted to meet the space limitations of the book) involves the full research process. Each part, preceded by its own introduction, examines actual applications of the method, illustrating its problems, principles, and potentials for a particular aspect of the research process.

Part I shows how observation can meet two criteria of relevance for many sociological designs—it can identify individuals *as members of groups* and it can trace their interaction *over time*. Part II, adopting the principle that productive research requires an interplay between data and theory, suggests interpretative procedures for adapting observation to far-reaching substantive interests and theoretical perspectives. Part III shifts the focus of attention to the practical problems of doing research, specifying some details of the observer's role and demonstrating both the insights obtainable and the epistemological and ethical difficulties involved. Noting the early distinction between experimentation and observing phenomena as they appear uncontrolled in nature, Part IV points out some implications of the varying degrees of systematic control between these polar extremes. These four parts show how the principles involved in observation relate to more general principles of sociological research. The two final parts (on measurement and analysis and on sampling) focus upon contributions available from other research methods which are stimulating more rigorous and wider application of observation designs. Such contributions include use of basic mathematical principles and computer technology, creation of new techniques of data gathering and analysis, and increased sophistication in employing historical materials.

The ingenuities of design implicit in the studies throughout the book herald the methodological possibilities of observation. Exploitation of these possibilities awaits only the integration of the observer's intimate view of human social life (cf., e.g., Blumer, 1969) with the enormously varied empirical procedures and the challenging new theoretical approaches now available.

NOTES

1. William James is reported to have predicted as early as 1890 that "circulars of questions" will be "ranked among the common pests of life" (quoted by Webb et al., 1966, p. 144).

2. Certain extensive or discursive findings from observation have found their way into monographic and other forms of publication, so that statistics based on journal articles may not be fully representative of the trends.

3. Useful dimensions for classifying the many complex types of observation are suggested by M. W. Riley's (1963, p. 18) paradigm of design alternatives.

4. The use of different methods may also be useful in providing special kinds of information needed at different points in the research process (see, e.g., Sieber, 1973).

PART I

Dynamic Studies
of Interaction

INTRODUCTION

To the extent that sociologists seek to understand social interaction, observation as a method of gathering data has two great strengths: its dynamic emphasis and its focus on people as they fit together within the collectivity. Especially because of these characteristics, the method is highly relevant to sociological theory. It treats the group not only *as undergoing* process and change, but also *as consisting* of interacting persons and subgroups who contribute to these processes. In these respects, observation may be contrasted with the widely used cross-sectional study, which is typically static—more naturally reflecting a single period of time[1]—and focused more on discrete individuals than on the group (Riley and Nelson, 1971).

The selections in Part I, which begin to suggest the variability of observation, serve to emphasize these two central characteristics. Like most selections in this book, they show how research observations can reflect the time sequence of events.[2] They also show how observation can reveal more than one level of the group simultaneously—the individual as he acts within the group context, the dyads that compose the larger group, or the entire group of identifiable members who initiate action and receive responses from one another (M. W. Riley, 1964, p. 1014).

These two potential virtues of observation are evidenced at the microlevel in the approach developed by *Bales*.[3] In respect to the first, Bales—and the many disciples who have adopted his "interaction process analysis" (IPA) for observing and comparing behavior in small problem-solving groups—records on a time dimension the entire sequence of acts in each group meeting. Thus he can examine the phases or stages of patterning in these acts. In respect to the second, analysis of the Bales data uses a matrix to make clear how each of the members (as the lower-level parts) contributes to the (higher-level) interaction of the group as a whole.

Whyte's study of street corner gangs, markedly different in certain obvious respects from the Bales approach, illustrates these same characteristics of continuing observation. First, from his three and a half years in Cornerville, Whyte is able to describe many dynamic aspects of gang life—the patterns and frequency of interaction between leaders and followers, the conditions under which such patterns break down, and the consequences of group interaction. Second, from his reports emerges a specific picture of the nature of Cornerville as a multilevel system (more complex than the Bales groups) in which corner gangs, rackets, police, and political organizations are all interdependent components. As a smaller unit within the community, the corner gang itself is seen as a hierarchy of personal relationships. It should be noted that Whyte's special interest is less in studying process per se than in abstracting from it the structure of the group—the *order* that implicitly governs the behavior of participants. That this technically "static" conceptual objective required uncovering the "dynamics" of the subject matter under study suggests the scope of theoretical concerns for which observation is methodologically appropriate.

Gans provides still another instance of these uses of observation. Living in Levittown over a period of years, he gains unusual insight into the process of development of a new community from its inception—in contradistinction to the Lynds' (1929) study of Middletown,[4] Hughes' (1943) studies of industrial towns, or Warner's Yankee City Series (of which the first was Warner and Lunt, 1941). By dealing in turn with the influx of initial settlers, the emerging groups and institutions, and the ultimate formation of a community, the study also draws attention to the multiple system levels of sociological concern. (Groundwork for this aspect of the community study was laid nearly a century ago by Henri de Tourville's "nomenclature," which extended LePlay's method [Part VI] to describe the relation of family to neighborhood, formal organization, community, province, and state [Sorokin, 1928, p. 64; Pitts, 1968, p. 88].)

Some Methodological Implications

Like the selections throughout this book, the studies in this part thus emphasize the potential of observation for uncovering both the dynamic processes of interaction and the internal structure of groups. For certain objectives, to be sure, such assets may be irrelevant. In order to explicate a group's status hierarchy, for example, Bales telescopes the time dimension (in a matrix), as does Whyte in drawing positional maps of the outcome of interaction. Similarly, if the conceptual focus is restricted to a single level, the multilevel aspect may not be pertinent, as in Bales' comparison between satisfied and dissatisfied groups. Fuller realization of the methodological potential might well result from increased efforts to *combine* the multilevel and dynamic aspects, as Bales might compare matrices at different phases of the interaction.

For each asset of a research method, there tend to be corresponding liabilities. Despite the dynamic aspect, a particular set of observations may not catch the critical event or endure to the conclusion of a behavioral sequence. In addition, even with teams of observers and batteries of recording devices, only comparatively small or simple groups lend themselves to simultaneous observation at all levels. Direct contact with the group itself brings hazards—questions of ethics or of reactive effects upon the action under study [to be discussed in Part III]. Nevertheless, a wide array of possible research designs provides the flexibility needed to maximize the assets of observation while offsetting and perhaps overcoming such difficulties.

NOTES

1. Cross-section surveys are not necessarily static, of course. For example, respondents can be asked to recall the past, sequences of cross sections can be compared over time, or panel analysis can be used. Removing individuals from the scene in order to question them, however, can interrupt the flow of activity under study.

2. The sociological observer typically spends more than a moment at the scene of interaction, though not always. In a dramatic example, Sudnow (1972, pp. 259-279) distinguishes between instantaneous recording, as in a camera shot, and the more natural enduring observation that traces the ongoing process.

3. For some later adaptations and applications, see, e.g., Bales (1970); Korsch and Negrete (1972).

4. The Lynds exemplify a different procedure for dynamic analysis by restudying the same community again several years later (Lynd and Lynd, 1937).

1
ROBERT F. BALES

SOME UNIFORMITIES OF BEHAVIOR IN · SMALL SOCIAL SYSTEMS

Introduction

... For several years at the Laboratory of Social Relations at Harvard a number of researchers have been engaged in the development of a method for the recording and analysis of social interaction. Up to the present time we have observed a variety of different kinds of groups, including some from other cultures, but our main experience has been with what could be called decision-making or problem-solving conferences of persons, ranging from two to ten, of our own culture. We are interested in the kinds of differences which appear under different experimental conditions. . . .

A Standard Diagnostic Task

One of our basic assumptions is that there are certain conditions which are present to an important degree not only in special kinds of groups doing special kinds of problems, but which are more or less inherent in the nature of the process of interaction or communication itself, whenever or wherever it takes place. In aggregates of cases

Reprinted in part from Guy E. Swanson, Theodore M. Newcomb, and Eugene L. Hartley, eds., *Readings in Social Psychology*, rev. ed. (New York: Holt, Rinehart and Winston, Inc., 1952), pp. 146-159.

14

where the special conditions associated with individual cases are varied enough to approximate randomness, one would expect the effects of those interaction system tendencies that are due to inherent conditions to become apparent. We have used averages of large numbers of cases to help us form hypotheses as to what such tendencies of interaction systems might be, and have then tried to set up conditions in the laboratory, in the form of a certain type of task, of personnel, etc., which will produce actual results like our averages.

Gradually we have evolved a laboratory task for groups which does tend to produce typical results in this sense. In this task the subjects are asked to consider themselves as members of a staff who have been requested by their superior to meet and consider the facts of a case, a human-relations tangle of some sort in his organization. The staff committee is asked to advise him as to why the people involved in the case are behaving as they do and what he should do about it. Each subject is given a summary of the case material. After each has read his summary, the typed copies of the case are collected by the experimenter. The manner of presentation is such that the subjects are made uncertain as to whether or not they possess exactly the same facts but are assured that each does possess an accurate, though perhaps incomplete, factual summary.

It should be noted that this particular concrete task has certain abstract characteristics which are important in eliciting a range of diversified behavior. It emphasizes certain *communication problems* (or conditions) which are present to some degree in all social interaction. The communication problems of *orientation, evaluation,* and *control* are each to a major degree unsolved at the beginning of the meeting and can typically be solved to some partly satisfactory degree for the members of the group during the period they are under observation. . . .

Description of the Method

A special room is available in which groups can meet and be observed from an observation room through a set of large one-way mirrors. Let us imagine we are observing a group of five persons who are meeting to come to a decision about a point of policy in a project

symbols 1-2 following Category 6, indicating an "attempted answer" to the previous question. As the chairman goes over the report the observer continues to score, getting a good many scores in Categories 6 and 7, but also occasional scores in other categories.

Phase 2. Emphasis on Problems of Evaluation: (deciding what attitudes should be taken toward the situation). As the chairman finishes reviewing the items on the report he may ask. "Have we been within bounds on our expenditures so far?" The observer puts down a score under Category 8.

Member 3 says, "It seems to me we have gone in pretty heavily for secretarial help." The observer puts down a score in Category 5.

Member 4 comes in with the remark, "Well I don't know. It seems to me. . . ." The observer puts down the symbols 4-3 in Category 10 to indicate the disagreement, and continues with scores in Category 5 as Member 4 makes his argument. The discussion continues to revolve around the analysis of expenditures, with a good many scores falling in Category 5, but also in others, particularly Categories 10 and 3, and interspersed with a number in Categories 6 and 7 as opinions are explained and supported by reference to facts.

Phase 3. Emphasis on Problems of Control: (deciding what to do about it). Finally the chairman says, "Well . . . what do you think we should do about that piece of equipment?" The observer scores 1-0 in Category 9. Member 2 says, "I think we should get it." The observer scores 2-0 in Category 4. As Member 2 begins to support his suggestion, Member 3 breaks in with a counterargument, and the discussion begins to grow heated, with more disagreement. Presently the observer notices that Member 5, who has said little up to this point, sighs heavily and begins to examine his fingernails. The observer puts down a score under Category 11.

In the meantime, Member 3, the chronic objector, comes through with a remark directed at Member 2. "Well, I never did agree about hiring that deadhead secretary. All she's got is looks, but I guess that's enough for Joe." The others laugh at this. The observer scores the first and second remarks under Category 12 as showing antagonism, and scores the laugh which follows as tension release in Category 2.

At this point Member 5 comes in quietly to sum up the argument, and by the time he finishes several heads are nodding. The observer scores both the nods and the audible agreements in Category 3. Member 3, the chronic objector, who is also the chronic joker, comes in with a joke at this point, and the joking and laughing continue for a minute or two, each member extending the joke a little. The observer continues to score in Category 2 as long as the laughing continues. As the members pick up their things one of them says, "Well, I think we got through that in good shape. Old Bill certainly puts in the right word at the right time, doesn't he?" The observer marks down two scores for the speaker under Category 1, shows solidarity, and after a few more similar remarks the meeting breaks up.

The idea that groups go through certain stages or phases in the process of solving problems, or that problem-solving would somehow be more effective if some prescribed order were followed, has been current in the literature for some time. However, the distinction between predicting an empirical order of phases as they will actually take place under some specific set of conditions, and prescribing an ideal order in terms of value judgments has not always been clearly drawn. It has typically not been recognized that different types of conditions or problems may result empirically in different sorts of phase movement. We have found that there are, indeed, *certain* conditions which must be quite carefully specified, under which a group problem-solving process essentially like that sketched above does tend to appear. These conditions can be set up experimentally in the laboratory, and have already been described above as the standard diagnostic task around which our other generalizations all revolve. . . .

Profiles

One of the important characteristics of interaction is the distribution of total number of acts among the twelve categories listed in Figure 1. A distribution of this kind, expressed in percentage rates based on the total number of acts, is called a profile. An illustrative and typical comparison of group profiles of two five-man groups working on the standard diagnostic task is shown in Table 1-1.

Different kinds of groups operating under different kinds of conditions produce different types of profiles. In the present illustration the "successful" group attained a higher rate of suggestions and more often followed these with positive reactions, rather than with negative reactions and questions, than did the "unsuccessful" group.

TABLE 1-1.

Profiles of "Satisfied" and "Dissatisfied" Groups on Case Discussion Task

| CATEGORY | MEETING PROFILES IN PERCENTAGE RATES | | | |
	SATISFIED[a]	DISSATISFIED[b]	AVERAGE OF THE TWO	AVERAGE RATES BY SECTIONS
1. Shows solidarity	.7	.8	.7	
2. Shows tension release	7.9	6.8	7.3	25.0
3. Agrees	24.9	9.6	17.0	
4. Gives suggestion	8.2	3.6	5.9	
5. Gives opinion	26.7	30.5	28.7	56.7
6. Gives orientation	22.4	21.9	22.1	
7. Asks for orientation	1.7	5.7	3.8	
8. Asks for opinion	1.7	2.2	2.0	6.9
9. Asks for suggestion	.5	1.6	1.1	
10. Disagrees	4.0	12.4	8.3	
11. Shows tension	1.0	2.6	1.8	11.4
12. Shows antagonism	.3	2.2	1.3	
Raw score total	719	767	1486	100.0

[a]The highest of sixteen groups, identified as HR2-2. The members rated their own satisfaction with their solution after the meeting at an average of 10.4 on a scale running from 0 to a highest possible rating of 12.
[b]The lowest of sixteen groups, identified as HR3-3. Comparable satisfaction rating in this group was 2.6.

The profiles produced by groups, however, are not completely and radically different from each other. The profile produced by the average of these two illustrative groups is more or less typical of averages of larger aggregates. "Attempted Answers"—that is, giving orientation, opinion, and suggestion—are nearly always more numerous than their cognate "Questions"—that is, asking for orientation, opinion, or suggestion. Similarly, "Positive Reactions"—that is, agreement, showing tension release, and solidarity—are usually more numerous than the "Negative Reactions" of showing disagreement, tension, and antagonism. Intuitively, one would feel that the process would surely be self-defeating and self-limiting if there were more questions than answers and more negative reactions than positive. . . .

Who-to-Whom Matrix

Another important direction of analysis deals with the way in which participation is distributed between members. The total number of different possible combinations of who is speaking and to whom for

ROBERT F. BALES

a given time period is called a matrix. Table 1-2 shows a matrix containing all the interaction initiated by and directed toward the members of eighteen different six-man groups.

TABLE 1-2.

Aggregate Matrix for Eighteen Sessions of Six-Man Groups, All Types of Activity

Rank of Person Originating Act	To Individuals of Each Rank						Total to Individuals	To Group As a Whole	Total Initiated
	1	2	3	4	5	6		0	
1		1,238	961	545	445	317	3,506	5,661	9,167
2	1,748		443	310	175	102	2,778	1,211	3,989
3	1,371	415		305	125	69	2,285	742	3,027
4	952	310	282		83	49	1,676	676	2,352
5	662	224	144	83		28	1,141	443	1,584
6	470	126	114	65	44		819	373	1,192
Total Received	5,203	2,313	1,944	1,308	872	565	12,205	9,106	21,311

The pattern of distribution for particular groups is different in detail under different conditions. For example, groups with no designated leader generally tend to have more equal participation than groups with designated leaders of higher status. However, in spite of these differences, the distribution of total amounts each member tends to address to the group as a whole, as well as the amounts men in each rank tend to talk to men in each other rank position seem to be subject to system-influences, which tend to produce similarities from group to group, and some regular gradations by group size.

These generalizations may be illustrated in part by reference to Table 1-2. Although this is an aggregate matrix for eighteen different groups, each of which has been rank-ordered before adding, it is sufficiently like those of particular groups to serve as an illustration. If the personnel for a particular group are arrayed in rank order according to the total amount they speak we then find that they are spoken to in amounts proportionate to their rank order. In general, each man receives back about half as much as he initiates in total. It will be remembered from the data in the profile that something like half of all interaction is "reactive" in a qualitative sense. Each man spends a certain portion of his time reacting to the initial acts of others. This amount of time differs, however, according to the rank of the member. . . .

Phase Movement

Changes in quality of activity as groups move through time in attempting to solve problems may be called phase patterns. The pattern of phases differs in detail under different conditions. However, these changes in quality seem to be subject to system-influences which produce similarities from group to group. An increase of task-oriented activities in the early parts of a meeting— that is, "Questions" and "Attempted Answers"—seems to constitute a disturbance of a system "equilibrium" which is later redressed by an increase in social-emotional activities—that is, both "Positive" and "Negative Reactions."

Part of our observations prior to the development of the standard diagnostic task were kept by time sequence. Each available meeting was divided into three equal parts, and the amount of each type of activity in each part of each meeting was determined. The meetings were divided into two kinds: those which were dealing with full-fledged problems (essentially problems of analysis and planning with the goal of group decision as described for the standard diagnostic task), and those dealing with more truncated or special-ized types of problems. Those groups dealing with full-fledged problems tended to show a typical phase movement through the meeting: the process tended to move qualitatively from a *relative* emphasis on attempts to solve problems of *orientation* ("what is it") to attempts to solve problems of *evaluation* ("how do we feel about it") and subsequently to attempts to solve problems of *control* ("what shall we do about it"). Concurrent with these transitions, the relative frequencies of both *negative reactions* (disagreement, tension, and antagonism), and *positive reactions* (agreement, tension release, and showing solidarity), tend to increase. The reasons why both negative and positive reactions have to increase are given below. It should be remembered that they are both "reactive." Figure 1-2 presents the summary data for all twenty-two group sessions examined in the phase study.

The underlying theory as to why the phase movement just described is characteristic of full-fledged conditions is again the same "system-equilbrium" rationale depending on the "interdependence of problems" in systems of social interaction. Consider first those problems immediately concerned with the task. An individual may be cognitively oriented to a situation and speak of it to others in cognitive terms without committing himself (or the other when the other agrees), either to evaluation of it or an attempt to control it. But in speaking to the other in evaluative terms he attempts to commit both himself and the other to some assumed previous orientation, and further, if he suggests a way to control the situation by joint cooperative action, he assumes a successful solution has been obtained for problems of both orientation and evaluation. When the problems of arriving at a common orientation and evaluation of the situation have not been substantially solved by the group members, attempts at control will meet with resistance on the part of the others and frustration on the part of the person attempting to exercise the control. Probably generally, unless there are contrary cultural, personality, or group organizational factors, the interacting persons tend to avoid or retreat from this frustration-producing type of interaction by "backtracking" toward orientation and evaluative analysis until the prior problems are solved.

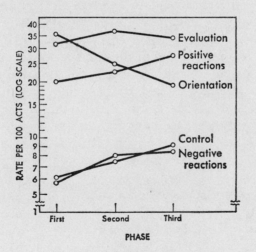

FIGURE 1-2. *Relative frequency of acts by type and phase based upon twenty-two sessions.*

In addition to their task problems, the members of any cooperating group have problems of their social and emotional relationships to solve and keep solved. Efforts to solve problems of orientation, evaluation, and control as involved in the task tend to lead to differentiation of the roles of the participants, both as to the functions they perform and their gross amounts of participation.

Some major features of this differentiation have already been described in the presentation of findings about the matrix. Both qualitative and quantitative types of differentiation tend to carry status implications which may threaten or disturb the existing order or balance of status relations among members. Disagreement and an attempt to change existing ideas and values may be necessary in the effort to solve the task problem but may lead, nevertheless, to personalized anxieties or antagonisms and impair the basic solidarity of the group.

This impairment, or the threat of it, we may assume, tends to grow more marked as the group passes from emphasis on the less demanding and more easily resolved problems of cognitive orientation on to problems of evaluation, and still more acute as it passes on to its heaviest emphasis on problems of control. Thus, a series of disturbances in the social-emotional relationships of the members tends to be set in motion by pressures arising initially from attempts to meet the demands of the external task or outer situation. These social-emotional problems tend to be expressed in a kind of status struggle as they grow more acute—hence the increasing rate of negative reactions.

However, at the extreme end of the final period, assuming that the members' attempts at control over the outer situation and over each other are successful and a final decision is reached, the rates in Categories 1, 2, and 3 also rise to their peak. In other words, the successfully recovering group tends to confirm its agreement and to release in diffuse ways the tensions built up in its prior task efforts, repairing the damage done to its state of consensus and social integration.

We note joking and laughter so frequently at the end of meetings that they might almost be taken as a signal that the group has completed what it considers to be a task effort, and is ready for disbandment or a new problem. This last-minute activity completes a cycle of operations involving a successful solution both of the task problems and social-emotional problems confronting the group. The apparent incongruity of predicting a peak for both negative and positive reactions in the third phase is thus explained. Negative reactions tend to give way to positive reactions in the final part of the third phase. The arbitrary division of the meeting into three equal periods of time is too crude to show the final dropping off of negative reactions in the third phase as solution is reached.

Conclusion

It may be that average tendencies like those presented can be taken as representative of typical social-system effects under full-fledged conditions. In experimental designs, then, where a full-fledged problem is used as the basic testing situation, deviations from empirical norms might be used as evidences of the effects of known or experimentally introduced conditions. For example, the experimental introduction of persistent difficulties of communication or orientation by placing together in the same group persons of widely different value standards might upset the profile, matrix, and phase sequence expected on the basis of the internal tendencies of the interaction system alone. Conversely, in using the method for clinical analysis or training of particular groups, groups might be set up under full-fledged conditions, and the deviations from the empirical norms used as diagnostic indicators of otherwise unknown characteristics of the group or the members.

The uniformities of the profile, matrix, and phase movement are all interdependent. They are manifest evidence that interaction is not a random collection of acts, but constitutes the observable process of a social system.

2

WILLIAM FOOTE WHYTE

STREET CORNER SOCIETY: THE SOCIAL STRUCTURE OF AN ITALIAN SLUM

Preface

This book is a report upon a three-and-a-half-year study of "Cornerville." My aim was to gain an intimate view of Cornerville life. My first problem, therefore, was to establish myself as a participant in the society so that I would have a position from which to observe. I began by going to live in Cornerville, finding a room with an Italian family. Since the mother and father of the family spoke no English, I began studying Italian. Conversations with them and practice with the Linguaphone enabled me to learn enough to talk fairly fluently with the older generation. As I became largely concerned with the second-generation men, who conducted their activities in English, Italian was not essential to me; but the fact that I made the effort to learn the language was important, since it gave the impression that I had a sincere and sympathetic interest in Cornerville people.

Staying with an Italian family gave me a view of family life and also provided important contacts with the community. Through the family I met a cousin of State Senator George Ravello's secretary. Through the cousin I met the secretary, and through the secretary I met Ravello. In this way I was able to establish myself in the politician's office at a time when he was running for Congress. He

Reprinted in part from William Foote Whyte, *Street Corner Society: The Social Structure of an Italian Slum* (Chicago: University of Chicago Press, 1943), pp. v-xi, 255-276.

had no opposition from within Cornerville in this campaign, which made it possible for me to work for him without losing standing with other local groups. During the campaign I did various odd jobs which were of no particular significance for the organization but which gave me an excuse for being around when things were happening. It was in this way that I found most of my material on politics.

I made my first contacts with the "corner boys" known as the Nortons through the Norton Street Settlement House. I subsequently learned that too close identification with the settlement would prevent me from becoming intimate with the rank and file of the people, but at this time I was fortunate in meeting corner boys who, while they had some contact with the settlement, also had a recognized position outside of it. Through the Nortons I came to know the college men of the Italian Community Club.

After I had lived eighteen months with the Italian family, I married, and my wife and I moved into a flat on Shelby Street. This opened for me a new field of contacts. One evening I went with the son of my Italian family to a banquet in honor of the local police lieutenant. There were three main groups of people present: policemen, politicians, and racketeers. My companion had met Tony Cataldo, a prominent local racketeer, and Tony had seen me around his district. We became acquainted in this way, and shortly thereafter Tony invited my wife and me to dinner at his house. We spent a number of evenings with the Cataldos and also came to know other members of the family. In order to study the influence of the racketeer upon a specific group of people, I joined the Cornerville Social and Athletic Club. Since the organization was located on Shelby Street, my contacts made it quite natural for me to join.

It was not enough simply to make the acquaintance of various groups of people. The sort of information that I sought required that I establish intimate social relations, and that presented special problems. Since illegal activities are prevalent in Cornerville, every newcomer is under suspicion. So that I would not be taken for a "G-man," I had to have some way of explaining my presence. I began by telling people that I was studying the history of Cornerville since the beginning of the Italian immigration, but I used this story only a few times. I found that in each group I met there was one man who directed the activities of his fellows and whose word carried authority. Without his support, I was excluded from the group; with his support, I was accepted. Since he had to take the responsibility of vouching for me, I made a practice of talking with him quite frankly about the questions in which I was interested. When his friends questioned him, he knew much more about me than they did, and he was therefore in a position to reassure them. In the course of my stay in Cornerville, several of these men came to have a very clear and detailed idea of the nature of my research, and this knowledge made it possible for them to help me by observing and discussing with me the sort of situations in which I was interested.

When I became accepted into a group, it was no longer necessary for me to explain what I was doing. Being accepted meant that I was a "good fellow" and that meant that whatever I was doing was all right. It became generally understood that I was writing a book about the old Italian customs in Cornerville, and occasionally I was asked, "How is your book coming?" I always replied that I was making progress but that there was still a lot for me to learn. No further answer was necessary, although I tried to give the impression that I was prepared to tell much more about my work than my questioner wanted to know.

The first few weeks of my association with any group brought in little information of value. Although my right to associate with the men was unquestioned, they could not feel at ease in my presence until they had become familiar with me. Therefore, I put in a great deal of time simply hanging around with them and participating in their various activities. I bowled, played baseball and softball, shot a little pool, played cards, and ate and drank with my Cornerville friends. This active participation gave me something in common with them so that we had other things to talk about besides the weather. It broke down the social barriers and made it possible for me to be taken into the intimate life of the group.

My aim was to be a friend to the people whom I was with, and I tried to act as a friend was supposed to act in that society. My friends helped me with my work, and I helped my friends as individuals in whatever way I could. I found it even more important to my social position to ask them to help me. I made it a rule that I should try to avoid influencing the actions of the group. I wanted to observe what the men did under ordinary circumstances; I did not want to lead them into different activities. I violated this rule several times; . . . but on the whole I held to it. Of course, my presence changed the situation for the group. I tried to minimize that change because it was much easier for me to study group activities if I could assume that my own influence had not been a significant factor in bringing about the actions I observed. Above all, I avoided making moral admonitions. I did not tell people that they were behaving improperly or suggest to them the way in which they should act. I was there to learn about Cornerville life, not to pass judgment upon it.

I was not immediately interested in broad generalizations upon the nature of Cornerville life. It seemed to me that any sound generalizations must be based upon detailed knowledge of social relations. Therefore, I concentrated my attention upon the inter-action of individuals in their groups. I was concerned not only with the "important events," because at the outset I had no basis for determining what was important except my own preconceived notions. I tried to keep my eyes and ears open to everything that went on between people in my presence. Frequently, I asked people to explain to me what had happened. Most of my interviewing was conducted informally while I was participating in group activities. I found that what people told me helped to explain what had happened and that what I observed helped to explain what people told me, so that it was helpful to observe and interview at the same time. In order to fill in the background in the history of the individual and of the group and to take up things which could best be discussed in private, I invited men to come separately and talk with me at my home. Much of the background of the Nortons and the Italian Community Club was gathered in this way.

It is customary for the sociologist to study the slum district in terms of "social disorganization" and to neglect to see that an area such as Cornerville has a complex and well-established organization of its own. I was interested in that organization. I found that in every group there was a hierarchical structure of social relations binding the individuals to one another and that the groups were also related hierarchically to one another. Where the group was formally organized into a political club, this was immediately apparent, but for informal groups it was no less true. While the relations in such groups were not formally prescribed, they could be clearly observed in the interactions of individuals. To determine the relative standing of members of the group, I paid particular attention to the origination of action. When the group or several of its members engaged in some common activity, I wanted to know who suggested what was to be done and whose agreement was necessary before the action could be carried out. Observation of this sort provided the basis for charts of hierarchical organization. . . .

The study of the Cornerville S. and A. Club presented some special problems. Since at times there were as many as fifty members, it was necessary to study the club through observing the groupings into which the men naturally divided themselves. Every afternoon or evening when I went into the club I looked around to see which members were grouped together, playing cards, listening to the radio, or talking. When the men were moving around, I could not retain all the movements; but, when they settled down, I counted the men present and fixed in my mind the spatial position of each individual in relation to the others. When I went home, I mapped the spatial positions of the members and indicated which ones were participating together. These maps showed quite clearly the main division between the two cliques and the subdivisions within each clique.

The events to be described will provide the evidence for assigning positions to the most prominent members of the Cornerville S. and A. Club. The relative positions of the minor members were discovered by observing which men took the initiative in group action when one of the top men was not present. . . .

My observations of interactions and of spatial positions would have been of no use to me if I had not made a permanent record of them. When I went to political rallies and campaign committee meetings, I was able to take notes on the spot; but on all other occasions I had to rely upon my memory until I could write in private. When I recorded conversations, I tried to put down in so far as possible the exact words that were said. Frequently, the phrase used carries a meaning which escapes any paraphrase, and therefore I felt that it was important to try for verbatim recordings. This is a skill which develops with practice. At first I found that I could remember only a few phrases used and give an impressionistic picture of the rest of the conversation; but, as I went on, I was able to record in greater and greater detail, so that I feel confident that the quotations I cite represent substantially what was actually said. I had the same experience in mapping spatial positions.

The stories of the Nortons and of the Cornerville S. and A. Club provide a body of information upon corner gangs, but they constitute only the smallest fraction of the total number of such groups to be found in Cornerville. So that I might be able to generalize upon the nature of the corner gang, I solicited the aid of several corner-boy leaders who discussed with me their own experiences and became interested in making the same sort of detailed observations that are found in my corner-boy stories. . . .

The corner boys do not explicitly recognize the structure of the gang, but it is implicit in all their actions. When, toward the end of my study, I discussed these matters with my informants, I made them conscious of the nature of their unreflective behavior. To that extent I changed the situation: the men talked to me about things that they had never formulated before. This did not mean that they were enabled to act more effectively. Doc, my chief informant, once told me:

> You've slowed me up plenty since you've been down here. Now when I do something, I have to think what Bill Whyte would want to know about it and how I can explain it. . . . Before I used to do these things by instinct.

This awareness, however, contributed toward building up a systematic picture of the corner gang. . . .

The life of the corner boy proceeds along regular and narrowly circumscribed channels. As Doc said to me:

> Fellows around here don't know what to do except within a radius of about three hundred yards. That's the truth, Bill. They come home from work, hang on the corner, go up to eat, back on the corner, up a show, and they come back to hang on the corner. If they're not on the corner, it's likely the boys there will know where you can find them. Most of them stick to one corner. It's only rarely that a fellow will change his corner.

The stable composition of the group and the lack of social assurance on the part of its members contribute toward producing a very high rate of social interaction within the group. The group structure is a product of these interactions.

Out of such interaction there arises a system of mutual obligations which is fundamental to group cohesion. If the men are to carry on their activities as a unit, there are many occasions when they must do favors for one another. The code of the corner boy requires him to help his friends when he can and to refrain from doing anything to harm them. When life in the group runs smoothly, the obligations binding members to one another are not explicitly recognized. Once Doc asked me to do something for him, and I said that he had done so much for me that I welcomed the chance to reciprocate. He objected: "I don't want it that way. I want you to do this for me because you're my friend. That's all."

It is only when the relationship breaks down that the underlying obligations are brought to light. While Alec and Frank were friends, I never heard either one of them discuss the services he was performing for the other, but when they had a falling-out over the group activities with the Aphrodite Club, each man complained to Doc that the other was not acting as he should in view of the services that had been done him. In other words, actions which were performed explicitly for the sake of friendship were revealed as being part of a system of mutual obligations.

Not all the corner boys live up to their obligations equally well, and this factor partly accounts for the differentiation in status among them. The man with a low status may violate his obligations without much change in his position. His fellows know that he has failed to discharge certain obligations in the past, and his position reflects his past performances. On the other hand, the leader is depended upon by all the members to meet his personal obligations. He cannot fail to do so without causing confusion and endangering his position. . . .

A man with a low position in the group is less flexible in his adjustments than the leader, who customarily deals with groups outside of his own. . . . However, no matter what the corner boy's position, he suffers when the manner of his interaction must undergo drastic changes. This is clearly illustrated in the case of . . . Doc's dizzy spells. . . .

Doc's dizzy spells came upon him when he was unemployed and had no spending money. He considered his unemployment the cause of his difficulties, and, in a sense, it was, but in order to understand the case it is necessary to inquire into the changes which unemployment necessitated in the activity of the individual. While no one enjoys being unemployed and without money, there are many Cornerville men who could adjust themselves to that situation without serious difficulties. Why was Doc so different? To say that he was a particularly sensitive person simply gives a name to the phenomenon and provides no answer. The observation of interactions provides the answer. Doc was accustomed to a high frequency of interaction with the members of his group and to frequent contacts with members of other groups. While he sometimes directly originated action in set events for the group, it was customary for one of the other members to originate action for him in a pair event, and then he would originate action in a set event.

That is, someone would suggest a course of action, and then Doc would get the boys together and organize group activity. The events of Doc's political campaign indicate that this pattern had broken down. Mike was continually telling Doc what to do about the campaign, and I was telling him what to do about seeing Mr. Smith and others to get a job. While we originated action for him with increasing frequency, he was not able to originate action in set events. Lacking money, he could not participate in group activities without accepting the support of others and letting them determine his course of action. Therefore, on many occasions he avoided associating with his friends—that is, his frequency of interaction was drastically reduced. At a time when he should have been going out to make contacts with other groups, he was unable to act according to the political pattern even with the groups that he knew, and he saw less and less of those outside his circle of closest friends. When he was alone, he did not get dizzy, but, when he was with a group of people and was unable to act in his customary manner, he fell prey to the dizzy spells. . . .

The type of explanation suggested to account for the difficulties of . . . Doc has the advantage that it rests upon the objective study of actions. A man's attitudes cannot be observed but instead must be inferred from his behavior. Since actions are directly subject to observation and may be recorded like other scientific data, it seems wise to try to understand man through studying his actions. This approach not only provides information upon the nature of informal group relations but it also offers a framework for the understanding of the individual's adjustment to his society. . . .

According to Cornerville people, society is made up of big people and little people—with intermediaries serving to bridge the gaps between them. The masses of Cornerville people are little people. They cannot approach the big people directly but must have an intermediary to intercede for them. They gain this intercession by establishing connections with the intermediary, by performing services for him, and thus making him obligated to them. The intermediary performs the same functions for the big man. The interactions of big shots, intermediaries, and little guys build up a hierarchy of personal relations based upon a system of reciprocal obligations.

Corner gangs such as the Nortons and the cliques of the Cornerville Social and Athletic Club fit in at the bottom of the hierarchy, although certain social distinctions are made between them. Corner-boy leaders like Doc, Dom Romano, and Carlo Tedesco served as intermediaries, representing the interests of their followers to the higher-ups. Chick and his college boys ranked above the corner boys, but they stood at the bottom of another hierarchy, which was controlled from outside the district. There are, of course, wide differences in rank between big shots. Viewed from the street corner of Shelby Street, Tony Cataldo was a big shot, and the relations of the corner-boy followers to him were regulated by their leaders. On the other hand, he served as an intermediary, dealing with big shots for the corner boys and trying to control the corner boys for the big shots. T. S., the racket boss, and George Ravello, the state senator, were the biggest men in Cornerville. T. S. handled those below him through his immediate subordinates. While Ravello refused to allow any formal distinctions to come between himself and the corner boys, the man at the bottom fared better when he approached the politician through an intermediary who had a connection than when he tried to bridge the gap alone.

The corner gang, the racket and police organizations, the political organization, and now the social structure have all been described and analyzed in terms of a hierarchy of personal relations based upon a system of reciprocal obligations. These are the fundamental elements out of which all Cornerville institutions are constructed. . . .

3
HERBERT J. GANS

THE LEVITTOWNERS:
WAYS OF LIFE AND POLITICS
IN A NEW SUBURBAN COMMUNITY

The Setting, Theory, and Method of the Study

THE SETTING

... In 1955, Levitt announced that he had purchased almost all of Willingboro Township, New Jersey, a sparsely settled agricultural area seventeen miles from Philadelphia. ... Three basic house types, costing from $11,500 to $14,500 would be built on the same street and organized into separate neighborhoods of about 1200 homes, each served by an elementary school, playground, and swimming pool. The complex of ten or twelve neighborhoods would be complemented by a set of community-wide facilities, including a large shopping center, some smaller ones, and of course high schools, a library, and parks; and some of these would be provided by the builder.

On a sunny Saturday in June 1958, Levittown was officially opened to potential purchasers, and that day my wife and I were among hundreds of others who looked over the houses. A few weeks later, the first group of about 100 purchasers was asked to come to Levittown to pick a lot, and we chose one in the middle of a short block—to make sure that we would literally be in the middle of things. During the second week of October, we were among the first 25 families who moved into the new community—none of them, I was pleased to discover, coming to study it. . . .

THE THEORY OF THE STUDY

. . . My first task was to determine the processes which transform a group of strangers into a community. . . . I intended to study how the community was planned: to what extent the plans were shaped by Levitt's goals and to what extent by the goals of the expected purchasers. For this purpose, I needed also to study the purchasers— why they were moving to Levittown and what aspirations they had for life in the new community. Once they had moved in, I wanted to observe the community formation process from the same perspective: how much specific groups were shaped by their founders, how much by their members, and how much by the group's function for the larger community. . . .

THE METHODS OF THE STUDY

. . .The main source of data was to be participant-observation. By living in the community for the first two years, I planned to observe the development of neighbor relations and social life and to be on hand when organizations and institutions were being set up. In addition to observing at public meetings, I would also be able to interview founders and members, and once having gotten to know them, follow their groups as they went through their birth pains. Meanwhile I would do much the same with churches, governmental public bodies, and political parties; I would talk to doctors, lawyers, local reporters, and the Levitt executives, as well. Eventually I would get to know all the important people and a sizable sample of other residents, and interview them from time to time as the community building process unfolded. The nature of everyday life I would discover principally on my own street, where I could observe my neighbors and myself in our roles as homeowners and block residents. These plans came to fruition, and I spent most of my days making the rounds of the community to find out what was happening, much like a reporter. For a year after organizations first sprang up, I went to at least one meeting every week night.

Although observation would also provide some data on the community's effects on people, and on their feelings about Levittown and their problems, it would not allow me to contact a large and random enough sample. Consequently, I planned to interview such a sample shortly before moving in, to find out what aspirations they were bringing to the community, and again two years later, to determine what intended and unintended changes had occurred in their lives. The shortage of funds made the sample smaller than I had wished, but forty-five respondents were interviewed twice, mainly by graduate students from the University of Pennsylvania. As the sample included too few former city dwellers for even a rudimentary statistical analysis, fifty-five ex-Philadelphians were interviewed as well, but only once. And being unable to persuade the builder to give me the names of purchasers before they moved in, I had to schedule the initial interview with the first sample shortly after they arrived. The builder did, however, send out a prearrival mail questionnaire for me, which ultimately went to 3100 purchasers (a record-breaking two thirds of whom filled it out), and provided much of the data on the Levittowners, their moving reasons, and aspirations. . . . Whenever I report statistical findings about people's behavior, the data come from the mail questionnaire . . . and from the interviews. . . .

. . .My previous participant-observation research had convinced me that my role in Levittown would be more an observer's than a participant's. Participating is undoubtedly the best way to discover what is really going on, but becoming a participant in one group automatically excludes the researcher from learning anything about what is going on in competing or opposing ones. Consequently, I decided I would participate only in the life of my own block and as a member of the public at meetings, but that otherwise my role would be that of an observer and informal interviewer.

As soon as I moved in, I told people I was on the faculty of the University of Pennsylvania and that I would do a study of the community formation process in Levittown. Having learned from previous experience that it is difficult to explain sociology meaningfully to people, I usually described my research as a historical study. I did not go into detail about it—I was rarely asked to—and I did not tell people on my block that I was keeping notes on their (and my) activities as homeowners and neighbors. To have done so would have made life unpleasant for them and for me. I disclaimed association with the mail questionnaire or the interviews on behavior change, fearing (probably unnecessarily) that I might be rejected as a participant-observer. Finally I did not tell people I had moved to Levittown in order to do the study. Actually, it would not have occurred to them that I was not simply interested in a good low-priced house and the chance to enjoy suburban living.

Aside from these deceptions, being a participant-observer was almost always enjoyable and often exciting. I liked most of the people I met and had no trouble in getting information from them. Identifying myself as a researcher did not inhibit them from talking, but then I asked few personal questions; being as curious as I about the evolution of a new community, they were willing and often eager to have me sit in at meetings, or interview them. After a while, I became a fixture in the community; people forgot I was there and went on with their business, even at private political gatherings. I was always welcomed at public meetings, especially when citizen attendance was low. Needing an audience, public officials were glad to forget I was there as a researcher. Indeed, I was once publicly praised for my steady attendance. . . .

The Levittowners—and Why They Came

. . .The people to be described are the first 3000 families who came to Levittown between October 1958 and June 1960.

These Levittowners were, like many other suburbanites, primarily young families who came to the new community to raise their children. At the time of their arrival in 1958-1960, almost four-fifths of the men were under forty; 44 percent were between the ages of thirty and forty. . . .

Most Levittowners were lower middle class. Most of the professionals were teachers and social workers; only 10 percent of them were doctors or lawyers. . . .I would guess that no more than 5 to 10 percent of the Levittowners could be considered upper middle class.

Conversely, most of the blue collar Levittowners were in the highest-skill, highest-status manual occupations, such as foremen, printers, electricians, and plumbers, and 10 percent had attended college. Many were trying to raise their children for middle class careers, and I suspect that the proportion of families who were workingclass in terms of family culture was smaller than the proportion working at blue collar trades—perhaps only 20 percent of the total population. Thus, about 75 percent of the community might be considered lower middle class, culturally speaking.

Thirty-seven percent of the families were Roman Catholic; 47 percent were Protestant—with Methodists, Lutherans, Presbyterians, and Baptists in the majority; and 14 percent were Jewish, the majority Conservative. . . .

ASPIRATIONS FOR LIFE IN LEVITTOWN

. . .Although only about a third of the people who filled out the mail questionnaire said they had given "a lot of thought" to what they wanted their life in Levittown to be like, 90 percent of all mail questionnaire respondents volunteered things they "especially looked forward to about (their) life in Levittown," and the list of aspirations was the same for those who had and those who had not thought seriously about the future.

Essentially, they wanted more comfortable and modern surroundings, but they did not want to change their old way of life or to make a new one in the new community. About half bought in Levittown because it was a new community, but their reasons indicate they were referring to the new house; about 40 percent wanted to make some changes in their lives, but the changes listed also had to do mainly with the house. . . .

. . .Altogether, about 95 percent of the respondents who volunteered aspirations hoped for improved individual, family, and social life; and less than 5 percent for identification with and activities in the wider community. . . .

The Beginnings of Group Life

. . .Among the Levittowners themselves, the first signs of group life began to appear even before they moved in. As they inspected the model homes, many were also inspecting the other people who were looking at the homes with them. . . .

. . .On moving day the first people to greet the new homeowners had not been their neighbors but an unending parade of milkmen, bread salesmen, and other merchants hoping to sign them up for home delivery until the shopping center was completed. At first, the constant callers were a bother, but when the moving-in chores were over, the salesmen became social intermediaries, telling people about their neighbors, and pointing out the ones with similar backgrounds or interests. Children, too, were a catalyst. . . .

The feeling of optimism that neighbors would be friendly was not enough; there had to be some sign that there would be no rejection. Women asked, "Are you settled yet?" If the answer was positive, then invitations could be exchanged to look at each others' houses. Being settled meant that the house was in sufficient shape to express the image that the women wanted to create among their neighbors. The men, knowing that they would be less dependent on their neighbors for social activities, could be more casual, although they did help their wives, working on the front lawn to make sure that the image outside was as good as that inside.

Once the image was ready, and an initial meeting produced no rejection, people were prepared to exchange information and to look for common backgrounds or interests that would bind them together. They described where they had come from, and their—or their husbands'—occupations, and went on to cover child-rearing methods and plans for fixing the house (women), the lawn, cars, and work (men). Every topic served either to bring people closer together or to pull them apart, by indicating where differences existed and what topics were taboo. For example, one of my neighbors was an Army pilot, and on our initial meeting—produced by a washout on our front lawns—we exchanged occupations. After I mentioned being a professor, he made a crack about another neighbor, a blue collar worker, to indicate that, although he referred to himself as "a glorified truck driver" he was, nevertheless, a white collar worker like me. He went on by talking about a relative who was studying for his Ph.D., but, aware that most professors were liberal and agnostic, he also let me know that he shared Southern race attitudes and was a fundamentalist Baptist. Disagreements would surely come up about race and religion, and if we were to be good neighbors, these subjects should not be discussed. . . .

. . . First encounters took anywhere from two weeks to a month or two; they were followed by a period of considerable informal visiting and entertaining, lasting perhaps two to six months. These visits provided companionship and mutual support in the early period of living in a new community, for a new house in a still almost rural area created not only loneliness but also a variety of problems which were solved by getting together and "sharing ideas."

INFORMAL CLUBS

As people decided how they felt about their nearby neighbors, a sorting and departure process developed. Those who had become friends set up block cliques, others moved into multiblock ones, and yet others looked for friends elsewhere, particularly for evening visiting. The earliest departures took place among social and cultural *minority groups*, especially working and upper middle class people, older ones, and Jews—and all others who felt themselves out of place among their neighbors and needed or wanted to find their social life elsewhere. With this departure, the community stratification process began in earnest. . . .

Some of the coffee-klatsch groups expanded into block clubs, involving a dozen neighbors on adjacent blocks, which met fort-nightly or monthly for conversation and/or cards, with individual members getting together in between. . . .

Most of the groups remained together for at least the three years that I was in touch with them. Some had become regular clubs when the group lost its initial enthusiasm and structure was needed as an adhesive. . . .

THE EVOLUTION OF SOCIAL LIFE

The development of social relationships reached an equilibrium rapidly, for 75 percent of the interview respondents reported having settled down both in the house and in the community within six months, and fully half indicated it took even less time than that. After two years in Levittown, 47 percent reported that they were doing about as much individual visiting with neighbors as they had after six months; 30 percent said they were doing more. . . .

Over time, the block social system had stabilized as well, ranging from close friendship among some to open hostility among a few, but mostly calling for friendly coexistence and occasional visiting among those who were not friends. . . .

ORGANIZATIONAL ORIGIN AND RESIDENTS' ASPIRATIONS

If the aspirations Levittowners volunteered before arrival had guided the founding process, most organizations would have been started internally by people to whom they were important. Civic groups would have outnumbered social clubs and both would have been surpassed by home-and-family-centered groups such as PTAs, Scouts, and Garden Clubs.

As it turned out, however, only 24 percent of the organizations emerging in the first two years were Internal, 31 percent were External, and the remaining 45 percent were Unintended. More were social than were civic. . . .

It is worthwhile asking, therefore, why the groups that sprang up were not those that people wanted before they came, why almost a third could be organized by outsiders who knew nothing about the new community, and whether the large number of Unintended groups, which sprang up on the spur of the moment, represented the impact of community conditions on the origin process.

One answer suffices for all three questions. How organizations were founded was ultimately less relevant than what happened to them once they were founded. No organization, however it started, could exist beyond the initial meeting without responding to some needs among the members it attracted, and these needs were not only more important than founders' or members' preoccupancy aspirations, but they developed largely after people had lived in Levittown for a while. . . .

Aside from the few civic groups, which tried to intervene in municipal affairs, and the men's service clubs, which provided "community-minded" activities for the lawyers, salesmen, realtors, and politicians who needed to advertise themselves in the community, the organizations were primarily *sorting* groups which divided and segregated people by their interests and ultimately, of course, by socio-economic, educational, and religious differences. On the block, people who shared a common space could not really express their diversity; the community sorting groups came into being for this purpose.

Men could divide and segregate themselves on the job, but the women had to do it in the community, and partly for this reason most organizations were sexually separated, with only some of those appealing to upper middle class people providing "coeducational" activities. The total array of women's groups offered the opportunity for extremely fine sorting. . . . Organizational programs reflected these diversities. The organizations of the college-educated stressed cultural activities and local or national political issues; those of the high school graduates scheduled fashion shows and lectures on beauty, home management, and child care. The highly educated shunned "gossip," their own version of it being buried in the discussion of social issues. Games, always major organizational sidelines, were also stratified, ranging from poker, pinochle, and hearts up to canasta, scrabble, and bridge. Municipal services and formal governmental institutions still being in a primitive stage, most groups combined social sorting with a variety of community service activities. The upper middle class groups put on candidates' night and community forums; the working class groups concentrated on sports for the children, firefighting, and Fourth of July ceremonies; the lower middle class groups' activities ranged from rolling bandages, running Miss Levittown contests, and collecting books for the library to helping the Superintendent of Schools.

Needless to say, the kinds of sorting groups that Levittown would require could not be determined until after people had lived there for a while and could see how many friends they could find on the block and what charitable and civic activities needed to be supplied. As a result, they could not have anticipated before arrival what kinds of organizations they would actually join. Likewise, the organizations could not anticipate their members' demands and needs in advance, but once they knew them, they adapted to them. . . .

Yet none of the sorting needs and community conditions were so distinctive as to require unique organizations. The ability of national groups to bend to local priorities helped, but even the local associations, 40 percent of the total, were modeled on similar organizations elsewhere and none was entirely original to Levittown. They were, rather, typical of those found in most other suburbs and communities of young families of similar class. In fact, although they considered themselves community-wide organizations, almost half of thirty-six for which membership addresses were available drew most of their people from one or two neighborhoods. Clearly, people cared less about the nominal purpose and scope of the group than to be with fellow residents who had come to Levittown at about the same time and were compatible in other ways. . . .

PRE-OCCUPANCY ASPIRATIONS AND COMMUNITY ORIGIN

. . . One of my initial hypotheses, that the origin of the community and the formation of particular groups and institutions would reflect the aspirations Levittowners expressed before arrival, was clearly not supported by what actually happened. Only a few residents aspired to community activities before they came, and Levittown's organizations were started instead by whatever External agencies were interested in the new community and by residents who had personal loyalties to a specific group. This would suggest that the aspirations and wishes of the mass of residents are irrelevant, and that a new community can be organized by individuals and even nonresidents who are determined to realize their own perferences, provided only that they have enough organizational know-how and persistence to put them over to the population.

It is true that almost anyone could start an organization in Levittown, but it is also true, and in the long run more important, that the organization's survival could only be assured by adapting it to the needs and wishes of its members, so that Levittowners could determine the fate of organizations by transforming what was started for them to their own preferences. . . .

. . . What brought a community into being in Levittown, then, was not the preoccupancy aspirations of the residents, but rather a complex process of external initiative and subsequent internal transformation that produced organizations and institutions which reflected the backgrounds and interests of the majority of the population. The new Levittowners had not thought much about their future community life before they arrived, but once they had settled down, they chose to enter the community being founded for them and then to alter it to meet their requirements. These choices were based less on explicit individual wishes than on requirements themselves generated by the community; that is, people went into and reshaped the organizations *on the basis of needs that had developed in the situation in which they found themselves in Levittown. The principal situation was the presence of the kinds of people with whom they lived, for insofar as Levittowners used organizations for sorting purposes and sorted themselves as they did, they were reacting to the population mix that had come about in Levittown.* Ultimately, then, the community evolved as it did because of the kinds of people who had decided, each on his own, to buy a house in Levittown, organizational and political life uniting them for cooperative ventures, segregating them for competitive ones, and bringing about class and other conflicts to determine which elements of the population mix would have power over the whole.

As a result, it would be absurd to argue that Levittown evolved out of a conspiracy, either on the part of a profit-seeking builder to entice buyers into his development or on the part of national organizations intent on adding to their membership rolls among an essentially captive audience. Indeed, few Levittowners objected that many of their organizations were national ones initiated from outside, and I am not sure that very many even noticed it. Not everyone was happy with what Levitt had wrought, and many were unhappy over the conflict generated by definitional struggles and by township politics, yet the events that made them unhappy were rarely conspiratorial or dictatorial measures, but almost always the outcomes of organizational and political compromises required by the need to establish a community quickly and to cope with the diverse requirements of that community. In the end, the community was an expression of the lower middle class culture of the majority, altered somewhat to accede to the demands of insistent minorities. . . .

The Methods of the Study

. . . Since sociological findings are the result of the researcher's methods, I must describe my specific methods and their shortcomings in more detail, . . . in order to give a fair picture of the reliability, validity, and limitations of the data. . . .

THE PARTICIPANT-OBSERVATION STUDIES

My major research activities as a participant-observer included the following:

1. As a home owner and a resident, I lived in the community and used its social and physical facilities like everyone else. I could study my own residence in the community and observe that of other Levittowners.

2. As a resident of a specific block, I could both act as a neighbor and observe my own actions, and also study my neighbors in their relationship to me and to other neighbors.

3. I attended meetings of all organizations about which I knew and at which I could be present without being overly visible. I also attended almost all meetings of public agencies and many of the meetings of social, civic, political, and cultural groups. I could not attend meetings of women's clubs, and I did not attend many religious functions (except in the Jewish community), partly because of lack of time, partly because people knew I was Jewish and I felt I would be intruding in a Christian religious service to no useful purpose. I did, however, attend at least one service in almost every church. I also attended other public gatherings, such as community ceremonies, social functions put on by organizations, high school football games, and local art shows, and even dropped in on a couple of teenage dances.

4. I conducted two types of informal interviews. I talked with people about specific events, for example, to find out the reasons for things that had happened at meetings I had observed. I also interviewed regularly a large number of informants in all major institutions and groups in the community. Like a newspaperman, I "made the rounds," checking regularly with one or more

informants in the governmental agencies, the voluntary associations, churches, and political parties. I also maintained continuing contact with ministers, doctors, lawyers, and realtors, the local newspapermen, Levitt executives, store managers, residents in different parts of the community, and some of the pre-Levittown residents as well. Keeping in contact with informants and keeping abreast of events took most of my research time.

5. I visited with people socially as a resident, and since Levittown was always an important topic of conversation, I was able to collect data on these occasions.

These activities cast me in three types of research roles: *total researcher, researcher-participant,* and *total participant.* As a total researcher I observed events in which I participated minimally or not at all, for example, as a silent audience member at public meetings. As a researcher-participant, I participated in an event but as a researcher rather than as a resident, for example, at most social gatherings. As a total participant, I acted spontaneously as a friend or neighbor and subsequently analyzed the activities in which I had so participated. The total participant role is the most honest one, and insofar as I was myself affected by the events in which I was participating, the most productive one for understanding a social situation. It is difficult to carry out, however, because it is almost impossible to lose consciousness of one's research role, and if one does lose it, one also becomes less observant of what is happening. Most of my data I gathered as a total researcher or researcher-participant, and only when I was involved in activities which I did not expect to produce relevant data would I relax into the total participant role.

Roles develop not only out of the participant-observer's activities, but also out of how people view him. When the researcher is very different from the people he studies, he is permanently an outsider, as I was in the Italian working class neighborhood I had studied in Boston. In Levittown, however, I had bought a house like everyone else, was about the same age as most of my neighbors, and was not different ethnically or in terms of income. Like them, I was a resident, home owner, neighbor, citizen, and friend—as well as a researcher, which resulted in some role conflicts, partly for myself, but also for the people I was studying.

One of these was on my own block, and as I noted in the Introduction, I decided from the start not to act like a researcher there. I kept my formal research activities on the block to a minimum and tried to be a total participant as often as I could. Even so, occasionally my neighbors were ambivalent about my role. Once, a neighbor invited my wife and me to a meeting of her church fellowship to show us what the church was like, but asked me to take no notes. . . . If I aroused suspicion, it was about getting to know too much of the less ethical or respectable aspects of community life. . . . Because I knew all the community's leaders, I aroused some status anxiety among my neighbors. To reduce their anxiety, I refrained from establishing social relations with community leaders. . . .

The various roles I took and the various roles in which I was seen undoubtedly affected the kinds of data I was given, but it is difficult for me to judge how. Since the participant-observer must "sell" himself to get his data, how he comes across as a person and a role player may influence what people tell him. . . . I became a bland and neutral person so as not to alienate people with different opinions but this *persona* also reduced my own activity in a relationship and gave the informant more opportunity to talk. Indeed, quite often I purposely "played dumb" in interviews, giving the impression I knew less than I actually did, so that people would give me a fuller description of their activities and their attitudes. Once I had obtained such a description, I could ask more specific questions, even about contradictions in the informant's description. . . .

The extent to which my own values affected my findings is also difficult to judge. Coming to Levittown with the hypothesis that the suburban critics were wrong may have blinded me to some contradictory data, but it also made me feel more sympathetic to the Levittowners and more receptive to how they thought and felt. So did my belief in pluralism and relativism. Yet none of these values caused me to overidentify with my sources of data. Overidentification is a major problem for the participant-observer, which may create such strong attachments to the population he studies that he fails to see undesirable elements in their behavior. The West Enders I lived with in my previous study were poorer than I and were facing destruction of their neighborhood by an urban renewal project which would eventually replace them with high-income tenants. They were underdogs, and I identified with them as such. The Levittowners were neither poor nor threatened, and I had no reason to feel sorry for them. . . .

The values (and feelings) which most affected my fieldwork concerned the deceptions required to be a participant-observer. They generated the guilt and anxiety I described in the Introduction, and

PART II

Interpretation

INTRODUCTION

Before scrutinizing in subsequent parts of the book the empirical methods of observation, let us consider the parallel but less well-codified methods by which observed data are interpreted (M. W. Riley, 1963, pp. 3-7, 26-29). Part I has pointed to the potential congruence between direct observation of interaction and the sociologist's conception of the group as a dynamic system of interdependent parts. Observation (structured or unstructured, with or without participation of the researcher) can often deal with the whole system in the round and with its dynamic processes, revealing patterns of action and changes of role structure which the actors themselves do not fully comprehend and cannot report directly in answer to questioning. Given this special theoretical congruence, does observation significantly constrain the researcher's choice of methods for interpreting his empirical data in the light of his conceptual model?

The studies included in Part II suggest that there are few such constraints, that gathering data by observation is largely independent of procedures for interpreting these data. Although interpretative procedures have been given far less methodological attention than empirical procedures, a wide range is explicated through actual use in these studies—from insight and creative imagination to deductive strategies and mathematical reasoning. The process of interpretation—the bringing together of theory and findings—commonly works back and forth between the conceptual model and the data being analyzed. However, depending upon the nature of his model and his objective, the investigator often emphasizes one or the other direction of the process. He can move from data to model—by adding new ideas to the model after he has completed the data-gathering phase of his research. Or he can go from model to data—by postulating in advance of data gathering what his findings would be if they accord closely with the assumptions of his conceptual model.

51

The first two selections, largely exploratory in objective, exemplify the movement *from data to model*. They use the research findings to suggest new ideas and hypotheses that might account for observed regularities in the data, and thereby amplify or specify the conceptual model with which the research began. *Coser's* generation of a theory relating authority to decision making, derived from three months of comparative observation of medical and surgical wards in a hospital, implies (but does not fully describe) some of the tools used by researchers in seeking theoretical clues: e.g., abstraction of relevant aspects of the data, generalization to wider situations, association of the phenomena studied with analogous phenomena that are better understood, or—following Weber's notion of *Verstehen* ([1922] 1947, p. 100)—empathy or insight into social relationships and processes. Many other observation studies make skillful use of such interpretative tools—Homans (1946) on a small warship, Turner (1947) on the disbursing officer in a bureaucracy, or Ball (1967) on an abortion clinic. The exploration by *Becker and Geer* of the socialization of medical students (cf. the prior work of Merton, Reader, and Kendall, 1957) culminates in a propositional statement concerning idealism under the strain of reality testing. Thus it suggests how the participant observer can start from exploration, obtain clues from his data to new ideas and hypotheses, and then go back to look for further data to test these hunches. (For additional methodological formulations, see, e.g.: Becker, 1958; Dalton, 1959; Glaser and Strauss, 1967; Weiss, 1968).

Several methods of moving in the other direction, *from model to data*, are shown in the next three selections. In providing the interpretation as part of the model in advance of the data gathering, the researcher typically determines what the expected findings would be if the assumptions of the conceptual model were in accord with the facts, sometimes using mathematical models or computer simulations (e.g., Coleman, 1964, p. 1050) as a precise language for formulating the interrelated ideas and implications. Then, once he has derived the implications of the conceptual model, his task is to obtain and examine the actual findings to see whether, for the particular conditions under study, they are consistent with the expected findings. *Cancian's* observations of interaction patterns among Indian families in Mexico typifies the testing of hypotheses, based in this instance on small group research and theories of self-other patterns. The elaborate situational simulation of police communication under stress, ingeniously conducted by *Drabek and Haas*, serves both to check observed data against the outcome of processes postulated from previous research and to provide further clues to emergent changes in structure and process. Of dramatic interest is the method used by the sociologist-mountaineer, *Emerson*, who demonstrates how, and with what difficulty, an explicit theory (of "goal-striving as a self-maintaining system, partially independent of environmental events") can be tested under the remarkably "natural" conditions of the 1963 ascent of Mt. Everest! Among the many other procedures for testing expected findings, Part IV of this book takes note of the classical experiment, and Part VI of the search for the single exception sufficient to disprove a presumed universal principle.

While particular inquiries differ in emphasizing either data or model as the mainspring of interpretation, in practice both data and model are usually interwoven in each study and the researcher works back and forth between the two. Ideally, this interweaving extends to cumulative studies that are specifically linked to interrelated ideas and propositions (cf., e.g., Hempel, 1952, p. 36; Berger et al., 1972, pp. ix-xxii). Although sociological research as yet reaches only occasionally toward such a scientific ideal, *Berger, Cohen, and Zelditch* demonstrate the potential.

Some Methodological Implications

Although selected as examples of observation, these studies should contribute also to the sorely needed general awareness of the barrier that often impedes fruitful interchange between theory and empirical research. They demonstrate that sociological understanding requires imagination and logic as well as technical skill. If there are special interpretative problems inherent in observation, in contrast to other means of assembling data, perhaps these problems derive from the "control effects" or "reactive effects" [see Part III] which, as Webb et al. point out (1966, p. 173), can interfere with ruling out rival hypotheses.

These studies also make clear that the reader cannot predict the nature of either interpretative or analytical procedures [described in Part V] from a knowledge of the data-gathering techniques. When interpretation moves from model to data, the researcher often uses systematic analysis, as in the studies by Cancian or by Drabek and Haas; alternatively, his analysis may take the form of pure description, as witness Whyte's qualitative analysis of a single case to negate the general hypothesis of the disorganization of the slum [Part I]. Conversely, when interpretation moves from data to model, many analysts proceed descriptively (e.g., Coser), but others may employ, for purposes of exploration, highly structured procedures of measurement and analysis [e.g., Short et al. in Part V].

The challenge, then, is to pursue some of the lines suggested here, to discover, try out in research, formulate, and codify general rules about interpretative procedures, and to strive for a more productive relationship of conceptual and empirical work.

4

ROSE LAUB COSER

AUTHORITY AND
DECISION MAKING IN A HOSPITAL:
A COMPARATIVE ANALYSIS

This paper presents a case analysis of the relationship between role behavior and social structure in two hospital wards. The analysis is based on daily observations made over a three-month period in the medical and surgical wards of a 360-bed research and teaching hospital on the Atlantic seaboard. Informal interviews, as well as a limited number of standardized interviews (10 each with house doctors and nurses), were used for the formulation of cues suggested by participant observation. Since only one hospital was studied, the comparisons to be made here—between the social structure of the medical team and that of the surgical team, and between the behavior of nurses on the two wards—should not be generalized beyond the case observed without further research. They are presented, however, with the aim of formulating hypotheses about the effect on role behavior of different types of authority structure in the hospital setting.

The surgical and the medical wards of this hospital were situated on two sides of the same floor, one floor each for men and women. An observer walking from one ward to the other, either on the male or on the female floor, would notice at first a superficial difference: joking as well as swearing, laughing as well as grumbling could be heard at the surgical nurses' station where some house doctors and some nurses gathered periodically. In contrast, on the medical ward the atmosphere can best be described as being more "polite." Joking and

Reprinted in part with permission from *American Sociological Review* 23 (February 1958): 56-63.

swearing were the exception; informal talk between doctors and nurses, if it occurred at all, was rare. Mainly medical students, who were not part of the formal ward organization, talked informally with nurses. On the surgical side, however, banter between doctors and nurses was a regular occurrence, and there one could also overhear from time to time a discussion between a nurse and some house doctor about a patient. Little if any of this occurred in the medical ward.

The behavior of the head nurse differed significantly on these two wards. While the medical nurse went through prescribed channels in her dealings with doctors, addressing herself to the interne whose orders she was expected to fill, the surgical nurse would talk to any doctor who was available, regardless of rank. She would more specifically ask that some decisions be made rather than trying to express her views through hints, which was the nurses' custom in the medical ward.

Moreover, in the surgical ward nurses participated much more fully in rounds than in the medical ward. . . .

In attempting to account for the different types of nurse-doctor relationship in the two wards, one could examine such factors as personality, character, and level of aspiration of the individuals. We propose, however, to discuss the phenomenon on the level of our observations, namely in terms of the network of social relations in the wards.

Social Structure of the Wards

Although the relationships in the surgical ward seemed to be easy-going, the social distance between the visiting doctor and the house doctors, and between the chief resident and those under him, was more marked among the surgeons. The contradiction between joviality and social distance was well expressed by a surgical interne; "It is not a very strict and formal atmosphere on our ward," he said, and then added: "Of course, the chief resident has everything; he's the despot, he decides who operates, so he takes the cases that he is interested in. The visiting doctor, of course, may propose to take a case over—he can overrule the chief resident."

To resolve this apparent contradiction, we must compare the

formal structure of authority with the *de facto* lines of decision-making. We will see that in the surgical ward the formal line of authority does not coincide with the actual line of decision-making; the process of decision-making, rather than the formal line of authority, apparently has an impact on the role of the nurse. . . .

[In both wards], the chief of service is responsible for the ward. He does not make any decisions for individual patients, however, but delegates his authority for the care of patients to the chief resident. The latter is responsible to the chief of service. In turn, the chief resident delegates the care of patients to the internes, each of whom is in charge of specific patients under the chief resident's continuous supervision. The internes pass on orders to the head nurse for the patients assigned to them. The assistant resident acts as supervisor and "consultant" to the internes.

The formal authority structure is essentially the same in both medical and surgical wards, with a simple organizational difference: there is no separation of tasks among the doctors for the male and female wards on the surgical side. . . . There, internes and residents walked up and down the steps to take care of their patients who were segregated by sex on two floors.

But the way in which the house doctors made use of the authority attached to their rank differed significantly in the two wards. In the medical ward, there was consistent delegation of authority down the line. The chief resident was heard saying on rounds to one or the other of the internes, "You make the final decision, he's your patient." Such remarks were not part of the pattern on the surgical ward, where the chief resident made the decisions. The medical house officers also based their decisions, to a large extent, on consensus, with the chief resident presiding and leading the discussion while the surgical house doctors received orders from the chief resident. The following incident was typical of the authority relations in the surgical ward:

An interne and an assistant resident were conversing about an incident that had transpired that morning, when the daughter of an elderly patient had created a scene at the nurse's station about the fact that she had been notified as late as the previous evening at eleven o'clock of her father's operation the next morning. When she came to see her father before the operation, he had already been taken to the operating room and the daughter was extremely upset about not being able to see him. The interne and the assistant resident felt that in the future something should be done to forestall similar reactions from patients' relatives; they thought that the chief resident was too busy to notify relatives in due time and that therefore they would take it upon themselves to notify a patient's relatives if the chief resident would give them sufficient advance notice. They decided to take up the problem with the chief resident at the next occasion, and did so that very afternoon. The chief resident's answer was curt: "I always notify the family on time," he said with an annoyed facial expression, and walked away. He did not wish to delegate authority in the matter, trivial though it may seem.

The chief resident's "despotism," to which the previously quoted interne referred, is part of the surgical ward's culture. Although his decision-making by fiat may seem, at first glance, to be a "bad habit," or due to a lack of knowledge about the advantages of delegation of authority and of agreement by consensus, it has its roots in the specific activity system of the surgical team which differs significantly from that of the medical team. We must bear in mind that responsibility for an operation, if performed by a house officer, lies with the chief resident or with the attending surgeon. They perform the important operations. As Stanton and Schwartz have pointed out, decision by consensus is time consuming. An emergency situation, in the operating room as elsewhere, is characterized precisely by the fact that a task must be performed in the minimum possible time. Whether in military operations or surgical operations, there can be no doubt about who makes decisions, that they must be made quickly and carried out unquestioningly and instantly.

The situation is quite different for the medical team. There the problems are those of diagnosis and of different possible avenues of treatment. Such problems require deliberation, and decisions are often tentative; the results of adopted therapeutic procedures are carefully observed and procedures may have to be modified in the process. All this demands careful consultation and deliberation, which are better accomplished through teamwork than through the unquestioned authority of a single person.

In his role as teacher of medical students, moreover, the person in authority teaches different lessons on the two wards: in the medical ward students and house officers are taught to think and reflect, while in the surgical ward the emphasis is on action and punctual performance. If this seems too sharp a distinction, and if it is objected that surgeons should learn to think also and medical doctors should learn to act as well, it must be borne in mind that the latter ideal situation is not always approximated, especially since the physicians themselves seem to have this image of the difference between medical and surgical men. The doctors on the medical ward, asked why they chose their field of specialization rather than surgery, said, for example: "Medicine is more of an intellectual challenge"; "I enjoy the kind of mental operation you go through"; "[Surgeons] want to act and they want results, sometimes they make a mess of it." The physicians on the surgical ward displayed a similar view of the differences between medicine and surgery and differed only concerning the value they gave the same traits. When asked why they chose to be surgeons, they said that they "like working with hands," that they "prefer something that is reasonably decisive," and that "[a medical] man probably doesn't want to work with his hands."

Thus the differences in task orientation and differences in self-images would seem to account in part for the main distinction between the two wards. This distinction can be summarized as follows: On the medical ward there is a scalar delegation of authority in a large area of decision-making, and the important decisions are generally made through consensus under the guidance of the visiting doctor or the chief resident. On the surgical ward there is little delegation of authority as far as decision-making is concerned and decisions about operations and important aspects of treatment of patients are made by fiat. . . .

The Nurse-Doctor Relationship

Under these circumstances surgical assistant residents and internes are more or less on the same level under the authority of the chief resident or the visiting doctor; this makes for a common bond between assistant residents and internes and the strengthening of internal solidarity. The relative absence of actual prestige-grading, notwithstanding the formal rank differences, as they were observed among those who were practically excluded from the decision-making process, tended to eliminate some of the spirit of competition among the junior members. Moreover, with only little authority delegated to them, they could not be consistently superior in position to the nurse. This "negative democratization," as Karl Mannheim has called it, encourages a colleague type of relationship between the nurses and doctors rather than a service relationship. Hence the banter and joking, which helped further to cancel out status differences, and the relative frequency of interaction to which we referred above.

Since authority was scarcely delegated, all house officers passed on orders to the nurse, who in turn communicated with all of them. Writing orders in the order book was not the task of internes only. This was confirmed by one of the internes who said: "Anyone on surgery writes in the order book," and the head nurse on one of the floors corroborated this situation when asked who gave her orders: "The internes, the residents also give orders, all give orders; we get orders all over the place and then you have to make your own compromise; you got to figure out what is most important."

Such a relation with the doctors puts the nurse in a strategic position. In using her own judgment about the importance of orders, she makes decisions about the care of patients, deciding to delay one action rather than another. This gives her a certain amount of power.

The position of the nurse in the surgical ward brings to mind Jules Henry's analysis of the social structure of a mental hospital. Henry discusses two types of social organization: the "pine-tree" type, in which authority is delegated downward step by step, as in the medical ward discussed above; . . . and the "oak-tree" type, in which orders come down to the same person through several channels, as in the surgical ward described here. . . . The latter type, Henry says, is a source of stresses and strains because the head nurse must follow orders coming from different directions that may or may not be compatible. This is probably true, to some extent, in the surgical ward described here, but it is accompanied by the fact that such a position gives the nurse more power and more active part in therapy.

The head nurse on the surgical floor, often facing the necessity of compromise, must know a great deal about the conditions of patients; she is constrained to contact patients frequently and to establish a closer relationship with them. This is all the more necessary since during a large part of the day, while surgery is being performed, the surgical staff is confined to the operating room with the exception of one interne on duty in the ward. The nurse must therefore be "on her toes," checking with the duty interne only if absolutely necessary, since he has his hands full. Her knowledge of the patients is thus greater than that of the nurses on the medical floor. A medical head nurse, although she tried to impress the observer with her own importance, admitted: "The nurse knows more about patients than the doctor on surgical. On the medical floor it's about even. . . . " The doctors, in turn, knowing that the nurse on the surgical floor has more contact with patients than they themselves, rely on her for information and reminders, in this way increasing her influence and decision-making role.

The doctors' expectations of the nurse differ according to ward. Asked to define a good nurse, the doctors on the surgical ward said that she should have foresight, intelligence, or that she must be a good assistant to the doctors, or that she should read. Some even noted that the same criteria apply to her as to a doctor. In contrast, the physicians on the medical ward emphasized her ability to "carry out orders" and "to do her routine work well." Only one of the medical internes declared: "Intellectual curiosity is rare but nice if you see it," thus implying that he wouldn't really expect it. Although our interviews with doctors are too few in number to draw any definite conclusions about expectations that medical doctors and surgeons have of nurses, the differences in their comments support our observations made elsewhere about some degree of autonomy and initiative among surgical nurses.

Moreover, where the rank hierarchy below the top decision-makers is not very strict and the delegation of authority not well-defined, informal relations are built across status lines. House doctors in the surgical ward sometimes abdicated their authority if they could rely on the nurse. According to a surgical nurse, "The doctors want to be called in an emergency only, if they know you and they feel you know what you're doing. . . . They let us *do* things first and then call the doctor, as long as we would keep him informed." A third-year student nurse in the surgical ward had this to say: "In this hospital we're not allowed to draw blood or give I.V. I do it occasionally but nobody knows. I do it just to help [the doctors] if there are no medical students around. . . . " Needless to say, such informal arrangements enhance the nurse's prestige and enlarge her realm of power. . . .

Ritualism or Innovation

Nurses on the surgical ward felt less tied to rules and regulations than nurses on the medical floor. This is illustrated by their reactions to the following story upon which they were asked to comment:

Interviewer: "I would like to tell you a story that happened in another hospital. An interne was called to the floor during the night to a patient who had a heart attack. He asked the nurse on the floor to get him a tank. She told him to ask an orderly. But there was no orderly around, and she still refused to get it for him. Do you think she had a right to refuse, or do you think he had the right to expect her to get it for him?"

All nurses agreed that the nurse is not supposed to leave the floor if there is no other nurse around. However, while the answers of four of the five medical nurses were unqualified (e.g., "I would never have gotten the tank, the doctor definitely should have gotten it," or "I wouldn't think of leaving the floor for a minute when I'm alone, this is unheard of"), all five surgical nurses made important qualifications (e.g., "she should have called the supervisor," or "she could have said, you keep your ears and eyes open while I get it," or "she could say, if you keep an eye open in the meantime, I'll run and get it"). In spite of the small number of respondents these figures lend support to our observations and other interview material according to which the surgical nurse is more accustomed than the medical nurse to "find a way out," to use her initiative, and is more ready to circumvent rules and regulations.

Nurses are often accused of being "ritualistic," of attaching more importance to routine and rules than to the ends for which they are designed to serve. While the nurses on the medical floor were accused fairly often by the internes of "merely clinging to rules" and "not willing or not able to think," the head nurses on the surgical floor were never the targets of such criticisms. Indeed, the surgical nurses seemed to be capable of innovation and were often relied upon by doctors to use their own judgment and to initiate action, as we have shown.

By relating the attitudes of the surgical nurses to the social structure of the ward, we have tried to confirm Merton's formulation in "Social Structure and Anomie," i.e., that "some social structures exert a definite pressure upon certain persons in the society to engage in nonconformist rather than conformist conduct." There is reason to believe that in the wards that we observed, "ritualism" or "innovation" is largely a function of the specific social structure rather than merely a "professional" or "character" trait. Nurses are often in a position in which the insistence on rules serves as a means to assert themselves and to display some degree of power. If their professional pride as well as their power and influence are enhanced by breaking through the routine, however, they seem to be ready to use informal means or to act as innovators to reach their goals.

If the relation of the nurse's position—and that of other occupational types, perhaps—to the structure of authority and decision-making is subject to the kinds of influence described in this case, problems of morale might well be considered in the light of their structural context.

5

HOWARD S. BECKER AND BLANCHE GEER

THE FATE OF IDEALISM
IN MEDICAL SCHOOL

In this paper, we attempt to describe the kind of idealism that characterizes the medical freshmen and to trace both the development of cynicism and the vicissitudes of that idealism in the course of the four years of medical training. Our main themes are that though they develop cynical feelings in specific situations directly associated with their medical school experience, the medical students never lose their original idealism about the practice of medicine; that the growth of both cynicism and idealism are not simple developments, but are instead complex transformations; and that the very notions "idealism" and "cynicism" need further analysis, and must be seen as situational in their expressions rather than as stable traits possessed by individuals in greater or lesser degree. Finally, we see the greater portion of these feelings as being collective rather than individual phenomena.

Our discussion is based on a study we are now conducting at a state medical school, in which we have carried on participant observation with students of all four years in all of the courses and clinical work to which they are exposed. We joined the students in their activites in school and after school and watched them at work in labs, on the hospital wards, and in the clinic. Often spending as much as a month with a small group of from five to fifteen students assigned to a particular activity, we came to know them well and were able to gather information in informal interviews and by overhearing the ordinary daily conversation of the group. In the

Reprinted in part with permission from *American Sociological Review* 23 (February 1958): 50-56.

course of our observation and interviewing we have gathered much information on the subject of idealism. Of necessity, we shall have to present the very briefest statement of our findings with little or no supporting evidence. . . .

The Freshmen

The medical students enter school with what we may think of as the idealistic notion, implicit in lay culture, that the practice of medicine is a wonderful thing and that they are going to devote their lives to service to mankind. They believe that medicine is made up of a great body of well-established facts that they will be taught from the first day on and that these facts will be of immediate practical use to them as physicians. They enter school expecting to work industriously and expecting that if they work hard enough they will be able to master this body of fact and thus become good doctors.

In several ways the first year of medical school does not live up to their expectations. They are disillusioned when they find they will not be near patients at all, that the first year will be just like another year of college. . . .

The freshmen are further disillusioned when the faculty tells them in a variety of ways that there is more to medicine than they can possibly learn. They realize it may be impossible for them to learn all they need to know in order to practice medicine properly. Their disillusionment becomes more profound when they discover that this statement of the faculty is literally true. . . .

. . . After a few tests have been taken, the student makes "what the faculty wants" the chief basis of his selection of what to learn, for he now has a better idea of what this is and also has become aware that it is possible to fail examinations and that he therefore must learn the expectations of the faculty if he wishes to stay in school. The fact that one group of students, that with the highest prestige in the class, took this view early and did well on examinations was decisive in swinging the whole class around to this position. The students were equally influenced to become "test-wise" by the fact that, although they had all been in the upper range in their colleges, the class average on the first examination was frighteningly low.

In becoming test-wise, the students begin to develop systems for discovering the faculty wishes and learning them. These systems are both methods for studying their texts and short-cuts that can be taken in laboratory work. . . . The interaction involved in the development of such systems and short-cuts helps to create a social group of a class which had previously been only an aggregation of smaller and less organized groups.

In this medical school, the students learn in this way to distinguish between the activities of the first year and their original view that everything that happens to them in medical school will be important. Thus they become cynical about the value of their activities in the first year. They feel that the real thing—learning which will help them to help mankind—has been postponed, perhaps until the second year, or perhaps even farther, at which time they will be able again to act on idealistic premises. They believe that what they do in their later years in school under supervision will be about the same thing they will do, as physicians, on their own; the first year had disappointed this expectation. . . .

A working consensus develops in the new consolidated group about the interpretation of their experience in medical school and its norms of conduct. This consensus, which we call *student culture*, focuses their attention almost completely on their day-to-day activities in school and obscures or sidetracks their earlier idealistic preoccupations. Cynicism, griping, and minor cheating become endemic, but the cynicism is specific to the educational situation, to the first year, and to only parts of it. Thus the students keep their cynicism separate from their idealistic feelings and by postponement protect their belief that medicine is a wonderful thing, that their school is a fine one, and that they will become good doctors.

Later Years

The sophomore year does not differ greatly from the freshman year. . . . During the third and fourth, or clinical years, teaching takes a new form. In place of lectures and laboratories, the students' work now consists of the study of actual patients admitted to the hospital or seen in the clinic. . . .

Contact with patients brings a new set of circumstances with which the student must deal. He no longer feels the great pressure created by tests, for he is told by the faculty, and this is confirmed by his daily experience, that examinations are now less important. His problems now become those of coping with a steady stream of patients in a way that will please the staff man under whom he is working, and of handling what is sometimes a tremendous load of clinical work so as to allow himself time for studying diseases and treatments that interest him and for play and family life.

The students earlier have expected that once they reach the clincal years they will be able to realize their idealistic ambitions to help people and to learn those things immediately useful in aiding people who are ill. But they find themselves working to understand cases as medical problems rather than working to help the sick and memorizing the relevant available facts so that these can be produced immediately for a questioning staff man. When they make ward rounds with a faculty member they are likely to be quizzed about any of the seemingly countless facts possibly related to the condition of the patient for whom they are "caring." . . .

The frustrations created by his position in the teaching hospital further divert the student from idealistic concerns. He finds himself low man in a hierarchy based on clinical experience, so that he is allowed very little of the medical responsibility he would like to assume. . . . The student culture accents these difficulties so that events (and especially those involving patients) are interpreted and reacted to as they push him toward or hold him back from further participation in this drama. He does not think in terms the layman might use.

As a result of the increasingly technical emphasis of his thinking the student appears cynical to the non-medical outsider, though from his own point of view he is simply seeing what is "really important." . . .

This is not to say that the students lose their original idealism. When issues of idealism are openly raised in a situation they define as appropriate, they respond as they might have when they were freshmen. But the influence of the student culture is such that questions which might bring forth this idealism are not brought up. Students are often assigned patients for examination and follow-up whose conditions might be expected to provoke idealistic crises. Students discuss such patients, however, with reference to the problems they create for the *student*: Patients with terminal diseases who are a long time dying, and patients with chronic diseases who show little change from week to week, are more likely to be viewed as creating extra work without extra compensation in knowledge or the opportunity to practice new skills than as examples of illness which raise questions about euthanasia. . . .

This apparent cynicism is a collective matter. Group activities are built around this kind of workaday perspective, constraining the students in two ways. First, they do not openly express the lay idealistic notions they may hold, for their culture does not sanction such expression; second, they are less likely to have thoughts of this deviant kind when they are engaged in group activity. The collective nature of this "cynicism" is indicated by the fact that students become more openly idealistic whenever they are removed from the influence of student culture—when they are alone with a sociologist as they near the finish of school and sense the approaching end of student life, for example, or when they are isolated from their classmates and therefore are less influenced by this culture. . . .

Their original medical idealism reasserts itself as the end of school approaches. Seniors show more interest than students in earlier years in serious ethical dilemmas of the kind they expect to face in practice. They have become aware of ethical problems laymen often see as crucial for the physician—whether it is right to keep patients with fatal diseases alive as long as possible, or what should be done if an influential patient demands an abortion—and worry about them. As they near graduation and student culture begins to break down as the soon-to-be doctors are about to go their separate ways, these questions are more and more openly discussed.

While in school, they have added to their earlier idealism a new and peculiarly professional idealism. Even though they know that few doctors live up to the standards they have been taught, they intend always to examine their patients thoroughly and to give treatment based on firm diagnosis rather than merely to relieve symptoms. This expansion and transformation of idealism appear most explicitly in their consideration of alternative careers, concerning both specialization and the kind of arrangements to be made for setting up practice. Many of their hypothetical choices aim at making it possible for them to be the kind of doctors their original idealism pictured. Many seniors consider specialty training so that they will be able to work in a limited field in which it will be more nearly possible to know all there is to know, thus avoiding the necessity of dealing in a more ignorant way with the wider range of problems general practice would present. In the same manner, they think of schemes to establish partnerships or other arrangements making it easier to avoid a work load which would prevent them from giving each patient the thorough examination and care they now see as ideal.

In other words, as school comes to an end, the cynicism specific to the school situation also comes to an end and their original and more general idealism about medicine comes to the fore again, though within a framework of more realistic alternatives. Their idealism is now more informed although no less selfless.

Discussion

We have used the words "idealism" and "cynicism" loosely in our description of the changeable state of mind of the medical student, playing on ambiguities we can now attempt to clear up. Retaining a core of common meaning, the dictionary definition, in our reference to the person's belief in the worth of his activity and the claims made for it, we have seen that this is not a generalized trait of the students we studied but rather an attitude which varies greatly, depending on the particular activity the worth of which is questioned and the situation in which the attitude is expressed.

This variability of the idealistic attitude suggests that in using such an element of personal perspective in sociological analysis one should not treat it as homogeneous but should make a determined search for subtypes which may arise under different conditions and have differing consequences. . . . The medical students can be viewed as both idealistic and cynical, depending on whether one has in mind their view of their school activities or the future they envision for themselves as doctors. Further, they might take one or another of these positions depending on whether their implied audience is made up of other students, their instructors, or the lay public.

A final complication arises because cynicism and idealism are not merely attributes of the actor, but are as dependent on the person doing the attributing as they are on the qualities of the individual to whom they are attributed. Though the student may see his own disregard of the unique personal troubles of a particular patient as proper scientific objectivity, the layman may view this objectivity as heartless cynicism.

Having made these analytic distinctions, we can now summarize the transformations of these characteristics as we have seen them occuring among medical students. Some of the students' determined idealism at the outset is reaction against the lay notion, of which they are uncomfortably aware, that doctors are money-hungry cynics; they counter this with an idealism of similar lay origin stressing the doctor's devotion to service. But this idealism soon meets a setback, as students find that it will not be relevant for awhile, since medical school has, it seems, little relation to the practice of medicine, as they see it. As it has not been refuted, but only shown to be temporarily beside the point, the students "agree" to set this idealism aside in favor of a realistic approach to the problem of getting through school. This approach, which we have labeled as the cynicism specific to the school experience, serves as protection for the earlier grandiose feelings about medicine by postponing their exposure to reality to a distance future. As that future approaches near the end of the four years and its possible mistreatment of their ideals moves closer, the students again worry about maintaining their integrity, this time in actual medical practice. They use some of the knowledge they have gained to plan careers which, it is hoped, can best bring their ideals to realization.

We can put this in propositional form by saying that when a man's ideals are challenged by outsiders and then further strained by reality, he may salvage them by postponing their application to a future time when conditions are expected to be more propitious.

6

FRANCESCA M. CANCIAN

INTERACTION PATTERNS
IN ZINACANTECO FAMILIES

In the research described below, a theory based on small group research is tested against the interaction record of ten families in Zinacantan, Mexico. Part of the theory is confirmed, indicating that some patterns of behavior are constant over cultures and types of groups. The data that do not conform to the theory are explained, in part, by the special attributes of family roles and of Zinacanteco culture.

Zinacantan is a community of about 8000 Maya Indians, located in the highlands of Chiapas, Mexico, near the Guatemalan border. About 10 per cent of the Zinacantecos live in a densely settled valley which is the ceremonial and political center of Zinacantan. The rest live in ten hamlets of varying sizes and compactness. Each hamlet contains several clusters of from two to 50 houses. "The clusters are composed mostly of patrilineally related kin. . . .

Hypotheses

The hypotheses presented below refer to a narrow segment of family life: patterns of affection, dominance and interaction rate among household members. . . . If the three dimensions are viewed in terms of self-other patterns, then common sense and previous research suggest the following hypotheses: (1) affection is responded to with

Reprinted in part with permission from *American Sociological Review* 29 (August 1964): 540-550.

affection; and (2) dominance elicits submission. The obvious hypothesis for activity is that, if time is not scarce, high interaction elicits high interaction. I did not gather the data necessary for testing this hypothesis, but my data were adequate for testing another, related hypothesis: (3) the greater the affection between two people, the higher the interaction rate.

The theory of self-other patterns also yields some interesting hypotheses about groups larger than dyads, if an additional assumption is made. The assumption is that, when two people interact, they learn both their own behavior and that of the other, and will tend to enact one of these two types of behavior with other people in similar situations. Thus, if two people are affectionate to each other, they will also be affectionate to other group members, and these others will then be affectionate to each other. If two people have a relationship of high dominance-high submission, each will be *either* highly dominant *or* highly submissive to other group members, and dyadic relations among these others will also be characterized by high dominance-high submission. The general prediction, then, is that all the dyadic relationships in a group will be the same. The specific hypotheses are that all the members of a group will exhibit: (4) the same degree of affection; (5) the same degree of dominance-submission; and (6) if time is not scarce, the same interaction rate. . . .

The Observer and the Families

I stayed in Zinacantan for a year before attempting to test the hypotheses. During this time I learned Tzotzil—the native Maya language, I also learned how to behave in a Zinacanteco household, became familiar with the norms of family life, and made friends. A year of preparation was adequate only because I could draw on the work of many other field workers in Zinacantan.

Collecting the interaction data from the ten families took three months. Most of this time was spent arranging a date for my visit when the family would be home alone and when no one was sick.

I stayed with each family for an average of four days and four nights. During this time I recorded the quality and quantity of interaction, and informally observed the family. In each household, the men and older boys were away in the lowlands harvesting corn when the data were collected. Given the time of year, it was inevitable that most of the older males would be absent. The major effect of their absence on family interaction seemed to be that the women and children were more relaxed, noisy and talkative.

I told the families that I wanted to record how the women worked and lived so that I could tell the people in my country, who didn't know how to make tortillas and weave. This explanation was generally accepted, and a few hours after I arrived the household seemed to slip back into its normal routine. I offered to pay for my food—about twice the amount it was worth—and half the families accepted the money.

The families were chosen according to predetermined criteria of household composition. Each household consisted of husband, wife and at least two children, including one child that was still nursing. Five households contained, in addition, the husband's parents. The other five households included a daughter between ten and sixteen years old, besides at least two other children. The size of the households, excluding men and older boys, varied from four to eight people.

It was difficult and time-consuming to locate households with both the appropriate composition and the willingness to let me stay with them for a few days. Therefore the sample was not randomly selected. All the families were friends of mine or of other field workers, or were relatives of these friends. The families seem to be atypical of Zinacantan in that wealthy families, residents of the two densely settled valleys, and men who speak fluent Spanish are overrepresented.

Method

In each family, I recorded the interaction rate for about nine hours, and scored the quality of interaction for a sample of about 1500 acts. The procedure for measuring interaction rate was to record how long each family dyad interacted in each of a series of five-minute periods. The presence or absence of each family member was also noted. For most families, interaction rate was recorded for nine consecutive hours. In some cases it was recorded on two separate days so as to follow the rule that each adult family member and at least one of the children should be present for at least five hours while interaction rate was being measured.

This procedure for measuring interaction rate appeared to be very satisfactory, given the technical problems encountered by one person observing and manually recording the interaction rate of as many as 28 dyads at a time.

The quality of interaction was recorded according to a category system devised by Richard Longabaugh and revised by myself. [Richard Longabaugh, "A Category System for Coding Interpersonal Behavior," *Sociometry* 26 (September 1963): 319-344.] The system contains 15 categories, formed by combining three resources (information, affection and dominance) with five modes of action (seek, give, deny, accept, reject). The resource "affection" was broadly defined to include all desired objects and behaviors except information and dominance, e.g., praise, bodily contact, food, toys. Acts were recorded by entering the initials of the initiator and recipient of each act under the appropriate category. Some acts were entered under two or more categories. . . .

In scoring the quality of interaction, each dyad was scored separately, since it was impossible to keep track of all the family members at once. For example, the interaction between mother and grandmother was scored for a certain time, then the interaction between mother and child, then between child and child. A predetermined, minimum number of acts was scored for each dyad, varying from 250 acts for "child-child" dyads, to 500 acts for "grandmother-mother" dyads. For each dyad, half of the interaction record was gathered while the dyad was off by itself, away from the other family members. The other half was gathered while the whole family was together in one group, usually at meal times: then I would record only the interaction of that dyad, and ignore the other family members.

The problems in this scoring system were no greater than in any system that demands a high degree of inference by the observer. The consistency of my scoring, however, is probably lower than in most studies, because I was working alone and did not have to communicate my criteria for classifying acts.

The three variables in the hypotheses—affection, dominance-submission and interaction rate—were operationally defined in terms of the category system and the record of interaction rate:

Affection score: Warmth from one person (P) to another (O) was defined as the percent of acts from P to O in the category "gives affection" minus the percent of acts from P to O in the category "deprives of affection." The percentages for both the affection score and the dominance-submission score were calculated on the base of the total number of acts from P to O.

Dominance-submission score: Dominance-submission from P to O was defined as the percent of acts from P to O in the category "gives dominance" plus those in the category "rejects dominance," minus "seeks dominance" and "accepts dominance." . . .

[As an example,] in Zinacanteco family groups of women and children, individuals dominate those younger than themselves. Henceforth, the dominance-submission score from the older member of a dyad to the younger will be called the *dominance score*, and the score from the younger member to the older, the *submission score*.

Interaction rate score: The interaction rate between P and O was defined as their average interaction rate score for the five-minute periods during which both were present.

The basic sample for testing the dyad hypotheses consists of 44 dyads in the ten families. . . .

Each member of every dyad was rated high or low on his affection score and on his dominance-submission score; and every dyad was rated high or low on its interaction rate score. The scores of individuals were rated high or low depending on whether they were above or below the mean for all *incumbents of that family role*. . . .

The effect of this procedure is to hold constant that part of the variation that can be attributed to role and to household composition. The hypotheses examined below thus do not refer to societal norms for family interaction nor do they refer to the effect of household types; rather, they refer to patterns of variation within these norms and types. Since these hypotheses attempt to predict behavior according to principles that apply across cultures and roles, family role and household type will be considered only to explain cases that deviate from the hypotheses. . . .

Prediction 1: If a family member, P, has a high affection score toward another family member, O, then O will have a high affection score toward P. If P has a low affection score toward O, then O will have a low affection score toward P.

The prediction is confirmed. The types of dyads with proportionately few deviant cases share two distinguishing features: (1) they consist of mother and her children; and (2) the status difference between the members of the dyad is large, compared to "daughter-child" and "grandmother-mother" dyads. Five of the six deviant cases occur among the 12 "daughter-child" and "grandmother-mother" dyads, and only one deviant case occurs among the 12 "mother-child" and "mother-daughter" dyads. . . .

TABLE 6-1.

Data For Prediction 1

		AFFECTION SCORE FROM OLDER DYAD MEMBER TO YOUNGER	
		High	Low
Affection Score	High	9	1
Younger to Older	Low	5	9

Summary and Conclusions

The interaction record of ten Indian families was used to test six hypotheses, four of which were supported.

1. The greater the affection from Person to Other, the greater the affection from Other to Person.
2. The greater the dominance from Person to Other, the greater the submission from Other to Person.
3. All the members of a group will exhibit the same degree of affection.
4. All the members of a group will exhibit the same degree of dominance-submission.

The two hypotheses on interaction rate were not supported by the data. . . .

7

THOMAS E. DRABEK AND J. EUGENE HAAS

LABORATORY SIMULATION
OF ORGANIZATIONAL STRESS

With a research focus on organizational stress, such as might be precipitated by natural disaster, an attempt was made to "bridge the gap" between the field and laboratory through "realistic simulation." Three teams of police communication room personnel participated in each of the three simulations with normal system demands. The teams then confronted system stress through a simulated disaster. Changes in team performance patterns under stress appeared related to strains existent in the system prior to stress and to incompatabilities between system structure and emergent system demands. Among the most important changes in group structure which increased system capacity was the gradual emergence of a display mechanism whereby intra-team activity became more shared.

. . . With a research focus on organizational stress such as might be precipitated by natural disaster, we began a research program in which we attempted to "bridge the gap" between the field and laboratory in the study of social systems. A research technique emerged which was labeled "realistic simulation." [Thomas E. Drabek and J. Eugene Haas, "Realism in Laboratory Simulation: Myth or Method?" *Social Forces* 45 (March 1967): 337-346.] Just as aerodynamics engineers use models (simulates) in wind tunnels (environment) to study aircraft design (theory) under varying environmental conditions, replica organizations can also be subjected to environmental change to test organizational theory. . . . Following a brief outline of some of the more relevant aspects of the conceptual framework by which the present research was guided, we will describe the simulation of the communication system of a metropolitan police organization and

Reprinted in part with permission from *American Sociological Review* 34 (April 1969): 223-238.

the types of findings which emerged when this system was subjected to stress.

Conceptual Framework

We define an organization as a relatively permanent and relatively complex interaction system. . . . As such, organizations are viewed as "open systems" in constant interaction with environmental elements which greatly vary in stability. When organizational incumbents are observed over a prolonged period of time, patterns in interaction can be noted. These interaction patterns, among organizational incumbents, as well as between incumbents and environmental elements, e.g., other organizations or "the public-at-large," are referred to as the performance structure. For analytical purposes organizational performance structures are viewed as being composed of a complex and interrelated set of processes such as task, communication, decision-making, and the like.

Three constructs are used to explain why these interaction patterns recur over time: normative structure, interpersonal structure and resource structure. Although these structures can be used to account for relatively stable behavior patterns, organizations, like all interaction systems, do change. And many types of system change can be explained by two additional constructs—strain and stress.

Organizational strain is defined as inconsistencies or discrepancies among structural elements. Many types of strains exist at varying levels in all organizations. We hypothesize that knowledge of strain can be used to explain certain types of organizational change. . . .

Organizational stress is the organizational state or condition indicated by the degree of discrepancy between organizational demands and capacity. Stress is viewed as a continuous variable and refers to the *state of the system* rather than to sets of stimuli or response patterns. Changes in either demands, capacity, or both, may alter the level of stress.

While this framework is viewed as applicable to all types of organizations, the interrelationships between these concepts can be illustrated most easily by analysis of extreme and sudden environmental change. For example, following community disasters, emergency organizations will confront sharp increases in demands and may simultaneously experience reduced capacity through the loss of personnel and/or vital equipment such as telephone service. Thus, disaster *per se* is not the source of stress, but rather it is the increase in the discrepancy between organizational demands and capacity which produces the condition of high stress.

The general hypothesis which emerges from this framework is, if there is organizational stress, then there will be change in organizational performance structure. In a global way the hypothesis was supported by field data. As organizations attempted to cope with sudden change in demands and capacity brought about by disaster, certain changes in performance structure occurred. For example, following the 1964 Alaska earthquake, the decision-making process was significantly modified in such organizations as the Anchorage Public Works Department. Many decisions were made at much lower levels than they would have been normally. Lines of authority were "breached" as upper echelon officials went directly to specialists or foremen for current information and advice. Similarly, many items were purchased without official authorization as ways of "cutting the red tape" were sought. Thus, using the concept of organizational capability, one can meaningfully interpret such coping behavior. That is, to meet emergent demands, alternative design structures were sought with greater capacities. However, most organizations lack adequate means to assess the consequences of their coping efforts. Hence, increased capacity often results, but the changes are erratic and often contradictory.

While numerous hypotheses were generated from this framework, many of which [were] supported by field data, our attempt was to devise a method whereby organizational stress might be studied in the laboratory. We hoped that the laboratory setting would precipitate increased conceptual precision and generate new hypotheses which could then be tested in the field.

Methodology

Upon trying to "bridge the gap" between the field and laboratory, we confronted the "realism" issue. Details of our analysis of this argument have been reported elsewhere (Drabek and Haas, 1967). In brief, we attempted to recast previous discussion by asking "What is it that makes an experiment, 'realistic'?" Pursuit of this question led us to conclude that synthesis of laboratory research could be accomplished only by recognizing that different relationships may exist between variables if tested under different experimental conditions. We concluded further that the "degree of realism" could be used as a means of identifying experimental characteristics.

This analysis also led to the identification of the major characteristics of a laboratory technique labeled "realistic simulation." In essence, this method requires: (1) a "real" group; (2) that this group be assigned tasks identical to those it normally encounters; (3) in a setting where ecological relationships are maintained; as well as (4) an environment, both physical and symbolic, identical to that with which the organization normally interacts; and finally, (5) subjects must not be aware that they are in an experiment. . . . Since different relationships may exist between variables under different sets of experimental conditions, interpretation of results will be more meaningful if comparisons are restricted to tests conducted under similar experimental conditions, at least until a more adequate knowledge of the effects of these variables is obtained.

The communication system of a metropolitan police department was selected as the system to be simulated. All three shifts of personnel from the police "radio room" participated in each of the three laboratory sessions in which demands were identical to what the system normally experienced (Sessions A, B, and C). These sessions were followed by a "stress" Session D, in which demands on the system were markedly changed through a simulated crash of a large jet aircraft into an apartment house complex. All twelve sessions were two hours each in length, including minimal time for orientation and debriefing. To prevent contamination, each shift received identical "exposure" on the same days.

Since the radio room teams were the key component of the communication system, they were isolated as the central objects of study. Simulation of the system then required construction of three additional elements: (1) construction of a physical facility that would function identically to the resource structure which characterized the teams' "natural habitat"; (2) duplication of the complex demand environment which provided input for team activity; and (3) establishment of apparatus with which to record team activity.

Prolonged observation of the police communication system easily permitted construction of a laboratory replica of the resource structure (see Figure 7-1). Recording of all interaction was rather easily accomplished given available facilities. All oral interaction was recorded on a 24-track audio tape recorder. Two television cameras were used interchangeably to video tape behavior of officers. After the experiment, additional data were collected through questionnaires, group debriefing sessions, and individual interviews.

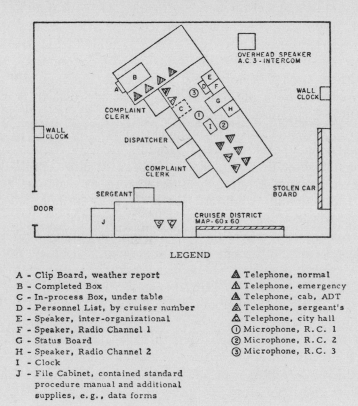

LEGEND

A - Clip Board, weather report
B - Completed Box
C - In-process Box, under table
D - Personnel List, by cruiser number
E - Speaker, inter-organizational
F - Speaker, Radio Channel 1
G - Status Board
H - Speaker, Radio Channel 2
I - Clock
J - File Cabinet, contained standard
     procedure manual and additional
     supplies, e.g., data forms

⚠ Telephone, normal
⚠ Telephone, emergency
⚠ Telephone, cab, ADT
⚠ Telephone, sergeant's
⚠ Telephone, city hall
① Microphone, R.C. 1
② Microphone, R.C. 2
③ Microphone, R.C. 3

FIGURE 7-1. *Laboratory design of simulated radio room.*

Duplication of the police team's environment was far more difficult. First, the basic communication flow was identified as follows: (1) outside caller reports incident; (2) complaint clerk secures and records necessary data using police code; (3) data form is passed to dispatcher who locates and assigns an appropriate cruiser; (4) data are transmitted to cruiser in code language; (5) data form is filed in "in-process" box; (6) after incident is "cleared," cruiser officer relays the type of disposition to dispatcher; and (7) dispatcher records disposition and then returns the data form to a complaint clerk who files it in the "completed" box. While much variation is possible, this pattern frequently occurs with little deviation. Prolonged observation was necessary to understand deviant patterns, e.g., robbery reports which activate notification of superior officers within the Uniform Division and the Detective Bureau. Direct observation was supplemented by: (1) analyzing training manuals; (2) listening to recorded radio and telephone police communication; and (3) observing in other areas of the organization.

Simulators were trained to activate positions of cruiser operators and telephone callers using language which police officers were familiar with and accustomed to. Thus, input calls and radio messages were entirely realistic. Calls were designed to correspond to police statistics as to the type of event, day of week, time of day, sex of caller, and geographical location of event. Since simulators had to "ad-lib" much of the telephone conversations, basic data were provided on each call as to who they were, address, phone number, nearby objects of identification, nature of complaint, etc. Recordings of actual police telephone conversations were invaluable in simulator training and constructing the 990 calls required for the three normal sessions. A total of over 900 other calls were constructed for the stress session to produce a sudden and extreme demand increase. These were largely based on recordings of telephone calls obtained from police departments in cities which recently had experienced large scale disasters. Cruiser simulators were similarly trained through the use of recorded police radio communication. For each call fed into the system, cruiser simulators had instructions as to how and when to report their actions. Inter-organizational communication, which was especially crucial during the stress session, was conducted by staff members who had recently interviewed officials at all major emergency organizations in the area. Lists of available extra-organizational equipment and personnel were constructed so that, during the simulation, police officers were forced to work within the constraints present in the community. Activities of all of these components were synchronized with a master script so that each simulator knew his assigned responsibilities at each instant. Physical placement of the police officers, simulators, recording equipment, and the like, is diagramed in Figure 7-2.

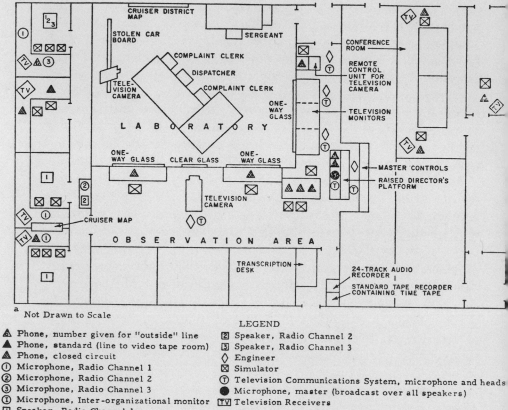

a Not Drawn to Scale

LEGEND

⚠ Phone, number given for "outside" line
▲ Phone, standard (line to video tape room)
⚠ Phone, closed circuit
① Microphone, Radio Channel 1
② Microphone, Radio Channel 2
③ Microphone, Radio Channel 3
① Microphone, Inter-organizational monitor
⑪ Speaker, Radio Channel 1

② Speaker, Radio Channel 2
③ Speaker, Radio Channel 3
◇ Engineer
⊠ Simulator
Ⓣ Television Communications System, microphone and heads
● Microphone, master (broadcast over all speakers)
📺 Television Receivers

FIGURE 7-2. *Total facility: design and personnel placement.*

These procedures produced a simulation which was an exact replica of the police communication system. All five of the criteria previously mentioned as identifying "realistic simulation" were met. A variety of data suggested that the "simulate" behaved exactly as its real counterpart in the non-stress sessions. Thus, behavior observed in the laboratory matched that which had been observed in police headquarters. In debriefing interviews, officers consistently indicated that they were unaware of any instances in which their work activity was modified by the simulation. Of course, to what degree their laboratory behavior under stress corresponded to their reaction to a stress event in their natural work setting remains problematic. However, at the time of the simulation, officers were unaware that they were in any type of a "stress experiment." Afterwards they expressed opinions that if they had been confronted with a similar event while at police headquarters, their behavior probably would have been identical to that exhibited in the laboratory. However, all emphasized that future behavior patterns would be slightly different, because of what they had learned through the simulation experience. In short, we concluded, as did the officers, that the behavior observed in the laboratory during normal and stress sessions was what would have been observed in the acutal police radio room if the same demands had been confronted.

Findings

WAS THERE ORGANIZATIONAL STRESS?

Organizational stress was defined as the state or condition indicated by the degree of discrepancy between organizational demands and capacity. A simulated plane crash was used to generate a sudden demand change along three axes: quantity, quality, and priority. The program was so constructed that the rate of call input could be raised from an average of two calls per minute to twenty-one calls per minute; i.e., it was felt that seven calls per minute per person answering would be more than enough to overload the system. Since only 21 percent of the total 1155 calls prepared for the stress period were processed by the "best" team, it was clear that the program was adequate. Yet, to what extent did the discrepancy between demands and capacity change? What was the level of organizational stress? . . .

Two types of strategies were used to derive indicators of stress. The first method was "indirect." . . . Telephone caller simulators recorded the number of seconds between the time they completed dialing a number and when an officer answered. Thus, the "lag time" was the time between a phone ringing (demand presented) and it being answered which was the first action required to meet it. If no answer was obtained within three minutes, simulators hung up and recorded a "No Answer" beside the call number. These were demands presented to the system which were never met. They . . . somewhat reflect the degree to which the demands exceeded the capacity of the system. . . . The "lag time" greatly increased during the high stress Session D. It can be concluded that the system was under greater stress during that period. . . .

The second approach used to assess stress levels was to devise crude indices for demands and capacity. There were three sources through which demands could reach the system: telephone, radio, and intercom. The number of demands at the end of a given period of time would be the sum originating from each source. . . .

Organizational capacity was defined as the maximum level of task or subtask performance that can be relatively sustained over time with a specified structural design. Team performance was indexed by assessing the number of demands which were met. Demands requiring action beyond that in the initial input exchange were not considered met until all necessary activity had been completed. For example, a call reporting a serious automobile accident was not considered "met" until a cruiser had been dispatched. Similarly, if the cruiser simulator reported back that an ambulance or wrecker was required, that demand was not considered met until the dispatcher made the actual assignment via radio. . . .

More intense organizational stress, as expressed by the increased discrepancy between demands and the projected team capacity (based on performance in Sessions A, B, and C), is evident in Session D. . . . Also noted during Session D was a sharp increase in the performance level.

Our next question then emerges: What, if any, structural changes occurred to permit these groups to increase their capacity under increased stress?

DID THE PERFORMANCE STRUCTURE CHANGE?

Organizational performance structure refers to patterning in interaction sequences. These interaction patterns become the central object of study when organizations are viewed as interaction systems. While performance structures may be conceptualized as several interrelated processes, three appeared most relevant to the analysis of this communication subsystem: (1) communication; (2) task; and (3) decision-making. Analysis was focused on each of these three areas guided by the general hypothesis that a change in performance structure follows an increase in organizational stress period.

Among the changes in the communication processes that we anticipated would occur as the degree of stress increased were: (1) increases in the *rates* of internal and external interaction; and (2) change in the *patterns* of internal and external interaction.

Data clearly indicated that internal interaction, i.e., among the officers in the laboratory, changed in both rate and pattern. Rate of internal interaction was assessed by counting: (1) number of interaction sequences in each session; and (2) number of words per minute. . . .

Pattern change occurred in several ways. First, it was suspected that the mode of interaction would be altered; i.e., fewer written communications would occur during the simulated disaster. This conclusion was supported. . . . Second, it was thought that initiator-receiver patterns would change, although the directions remained unspecified. Data . . . indicated little change in the receiver pattern. The dispatcher was the major receiver during both normal and stress session. However, the initiator pattern . . . changed sharply. The sergeant consistently emerged as the major initiator during high stress in all three groups.

Two types of external systems for the communication team must be differentiated: (1) other officers within their police organization; and (2) officials in other organizations whose activities become highly interdependent with the police during community disasters. The rate of team-initiated interaction with other members of their organization did not appear to increase under stress, using number of interaction sequences per minute as the index. . . . However, this may have been due largely to the volume of radio traffic generated by the simulators designed to overload the system. But there was a major change in the pattern of this interaction which was clearly revealed by using number of words per minute as an index. . . . Thus, although the number of interaction sequences initiated by the teams did not increase during stress, the length of these interactions increased sharply.

Team-initiated interaction with external organizations (inter-organizational) greatly increased during the simulated disaster. . . . Calls were placed to other police organizations, e.g., state police, county sheriff's office, and suburban units; ambulance firms; hospitals; and a variety of private organizations, as officers attempted in a small way to coordinate the massive resources available in the community. Thus, it was clear that the communication processes, both internal and external, greatly changed as the level of stress increased.

We hypothesized that response to the simulated disaster would result in increased *rates* of task performance and rather substantial changes in the *patterns* of task performance. As indicated earlier in the discussion of group capacity, during the high stress session performance of all groups increased. One specific measure of task performance was the number of calls answered per minute. . . . All three groups increased their rate of task performance during the high stress Session D.

As output levels increased three important changes in the pattern of task performance occurred. First, officers reduced the average length of time for telephone conversations. . . . Second, they increasingly limited their activity to following up calls that were of highest priority. The simulation program was so designed that routine requests continued at a normal rate during the disaster. However, cruisers were dispatched to relatively few of these requests during Session D. . . . And when cruisers were dispatched, it was only for incidents of the highest priority, e.g., personal injury auto accidents, a cutting, shooting, and the like.

Third, and finally, officers sought out alternative modes of task accomplishment. This was done in two principal ways: (1) Many callers were encouraged to handle the request themselves even in some extreme emergencies. For example, detailed instructions were given to a rather frantic mother who had just spilled hot grease all over her young son. The officer explained that ambulances were not available, gave explicit first aid instructions, and suggested that she find a neighbor to provide transportation. (2) And somewhat implied in the above example, officers "expanded" their organization by calling upon external resources availabile in the community. Frequency of team-initiated inter-organizational interaction was previously [reported]. Many of these efforts were aimed at mobilizing organizational action which would hopefully meet specific demands made on the police. All of these findings were interpreted as supporting the more general hypothesis that as the degree of organizational stress increases, task processes will change.

Decision-making processes also changed during the response to the simulated disaster. Under normal demand loads, each officer functioned rather autonomously. Complaint clerks received requests through telephones, evaluated the requests, and then wrote cruiser request cards for the dispatcher when required by the call. However, during Session D, officers began to ask each other for information before making decisions as to how to handle calls. . . . Thus, there was a much greater rate of consultation before decisions were made.

This consultation pattern changed greatly under increased stress.

Of all requests for information received in normal sessions, about one-third were made by dispatchers. During the simulated disaster, the proportion of information requests by dispatchers decreased dramatically in all three groups. . . . In contrast, sergeants, who accounted for about one-fifth of all information requests normally, increased their requests to about one-third of the total. Dispatchers also consistently demonstrated a further pattern change in the position to which information requests were directed. Nearly all such requests by dispatchers were directed to complaint clerks in sessions A, B, and C. In session D, most dispatcher requests for information were directed to sergeants. . . . These data were interpreted as supporting the hypothesis that change in decision-making processes would occur when there was increased organizational stress.

In summary, hypotheses related to communication, task, and decision-making processes strongly supported the general hypothesis that when there is organizational stress, change in performance structure will occur. Why did these changes occur and not others? This question will be briefly explored in a discussion of the experimental results.

Discussion

It should be emphasized at the outset that the communication system did continue to function under stress. In fact, in comparison to the kinds of changes which occurred in the simulated environment, the police system changed little. . . . Normally the system was an efficient "pipe line," and it did permit officers to cope reasonably well during the simulated disaster. However, there were changes in the performance structure and they were not random or unrelated.

The conceptual framework, which was outlined briefly at the outset, suggests some helpful interpretations as to why the coping behavior of these groups assumed the forms observed. The concept of organizational strain was emphasized. We have hypothesized that as the degree of organizational stress increases, performance structure change will vary directly with the intensity and location of organizational strain. There were two major types of strain in the communication system under normal demand loads, and many of the changes which occurred under stress appear to be directly related to them.

The resource structure emphasized a functional division of labor, i.e., complaint clerks were to receive telephone calls, and dispatchers were to communicate with cruisers. An offical norm prohibiting oral communication with the dispatcher was mildly enforced so that cruiser radio messages would not be missed. In fact, some consideration had been given by police officials in designing a new facility in which dispatchers would be physically separated from complaint clerks. This idea was based on a highly mechanical analysis of the functioning of the system. If separated, then each position incumbent would not be "impaired" by "irrelevant noise." Yet, oral communication did take place. Usually this interaction was directed at providing additional information which did not appear on the dispatch cards. Furthermore, given the ecological arrangement of equipment in use at the time, the complaint clerks could and did consistently observe the dispatcher's status board which indicated cruiser availability. The handling of the public's requests was directly affected by this information source. For example, if all cruisers in the geographical area where the call was placed were busy, complaint clerks might try to handle the call themselves by encouraging the caller to solve his own problem, interrogating the caller in detail so as to better assess call priority, suggesting that the police were very busy right then and requesting the caller to call back if the situation got worse, etc.

What was lacking in the resource structure was any type of "display" mechanism whereby information arriving through telephone, radio, and intercom could be shared more efficiently. Oral interaction among the officers, viewed as undesirable and unnecessary, partially performed this latent function. Also, officers demonstrated an uncanny ability to engage in telephone conversation and ascertain police activity by simultaneously "listening in" on the radio exchanges and segments of telephone conversations of other complaint clerks and sergeants.

During the simulated disaster (Session D), the large increase in information requiring processing and qualitative changes in the types of information being fed into the system, greatly intensified the need for the "display function." The strain existed at time one, but a partial solution had evolved over time. Under increased stress, many of the observed changes in performance structure were directly related to this area of strain. Emergence of the sergeants as major initiators of oral interaction and the chief receivers of information requests from dispatchers was discussed above. Thus, sergeants moved to the center of the team, received information from all sources, and dispersed it among the team members. Officers were now too busy with their immediate responsibilities to "listen-in" on other conversations. Such activity was further curbed as the noise level greatly increased due to the almost continuous simultaneous interaction. Yet, each officer needed information obtained by other team members, as to emergent traffic patterns, hospital loads, extra-organizational items required at the scene such as blood, and specialized equipment. Initial actions by sergeants were to assist complaint clerks in answering phones. Often, when backlogs occurred, they would assist for a few minutes until the team caught up. In Session D, sergeants gradually became attached to the dispatcher and performed the display function which became increasingly critical as the simulated disaster progressed. Keeping track of cruiser status became increasingly difficult for the dispatcher alone. Availability of extra-organizational personnel and equipment further complicated his task. Also, messages to or from extra-organizational officials were circulated through the police system, which gradually emerged as the major communication system for the total community.

A second source of strain during normal sessions was the code language used. Types of events had code numbers, e.g., auto-accident, 10-4; personal injury auto-accident, 10-5. Often additional information was needed to supplement address and code for type of event. This is not to suggest that the code did not increase communication effectiveness as it clearly did. However, unusual events required additional explanation, which was often too cumbersome to write on the back of a cruiser dispatch card.

Many of the findings reported above can be interpreted as being related to the inappropriateness of the police code during the simulated disaster. For example, . . . the length of interactions between the communication teams and other organizational members increased in Session D. Computation of the number of words used in such interactions specifically indicated that such exchanges were longer. As might be suspected, this was directly due to the general decrease in code usage during Session D. . . . Written communication, highly dependent upon code usage, dramatically decreased during Session D. . . . Thus, the qualitative demand change curtailed the use of one of the most important resources—the police code. Many of the observed changes in group structure can be directly related to this source of strain which remained relatively unimportant under normal demand requirements, but which became crucial during the simulated disaster.

In summary, we have described our efforts to use "realistic simulation" as a method to study system stress. While the method is clearly no panacea, it remains relatively unexplored and appears to possess much potential. Drawing upon a general theoretical framework, crude indices were constructed for the measurement of organizational stress. The general hypothesis was supported: as the degree of organizational stress increases, there will be change in organizational performance structures. And the location of these changes often appeared to be directly related to strains in the system prior to increased stress. Of course, these substantive findings should be viewed as suggestive since only three experimental groups were used. While probably not relevant to all or even most types of organizations, these findings do offer much insight into how information processing centers may change under stress.

8

RICHARD M. EMERSON

MOUNT EVEREST: A CASE STUDY OF COMMUNICATION FEEDBACK AND SUSTAINED GROUP GOAL STRIVING

In the spring of 1963, the American Mount Everest Expedition launched the first serious American effort to climb the world's highest peak. Most of the research conducted on such expeditions has focused either upon the novel environment or upon physiological adaptation to high altitude. Since the opportunities for behavioral study have been relatively neglected, this expedition chose to emphasize psychology and sociology along with physiology, forming an integrated core of human studies.

This study was designed to examine the plausibility of a theory of group effort as a self-maintaining system, in a natural field setting. The research was conducted on Mount Everest in the hope that relevant principles would be thrown into bold relief in such an adverse environment, during a prolonged and effectively isolated group effort. The particulars of mountaineering and its "special" motivation provided a vehicle for the study, but were otherwise irrelevant.

Theory: Group Goal Striving as a Self-maintaining System

The theoretical basis of the study builds upon principles concerning "level of aspiration." In general, it has been shown that success

Reprinted in part with permission from *Sociometry* 29 (September 1966): 213-227.

experienced at time 1 is associated with increased level of aspiration at time 2; and conversely, experienced failure is associated with decrease in aspiration level. . . .

Most of these findings can be handled under a single principle: *goals tend to be defined in regions of uncertain outcome*. Changes in aspiration level become a special case involving goal redefintion. Success reduces uncertainty, and goals are redefined upward into a region of uncertain goal outcome. Failure likewise reduces uncertainty, and goals are redefined downward, again into a region of uncertainty.

This interpretation of level of aspiration studies suggests that *uncertainty about goal outcome* might be a crucial variable relating to sustained group goal striving. At the same time, uncertainty should be a function of patterns of selective communication in group problem solving. If so, this concept will provide an important theoretical link between distinctly psychological and distinctly social processes.

MOTIVATION IN PROBLEM-SOLVING GROUPS

We begin by specifying three psychological variables along which group members can be described.

Goal-oriented motivation (M). It is assumed that at any point in time each member of a group has some degree of motivation toward a group goal. Such motivation is assumed to be a dispositional property, and it is assumed to vary across relatively large time periods.

Energy mobilization (E). At any point in time each group member is assumed to have some proportion of his available energy mobilized in immediate goal-relevant behavior, be it action, thought, or fantasy. E is not a dispositional property, and it is assumed to vary across relatively short time periods.

Uncertainty of goal outcome (U). It is assumed that at any point in time each group member can provide a subjective probability estimate of eventual success or failure. Uncertainty (U) can vary toward certainty of success (optimism) or toward certainty of failure (pessimism). U is assumed to be a cognitive state reflecting an assessment of the environment, including group resources. Hence, U is thought to be a function of goal-relevant *information* obtained through perception and communication.

Drawing upon our reasoning about level of aspiration, these three variables can be organized into a miniature theory of goal striving and environmental assessment:

Hypothesis 1. M fixes the upper limit of E, as a necessary but not sufficient condition for E.

Hypothesis 2. M varies directly with U over long time periods. (Prolonged certainty of *either* success or failure reduces goal-oriented motivation. Prolonged uncertainty increases or maintains motivation.)

Hypothesis 3. E varies directly with U over short time periods, holding M constant and greater than zero.

This system of task-motivation places uncertainty about goal outcome in a most strategic position. Being an assessment of the environment, it opens motivation to environmental influence, linking information input with motivation and energy output. Furthermore, it opens the motivation system to influence from group processes, for much of the information input may be selectively amplified or dampened by patterns of communication. Our theory thus moves to a social level, focusing upon the selective flow of information in communication processes.

ROLE-RELATIONS AND SELECTIVE COMMUNICATION

A sharp distinction can be made between "group norms" and "role prescriptions." Behavior which must be performed by *all* members in order to maximize the likelihood of group goal-achievement tends to become the content of group norms. By contrast, behavior which moves all members toward goal-achievement when performed *only* by *one* or some members, tends to become the content of role prescriptions. Such behavior will be valued when performed by someone, but devalued if additional persons perform it. Thus, it appears that the division of labor in role-relations evolves around a broad principle: the reduction of *behavioral redundance* in collective effort.

It is clear that task-oriented or goal-relevant communication should follow this principle. The goal-relevant information selected for communication in group problem solving should avoid informational or *implicational redundancy*. Thus, we suggest that group goal-oriented communication is often organized as a communicator-communicatee role-relation, with implicit social expectations: "When you assume the role of communicator, provide *new* information at least, and *new implication* if possible." Finally, it seems intuitively

93

reasonable that such implict role-expectations should be evoked primarily under conditions of high task motivation in the group.

Given these guiding hunches, specific hypotheses concerning selective communication can be established. Any item of information which implies eventual success will be labeled "optimistic" and information implying eventual failure will be called "pessimistic" information.

Hypothesis 4. When the environment contains predominantly optimistic (pessimistic) information, initiating communication will contain predominantly pessimistic (optimistic) information, holding M constant and greater than zero.

Hypothesis 5. Reactive communication will involve predominantly negative feedback, holding M constant and greater than zero (i.e., an optimistic or pessimistic statement will evoke a pessimistic or optimistic reply, respectively).

Hypothesis 6. The strength of the relations in Hypotheses 4 and 5 varies directly with M.

Hypotheses 1 through 6 describe group goal striving as a self-maintaining system, partially independent of environmental events, and with role-relations in communication playing a strategic part. The system is open at two important points. First, some initial motivation is assumed, and therefore competing motives involving alternative goals might intervene. Second, the system is open to goal-relevant information received directly from the environment rather than through communication. Hypotheses 4 and 5 describe communication processes which counteract environmentally provided information. Hence, this self-maintaining system will tend to "tighten" as members become increasingly dependent upon, or attentive to, one another as sources of information.

The Research Setting

Expeditionary mountaineering provides an ideal setting for this research for a variety of reasons. Most important, member motivation is initially very high, yet the endeavor can drag out over a long time period, during which sustaining processes can be studied. The environment is not only problematic but exceedingly punishing as well, pressing hard against the climber's will to continue. High altitude alone exacts a very heavy toll from a person's energy and resources, both physical and mental. Thus, goal-oriented motivation and social processes which might sustain it must compete with powerful opponents in this setting.

After a 30-day march of about 180 miles through the mountains of Nepal, the ascent of Everest began at the mountain's base, at an elevation just under 18,000 feet. The team consisted of Western mountaineers and Nepalese-Tibetan Sherpas. The role of the Sherpa in this team did not include policy, strategy, or decision making to any important degree. All Western climbers did participate in these functions in varying degrees, with principal responsibility in the hands of a designated leader and subgroup leaders.

The ascent began with a complex and dangerous operation moving supplies up through an "ice fall" for about 2000 vertical feet. This ice fall descends from a high glacial basin at 21,500 feet, tightly enclosed among three major peaks (Everest, 29,028 feet; Lhotse, 27,890 feet; Nuptse, 25,850 feet). A heavily supplied advance base camp (Camp 2) was located in this basin at 21,500 feet providing access to several potential expedition goals.

SOME PARTICIPANT OBSERVATIONS

This study differs from traditional case-field studies in three important ways: (1) a specific set of hypotheses was fully formulated before entering the field; (2) field observations of the behavior of specific subjects were hampered by restrictions upon personnel movements on the mountain; and (3) unstructured participant observation might be even less reliable than usual, due to intense environmental stress, including anoxia. For these reasons, an effort was made to adapt more structured research procedures for use in this field situation, as a supplement to participant observation. Before reporting the more structured techniques used, some participant observations relevant to our hypotheses regarding group goals are in order.

The summit of Everest could be approached via the *South Col*, the route successfully used by a British and by a Swiss expedition. This known and tested route clearly gave the greatest assurance of success on Everest. In addition, Camp 2 might provide access to the little known, but assuredly difficult, *West Ridge* of Everest. Finally, both Lhotse and Nuptse could be approached from this camp. Thus, from Camp 2 the Expedition could distribute or concentrate its resources across any combination of these four potential goals. The most *uncertain* of these was clearly the *West Ridge*.

When climbers were invited to join this expedition, its stated objectives were *Nuptes, Lhotse* and Everest by the *South Col.* The *West Ridge* of Everest was not involved. Some members had given private thought to the West Ridge before leaving for Nepal. However, once the team was together and members could communicate, the West Ridge (WR) became an increasingly frequent and engaging topic of group discussion. By the time the expedition had moved 20 days along its march toward the mountain, the WR had a firm hold on the climbers' imaginations; Lhotse and Nuptse had drifted to peripheral interest; and the group had formed into two teams, one for the WR and one for the South Col route on Everest. During this period there was lively exchange of opinion and information about the WR, but no new information could be added to the pool. The emerging motivation for the WR can be seen in a special request radioed back to civilization, asking to have a particular book (which might contain photos of the WR) sent on to the group by runner! A reconnaissance of the WR was planned and placed *first* on the climbing agenda.

To a participant observer, there can be little doubt but that uncertain outcome combined with group interaction played a very large part in mobilizing member motivation for the WR.

Even so, the South Col approach to Everest remained the first goal. A heavily sponsored expedition to climb Mt. Everest had to climb that mountain, one way or another, if at all possible, and consequently the South Col had to have first priority in expedition policy. In addition, any WR effort, splitting the group's resources as it would (and did), could not be allowed to jeopardize the Col endeavor. But the WR aroused too much enthusiasm to be ignored, and conflict became a built-in feature of the expedition. The expedition leaders will testify to the problems encountered in trying to manage the "pathological motivation" of the WR Team, whose undertaking was seen as a potential threat to overall expedition commitments if it should be pursued *too* vigorously.

With the above observation as background, communication within and between teams will be examined using more structured data.

SUBJECTS

The group under study consisted of 19 Western climbers working as a team (18 subjects and a participant observer). This group was divided into the WR Team and the Col Team, the division having formed through personal choice. The WR Team began with six climbers, including the investigator. One was killed in an ice-fall avalanche early in the climb, leaving five members, *four* of whom are subjects in the study. The Col Team, as defined here, consists of a core of five American climbers, comparable with the WR Team in size and involvement in the climbing process. The remaining members served largely with the Col Team in various roles more marginal to the climbing process. They are classified together in this study as the *Peripheral* Group. Inadequate data were obtained from one of these, the only non-American member, and Dr. Lester [the Expedition psychologist] was not viewed as a subject, due to his role in psychological research. Thus, we have 15 subjects: Col Team, 5; WR Team, 4; and Peripheral, 6.

RESEARCH DESIGN

The research was designed as a longitudinal case study. Data were obtained from February 20 through May 22, 1963, when the WR Team reached the summit, a period of 92 days covering a 30-day approach march and a 62-day assault on the mountain. An important phase ended after the seventieth day, when the Col Team succeeded in reaching the summit. The demanding conditions to be encountered during the assault phase required that research procedures be woven into normal expedition routine as unobtrusively as possible. As a result, research procedures were organized into four data-gathering routines which could be committed largely to habit.

1. *The diary routine.* Subjects were provided a specially prepared diary book for personal use as well as research recording. Each pair of facing pages was allocated for one day's entries. Some of the questions occured every day. For example, "Tomorrow I (should, will, would like to) _____." (Illustrative responses would be "*should*: carry a load to Camp 3," or "*would like to*: sack out another day.") This item was designed to tap E, energy mobilization. Some items occurred every second day, such as subjective probability estimates of success or failure on each objective. Still other items occurred every fourth or eighth day, whereupon the cycle repeated itself throughout the diary book.

2. *The stimulus-statement routine.* Working as a participant observer, the investigator inserted "stimulus-statements" into natural discussion with individual subjects and recorded the immediate

feedback he received, either on tape or in field notes. After the opportunity to make such a statement occurred, the statement itself was then designed in context to convey either *optimistic* or *pessimistic* information. The number of each type was balanced for each subject and approximately alternated in sequence.

The design called for equal frequencies of stimulus-statements across subjects, but this proved impossible in the field, due to personnel movements on the mountain. Subjects were to remain unaware of this procedure, and postexpedition discussions, as well as behavior at the time, indicate that subjects were not cognizant of this method.

3. *Recorded group discussion.* Tape recordings were made of group planning sessions, reconnaissance reports, and smaller "bull sessions" where possible. Technical difficulties with recorders and battery power at low temperatures (almost constantly below freezing and frequently well below zero) severely hampered this routine.

4. *Recorded radio communications.* A Walkie Recordall with voice activated on-off control succeeded in recording all inter-camp communication semi-automatically. Unfortunately, the amount of radio communication devoted to environmental assessment was very small. The demands of logistic co-ordination through radio contact left little room for the kind of communication of interest in this study.

Results

The data presented are organized around a South Col-West Ridge comparison because this separation within the expedition provides clear-cut variation on our main variable, *uncertainty* about goal-outcome. Figures 8-1 and 8-2 portray the large difference between these two goals with respect to likely outcome. Every second day, the climber was asked in his diary to make both *high* and *low* realistic estimates of the probability of success on each of the expedition's goals. A rating of "5" was defined as "absolutely certain to succeed," a "-5" meaning certainty of failure. Figure 8-1 shows the South Col perceived to be well into the "success" region, with a slight tendency to become more certain of success through time. In Figure 8-2, the West Ridge is clearly in the region of maximum "uncertainty," with a pronounced tendency toward growing "pessimism" through time.

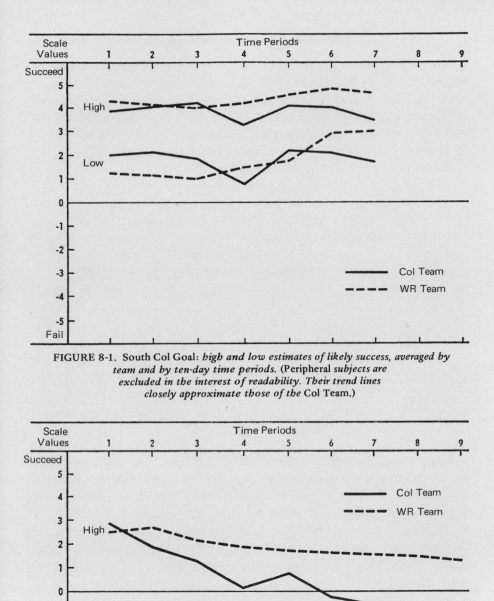

FIGURE 8-1. South Col Goal: *high and low estimates of likely success, averaged by team and by ten-day time periods. (Peripheral subjects are excluded in the interest of readability. Their trend lines closely approximate those of the* Col Team.)

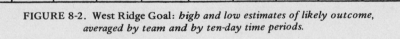

FIGURE 8-2. West Ridge Goal: *high and low estimates of likely outcome, averaged by team and by ten-day time periods.*

1. *Hypothesis 4.* In the diary, subjects encountered the following question: "If I were talking with _____ about chances of failure or success on _____, I would point out (or ask): _____." He chose some person as target, some goal as subject and composed his would-be message. Table 8-1 presents these quasi-communication data by team or origin, goal spoken of and information contained.

TABLE 8-1.

Number of Quasi-Communication Messages About the Col and WR, by Team of Origin and Import of Information

FROM	ABOUT	INFORMATION:			TOTAL
		OPTIMISTIC	PESSIMISTIC	OTHER	
Col Team	Col	(2	20)*	3	25
Col Team	WR	5	13	7	25
WR Team	Col	4	6	5	15
WR Team	WR	(20	21)**	15	56
Peripheral	Col	6	17	7	30
Peripheral	WR	5	23	12	40
TOTAL		42	100	49	191

Note: Some messages (classified "other") could not be coded as containing "optimistic" or "pessimistic" information. Most common were messages advocating decisions.

*χ^2 = 4.42; P < .05.
**χ^2 = 7.25; P < .01.

Concerning messages about the South Col, we find a rather pronounced tendency to select "pessimistic" information about a goal which is seen as promising success. This is in accord with Hypothesis 4, and clearly indicates that information communicated is not simply a reflection of the opinions held by the communicator. Moreover, the proportion of "pessimistic" messages about the Col is largest from the Col Team, supporting Hypothesis 6 which views *goal-oriented motivation* as a necessary condition for the predicted communication patterns.

Concerning messages about the WR, Hypothesis 4 predicts balanced attention to pessimistic and optimistic information. We find a balance from the WR Team, but messages from the Col Team and its peripheral members are predominantly pessimistic. Motivation for the WR on the part of Col and Peripheral members was *very low*. Hence, the motivational qualifier *might* explain this, but from participant observation we suspect there is more to it. It is well to recall that the WR undertaking was perceived as a threat to the Col enterprise. Hence, it might involve the difference between conveying information to *convince*, as in debate, versus conveying information to *explore*, as in joint problem solving.

2. *Hypothesis 5: Communication Feedback.* The quasi-communication data concern the selection of messages by an initiating sender and relate only to Hypothesis 4. Hypothesis 5 deals with the patterning of *return* communication (feedback). The stimulus statement routine was a method devised specifically to isolate and obtain data on feedback. The statement and the *immediate* reply were recorded on tape, or in field notes at the first opportunity. For example:

Statement A: "We have a real good time-jump on the mountain."
Reply A: "Uh huh—and the weather hasn't been terribly bad. I expected worse."
  (Positive feedback)
Statement B: "We're about a month ahead of any previous expedition on this mountain."
Reply B: "Sure, but we have a bigger job. It's how we use the time." (Negative feedback)

Table 8-2 presents the feedback data classified by information in the statement, information in the reply, team affiliation of subject, and goal (WR or Col) spoken of. Peripheral and Col Team members were pooled to increase the N.

TABLE 8-2.

Communication Feedback to "Optimistic" and "Pessimistic" Stimulus Statements, Concerning Goals with Varying Degrees of Uncertainty and Motivation

| | | | RESPONSE | | PERCENT NEGATIVE FEEDBACK | PREVAILING CONDITIONS: | |
SUBJECT	GOAL	STIMULUS	OPTI-MISTIC	PESSI-MISTIC		OUTCOME	MOTIVATION
West Ridge	West Ridge	Optim	6	32	84.2		
		Pessim	31	7	81.6	Uncertain	Very high
West Ridge	South Col	Optim	5	15	75.0	Success likely	
		Pessim	11	8	57.9		High
South Col	South Col	Optim	4	20	83.3	Success likely	
		Pessim	15	9	62.5		Very high
South Col	West Ridge	Optim	2	11	84.6	Failure likely	
		Pessim	3	8	27.3		Low
TOTAL		Optim	17	78	82.1		
		Pessim	60	32	65.2		

Note: Only the Col Team concerning the WR falls short of significance at the .05 level by Chi Square.

Looking first at the totals, we find: (a) pessimistic replies outnumber optimistic (similar to Table 8-1, suggesting a tendency to focus upon the "problematic" in problem solving); and (b) negative feedback prevails in response to *both* optimistic and pessimistic statements. Concerning feedback from the WR Team about either goal, and from the Col Team about *their own* goal, the data support Hypothesis 5. However, concerning feedback from the Col Team about the WR, the data do not support our hypothesis, if M is ignored. Response from Col and Peripheral members was largely pessimistic to both forms of stimulus statement about the WR. Again, we could invoke the motivational qualifier as an out, but again our reasoning must include the possibility of a process involving *inter* group communication. With the WR seen as a threat to the Col enterprise, but not vice versa, these data strongly suggest that Hypotheses 4 and 5 are true only under conditions of *collaborative* problem solving.

3. *Uncertainty of Outcome Over Time.* Our theory *assumes* that the communication processes described here tend to sustain uncertainty. From this assumption it follows that: (1) uncertainty about outcome on the Col should be sustained over time more in the Col Team than in the WR Team; and (2) uncertainty about the outcome on the WR should be sustained more in the WR Team than in the Col Team. A glance at Figures 8-1 and 8-2 will show that these predictions correspond with the data. These trend lines show both teams tending to maintain uncertainty about their *own* goal, compared with the other team. Participant observation strongly supports this interpretation concerning the WR. Indeed, the WR Team grew progressively more upset with other expedition members for seemingly writing the WR off as impossible; and their high motivation was judged "pathological" not for being high but for being ill-founded. Concerning the South Col, however, I cannot claim as much support from participant observation even though many anecdotes could be provided here as well. Even so, while sustained uncertainty is predicted from our theory, many other possible explanations could be offered, and this link in our theory must await experimental study.

4. *Hypothesis 2: Uncertainty and Motivation.* Hypothesis 2 states that goal-oriented motivation is aroused and sustained by prolonged uncertainty of outcome. We have given an anecdotal account of the emergence of motivation toward the uncertain WR in the course of

expedition goal setting. While participant observation produced compelling impressions, diary self-ratings failed to show any real difference between Col and WR Teams on motivation for their *own* respective goals. However, on *energy mobilization* there was a pronounced difference.

5. *Hypothesis 3: Uncertainty and Energy Mobilization.* Subjects filled in their diaries at the end of the day. As a result, every afternoon or evening they encountered a question about the next day: "Tomorrow I (should, will, would like to)_____." These open-end responses were subsequently coded from -5 to 5 on a scale of "escape" versus "approach" relevant to group goals. References to personal health (*"would like to:* get this sinus condition cleared up") were coded "0." References to personal hygiene (*"will:* clean the dead skin off my feet") were coded -1, with lower minus codes reserved for more overt escape (*"would like to:* stay in the sack," etc.). Low positive codes were used for routine task-relevant actions (*"will:* accompany Sherpas to dump"), and higher codes for nonroutine action requiring initiative (*"will:* recalculate oxygen logistics"). In these data we are dealing with energy mobilization at the level of thought, planning, and fantasy at the *end* of a day's activities.

Coding was performed by the investigator, using all knowledge available as context. Hence, it was not a "blind" coding. Dr. Lester, the Expedition psychologist, was given the same responses for blind coding out of context. The two coding agree A = .83. Table 8-3 presents results using the first coding. For every time period after time 1, group means all ordered the same: WR > Col > peripheral, with differences increasing across time.

TABLE 8-3.

Goal-Oriented Energy Mobilization: As Seen in Plans and Desires Concerning the Next Day's Work, by Team and by Time Period

TEAM	TEN-DAY TIME PERIODS								
	1	2	3	4	5	6	7	8	9
WR	0.77	0.41	1.42	1.40	2.39	2.53	1.90	1.93	2.76
Col	0.77	0.38	1.19	1.07	1.08	0.79	1.28	–	–
Peripheral	0.44	0.10	0.58	0.74	0.64	0.48	0.08	–	–

Note: The Col and Peripheral teams completed their mission by the end of the 70th day.

Do such "projective" diary respones correspond with behavioral observation? Dr. Lester spent five consecutive weeks at Camp 2, the main center of expedition activity. He was later asked to rate each person with whom he had extensive contact during that time. He considered their behavior during "leisure" time, when expedition routine did not govern their behavior. Under such instructions he rated them on goal-oriented energy mobilization. Ratings could be made for 13 individuals, and these ratings correlate with coded diary responses for the same period, rho = .64.

Energy mobilization is a far more important and meaningful variable than the more abstract "motivation," as defined above, especially in the context of this research. A climber at 24,000 feet, where the most simple act requires enormous will, can honestly say he "wants" to climb Everest "very much" and still fail to get out of his sleeping bag soon enough to get crucial work underway. Hypothesis 5, linking energy mobilization to uncertainty of outcome, finds considerable support in participant observations. Space will allow for one illustration of these incidents. Figure 8-1 shows a marked increase in certainty of success for the Col Team during periods 5 and 6. These periods correspond with success in route preparation to the point on the mountain from which the Col Team could launch its final effort. There followed the task of supplying camps along this route. This job was left almost exclusively in the hands of the Sherpas, while the Col Team climbers remained waiting at Camp 2. This procedure is *known to be* poor policy. Its result was logistic confusion during the final assault via the Col and the near failure of the assault itself.

In a postexpedition questionnaire designed specifically to validate such observations, nine out of thirteen respondents mentioned failure to accompany and supervise this supply build-up in response to the open-end question: "What are some of the things we did wrong?"

Summary

Theory suggested that goals tend to be defined in "regions of uncertainty," and that goal-oriented motivation is maximized and maintained over time as a function of prolonged uncertainty. Energy mobilized in goal striving is seen to be a function of *uncertainty* at any point in time. Theory further suggested that specific patterns of information flow in communication emerge, given motivation greater than zero. These patterns involve: (a) information which counteracts the prevailing information in the environment, notably in initiated communications; and (b) a high incidence of *negative feedback* which tends to offset the information currently flowing in communication. These patterns are thought to result from implicit role-relations in communication. The net effect of such selective communication would be group goal striving as a self-maintaining system.

In this case study, evidence provides some support for certain points in the theory: (1) Communication tended to counter the prevailing information in the environment (quasi-communication data), and feedback was predominantly negative, especially under conditions of high motivation; (2) in assessments of likely goal-outcome, uncertainty appears to be sustained *possibly* as a result of such communication; and (3) energy mobilized in goal striving appears to be increased under conditions of uncertain outcome.

While this study might be fortified somewhat by its longitudinal character, it remains a completely uncontrolled field study, hardly suited for empirical demonstration of directional relations from communication to uncertainty to motivation and back to communication. Hence, controlled studies are planned with these field data as background.

9

JOSEPH BERGER, BERNARD P. COHEN, AND MORRIS ZELDITCH, JR.

STATUS CHARACTERISTICS
AND SOCIAL INTERACTION

Background and Statement of the Problem

This paper studies how status characteristics organize social interaction. . . .

Many studies in the "small groups" literature deal with this problem: that is, they observe some interaction measure, such as participation or influence, in groups whose members differ in status categories. For example, Caudill finds that positions in the occupational hierarchy of a psychiatric hospital determine participation rates in ward rounds. The ward administrator participates more than the chief resident, the chief resident more than other residents, the most passive resident more than the most aggressive nurse. . . . Or Torrance finds that positions in a B-26 air crew influence group decisions. Pilots influence decisions more than navigators, navigators more than gunners; and this is true even when the pilot's opinion is objectively incorrect; and when the group task is unrelated to B-26 air crew activities. In juries, sex and occupation determine participation, election to foreman, and evaluation of juror competence. In biracial work groups whites initiate more interactions than blacks, talk more to other whites than blacks, and even blacks talk more to whites than other blacks. . . .

First, we will examine what all this research adds up to; that is, describe the phenomenon in general. Second, we will explain the results of this research; that is, show them as consequences of some

Reprinted in part with permission from *American Sociological Review* 37 (June 1972): 241-255.

more general theory. Part of the paper, therefore, constructs the required theory. Third, with the theory formulated, we review research designed to test, refine, and extend it.

Generalization of Research Results

... The principal findings of this research may be reduced to the following empirical generalization:

When a task-oriented group is differentiated with respect to some external status characteristic, this status difference determines the observable power and prestige within the group whether or not the external status characteristic is related to the group task.

The Problem of Explanation and Constructing a Theory

Our problem now is how to derive the above generalization from some more general theoretical formulation. To be useful, that is to increase understanding of this phenomenon and provide a basis for refining and extending knowledge of it, this theory should satisfy at least the following four requirements: (1) it should stipulate the sufficient conditions for a status organizing process to occur: (2) it should specify what about status characteristics determines behavior; (3) it should specify what behaviors are determined by status characteristics; (4) it should describe the mechanisms by which status characteristics determine behavior.

We will formulate our theory from the point of view of an actor, p, oriented to at least two social objects, himself, p', and another, o. P faces a task, T, with at least two outcomes, T_a and T_b, *differentially evaluated:* One outcome constitutes "success," the other, "failure." The individuals for whom T is a task are task-focused; that is, motivated to achieve the successful outcome. They are also *collectively-oriented,* that is, they believe it both legitimate and necessary to take others' behavior into account. It is assumed that possessing the state x of some performance characteristic C^* increases the individual's likelihood of achieving "success" at the task, while possessing the complementary state of C^* increases the individual's likelihood of "failure" at the task. In other words, C* is *instrumental* to T. (To simplify analysis, we treat all characteristics as dichotomies. Hence the characteristic C* has only the states C_a* and C_b*. If they are differentially evaluated, we say that one is positively and one negatively evaluated.) Who possesses the state x of C* may not be known to p. Call a task situation having these properties S*. We assume that in S* the social objects p' and o are described by states of a diffuse status characteristic, D, and only by D. A characteristic is a diffuse status characteristic for p if it has three properties:

1. The states of D are differentially evaluated.
2. To each state x of D there corresponds a distinct set γ_x of states of specific, evaluated characteristics associated with D_x.
3. To each state x of D there corresponds a distinct general expectation state, GES_x, having the same evaluation as the state D_x.

The task situation S,* then, is one having a valued task T; a characteristic C* instrumental to T; individuals task-focused and collectively-oriented; and individuals possessing the states of one, and only one, diffuse status characteristic D.

Status characteristics do not operate in every situation: We need, therefore, to formulate conditions under which individuals base their behavior toward one another on them. When they do we say the status characteristic . . . D is *activated* in S* if and only if p attributes in S* the states GES_x and/or the sets of states γ_x to p' and o which are consistent with their states of D. . . .

[These concepts are assumed to operate in such a way as to conform to] the following result:

Basic Result. (Order-equivalence of Status Definitions) Given S*, and a D culturally neither associated with nor dissociated from C*, p's position relative to o in the observed power and prestige order will be a direct function of their relative states of D, provided any of the following is true in S*:

1. if D is the only social basis of discrimination;
2. if D is the only social basis of discrimination and has been activated;
3. if D is a social basis of discrimination, has been activated, and any of its components are relevant to C*;
4. if D is a social basis of discrimination, has been activated, and has had relevant states of C* assigned to it consistently;

and for a diffuse status characteristic, $\hat{D}$, whose states have been culturally associated consistently with states of C*,

5. if $\hat{D}$ is a social basis of discrimination and has been activated.

Thus, the ordering effect of a status characteristic is independent of the amount of status definition originally occurring in S^*. That is, the mean probability of an action opportunity, performance output, positive reward action, or exercise of and resistance to influence is greater for the higher as compared to lower status individuals in each of these situations. Line (1) is a situation that is initially only minimally defined; that is, initially states of D and C^* and expectations of p's behavior are unrelated. Specifically, group members know only that p' is a D_a and o is a D_b and that this status difference has not been culturally related to their immediate task. Line (4), however, is maximally defined at the outset; that is, task-expectations are initially assigned to p' and o consistent with their states of D. Here, p' is known or believed initially to be a D_a and o to be a D_b; this specific p' is superior to this specific o on a set of characteristics $C_1, C_2, \ldots C_n$ (some members of the set of characteristics associated with D); and this specific p' is expected to be and is believed to be superior to this specific o with respect to C^*, the characteristic instrumental to their immediate task. Line (5) also describes a situation maximally defined initially, but in this case the maximal definition results from the fact that task-expectation differences have been previously culturally associated with status differences. That is, members of the group know that p' is a D_a; that o is a D_b; that this particular p' is superior to this particular o on a set of characteristics $C_1 C_2, \ldots C_n$ (some members of the set of characteristics associated with D); *and* believe that C^*, the characteristic instrumental to their task, is included in this set. The basic result claims the equivalence of these status situations: The distribution of action opportunities, performance outputs, reward actions, and influence is in all ordered in terms of relative states of D. This result does not claim that the magnitude of differences between high and low positions in the power-prestige order is necessarily the same in all cases; increasing amounts of status definition may strengthen the effect. But the order of the differences in the mean probabilities of various actions forming the observed power and prestige order between high and low states of D is preserved. Furthermore, this effect does not depend on whether or not states of C^* and D were previously associated. In line (5) our basic result covers a case in which $\hat{D}$ and C^* had been associated but in lines (1)-(4) no prior association of D and C* is assumed. Again, our basic result claims these situations are equivalent: The distribution of action opportunities, performance outputs, reward actions, and influence will be ordered in both cases in terms of relative states of D.

The order equivalence result makes it evident that the theory explains the results of previous experiments all of which are covered by it. One might validly object that the theory's conditions are simpler than those of previous experiments, and require much interpretation to match theory to experiment. It is for this reason that we subjected the theory to more direct tests which are described in [the following] section. But otherwise, the results of these experiments follow from our theory's concepts and assumptions in a fairly straightforward manner. . . .

Direct Experimental Tests of the Theory

While we argue that our theory enables us to explain much that is known about the status organizing process in task-oriented groups, this argument involves considerable interpretation of what is taking place in the wide variety of situations in which the process has been investigated. These situations are typically complex, involving more features than are necessary according to our theory to activate the process. This makes such experiments easily subject to alternative explanations. Furthermore, they are not systematically informative for the whole range of situations in which, according to our theory, status organizing processes will take place. We must therefore obtain more direct tests of our theory in situations involving no more and no less than the conditions it stipulates.

In this section we describe two such tests. Both take place in a standardized experimental situation whose techniques and procedures are designed to operationalize the theory's conditions and the components of an observable power and prestige order.

This situation has a manipulation phase and a decision-making phase:

In the manipulation phase, subjects are placed in an expectation-state, either by testing their ability directly or by giving them status information. The actual status of the subjects is always the same. They are kept apart during the experiment, for complete control over their status information. If both have the state D_x, each is told that one is D_x but the other has some state of D. For example, if both are Air Force staff sergeants, each is told that one is a staff sergeant and the other a captain; or that one is a staff sergeant and the other an airman third class. Each subject assumes that his counterpart has the other state of D.

In the decision phase, pairs of subjects repeat n identical decision-making trials, each of which requires a binary choice. The choice is made in three stages, the first of which is the subject's initial choice between alternatives made independently, without knowing his partner's choice. Subjects then communicate these choices to their partner, after which each makes a final choice.

Subjects are instructed to make what they feel is the correct preliminary choice and, after taking the other subject's choice into consideration, to make what they feel is the correct final choice. They are told repeatedly that whether initial choices coincide with final choices is unimportant, that using others' advice is both legitimate and necessary, and that the correct final choice is of prime importance.

The task consists of a sequence of almost identical large rectangles made up of smaller black and white rectangles. The subject must decide whether each rectangle contains more white or black area. The task is ambiguous: The probability of a white-response for each stimulus is close to .50, and the decision on any given trial is independent of decisions on preceding trials. However, the subject is told that there is always a correct response, and success is defined by a set of standards giving scores (number of correct responses) typical of subjects like himself. The experimenter describes the task ability as "contrast sensitivity" or "spatial" judgment ability, and tells the subject that it is not related to artistic or mathematical ability. In other words, he attempts to preclude the subject's having prior expectations about the ability.

The experimenter totally manipulates communication between subjects. He does so by an Interaction Control Machine (ICOM) consisting of subject-consoles, a host experimenter panel, and a master control unit. Each subject, partitioned off from other subjects, sits before a subject-console having various buttons and lights. When he makes a decision he pushes the buttons; he receives information from the lights. All circuits pass through the master control unit, so the experimenter can manipulate communication from subject to subject.

The structure of the experimental trial, together with the control exercised through ICOM, makes the action opportunities and performance outputs of all subjects equal; ICOM controls all reward actions, that is, all communicated evaluations, and therefore all subject agreements or disagreements. A precise measure of the subject's power and prestige position is obtained by studying the probability that one subject influences or is influenced by another. If the subject changes his final choice, he is said to make an *O-response;* if not, he is said to make an *S-* or *stay response.* The probability of an S-response measures the exercise of influence in the situation.

A postsession interview follows the manipulation and decision-making phases. This interview is used to eliminate subjects who are definitely suspicious, and claim to act on their suspicions; subjects who differentiate themselves from their partner on some basis other than the status characteristics—who, for example, manage to see the other subject when the other is from a visible minority group; and subjects who are unable to understand the instructions or to hear or understand the status manipulations of the experiment.

The first experiment testing the status characteristics theory was carried out by Moore, using the standardized experimental setting described above. Moore found that subjects who believed themselves better educated than their partner had a higher probability of an S-response; i.e., were less readily influenced, than those who believed themselves less well educated. Furthermore, and perhaps more important, Moore found no significant difference between subjects who already associated the task ability with the status characteristic and those who did not.

For this experiment, Moore used 85 junior college students. To create a high-low condition Moore informed 45 of them that one of the two subjects in the experiment was from the junior college from which both in fact came, while the other was from a nearby high school. Both subjects believed themselves to have higher status and their partner to have lower status. To create a low-high condition, Moore informed the remaining 40 that one of the two subjects was from the junior college from which both came, but the other from a nearby four-year private university, Stanford. In addition, 22 of the 45 high-low subjects were informed that those from the junior college consistently did better at the task they were to perform than subjects from the nearby high school. Similarly 20 of the 40 low-high subjects were informed that those from Stanford consistently did

better at such tasks. These two instructions experimentally associated the status and performance characteristics. Moore found that
if a performance-characteristic is previously associated with a status
characteristic, and the latter discriminates between p' and o, the
probability that S yields to his partner's influence is an inverse
function of this status. If the performance-characteristic is not
previously associated with a status characteristic, but not dissociated
from it, the probability that a subject yields to his partner's influence
is again an inverse function of his status, and to about the same
degree. Thus, this experiment confirms two of our theory's predictions. . . . [Further experimentation is shown to confirm the remaining assumptions of the theory.]

Refining and Extending the Theory

Our further research has had two objectives: First, to refine the
theory by increasing its precision; second, to extend it by increasing
its generality. Both go beyond what is conventionally meant by
testing the theory. To test a theory is to confirm or disconfirm some
hypothesis that in a strict sense derives from it. The experiments
described in the preceding section are in this sense properly called
tests of the theory. But for the most part, the research that now
concerns us does not test hypotheses that derive rigorously from the
theory. Rather, the theory provides the basis for this research in the
sense that it poses the research's problems and provides the concepts
and theoretical arguments used to treat them. Thus, the theory
guides and organizes this research and its results show as modifications in the way the theory is formulated.

We will describe six further experiments which fall into three basic
groups: the first group equates, as well as differentiates, the statuses
of individuals; the second makes specific (as opposed to diffuse)
status characteristics that are initially irrelevant, relevant to a group's
task; the third provides subjects with information about multiple
statuses, some of which is inconsistent. . . . [Only the third group of
experiments is presented in this selection.]

(3) Multiple-characteristic status situations. When two or more
status characteristics are activated they may be inconsistent; most
theories of status characteristics have been written about such

113

situations. . . . Such situations are typically assumed to be tense and awkward, but how they are resolved is not so clear. Does the individual define the situation with respect to one characteristic, neglecting, suppressing, or denying the other's significance? A balance theory in which inconsistency is reduced, might suggest this. Or does the individual "average" all available information, forming expectations for self and other somewhere between those formed if all characteristics are high or low?

Two experiments by Berger and [others] show that subjects combine rather than balance status information. These experiments artificially construct two equally weighted specific status characteristics, each of which is made equally relevant to the contrast sensitivity task. When the characteristics are made inconsistent, subjects have a probability of an S-response lower than subjects who are consistently high, but higher than subjects who are consistently low. Furthermore, a subject high on one characteristic and low on another has a lower probability of an S-response when his partner is high on both than when his partner is low on one but high on the other (and similarly for the obverse). This further supports the finding that a combined hierarchy is formed from inconsistent status information.

These two experiments provide information important to extending the generality of the original theory; for, if the result survives further tests, the theory can be extended to situations defined by any number of characteristics.

Summary and Conclusion

The research described in this paper can be summarized as follows:

1. First, we constructed an abstract empirical generalization from an analysis of investigations of the distribution of participation, prestige, and influence in decision-making groups that are initially different in status categories: When task-oriented groups are differentiated by some external status characteristic, differences between individuals in status determine the observable power and prestige order of the group, whether the status characteristic is previously associated with the task or not.

2. Second, we formulated a theory that explains this generalization. Different evaluations, different specific expectations, and different general expectations are associated with the states of status characteristics. These three

properties are called into play when two or more individuals are committed to some outcome, must take each other into account in achieving this outcome, and have no other or prior basis for inferring who can better achieve this outcome. They are called into play even if no prior association exists between status characteristics and instrumental-task characteristics, so long as nothing prevents connecting the two. Becoming in this way relevant to the immediate task situation, expectations for performance in the particular situation are formed consistent with the status characteristic. Once formed, such performance-expectations are known to determine the distribution of opportunities to perform, the rate of performance outputs, the likelihood that a performance output is positively rewarded, and the exercise of influence.

3.   Third, we tested directly the assumptions made by this explanation. The argument's structure enabled us to test each independently. These tests confirmed the basic assumptions of the status characteristics formulation.

4.   Fourth, we refined and extended the theory. Further experiments show that: (a) Under certain circumstances, other status elements can be used to organize the distribution of power and prestige in the group. (b) Given information about two relevant characteristics, subjects combine it even if it is inconsistent; creating a power and prestige hierarchy that places inconsistent individuals between those consistently high and those consistently low. (c) Information that equates the status of subjects is combined with other information in the same way; so that in certain circumstances, if subjects are equal in status, the effect of a status characteristic that discriminates between them is reduced. Our current work involves reformulating the theory to account for these results.

PART III

Data Gathering

INTRODUCTION

How are observations made? Many different answers to this question pervade the studies in this book. As a means of simplifying our examination of the data-gathering process, this part focuses on three decisions confronting the observer as to the nature and performance of his role: (1) the extent to which he participates directly in the action under study; (2) whether and how he conceals or reveals his presence as a researcher; and (3) how often he relies on observation alone without recourse to other means of assembling information. Each decision has important implications, both ethical and cognitive (in terms of the meaning and accuracy of the findings).

First, in regard to participation, there are varying degrees to which the observer may elect to take a part (see such commentaries as those by Gold, 1958; Wax, 1972). In the study by *Lang and Lang,* the observers were trained as full participants, since their aim was to experience the MacArthur Day parade in the same way as other members of the crowd. *Humphreys* tried out several roles until he found one—that of "lookout"—that would legitimize his presence without involving him directly in the homosexual acts under scrutiny. By contrast, in a study of "swinging in wedlock," Charles and Rebecca Palson (1972, p. 29) found that obtaining their important insights required personal experiencing of "some of the same things that our informants did" (cf. Huesler's 1970 account of her own role as patient in an insane asylum). At the opposite extreme, some observers try to avoid all participation—Bales [Part I], for example, concealed behind a one-way mirror, cannot even exchange glances with his subjects.

Taking part in the observation may be highly effective in developing a remarkably full understanding. Nevertheless, it is subject to two major types of errors possible in data gathering: (1) an unwanted and unsystematic *control effect* over the system under study, so that the research itself has the consequence of changing the facts; and (2) a *biased viewpoint,* or the researcher's misperception of the facts, because of his own personality and the role he plays in the research (M. W. Riley, 1964, p. 1001). Neither of these contaminants is peculiar to observation, though each is related to the method in special ways. *Control effect* can confound the findings of participant observation because the observer himself is directly on the scene—and the addition of a new member, even in some presumably peripheral role, may affect the entire structure of interdependent parts in the group being observed. In certain forms of questioning, by contrast [see Introduction, pp. 6-9], as in the single cross section survey, the researcher cannot change through his ex post facto interviewing those actions which have already taken place (though he may, of course, obtain a biased view by changing respondent reports of those actions).

Unlike control effect (which changes the action under study), *biased viewpoint* is a potential limitation distorting the observer's perception of this action. Not only does his personality influence what he observes, but he also tends to perceive the action more narrowly as he becomes immersed in one role. While this may provide him with a fuller comprehension of the particular role, he may himself alter the role or be altered by it (cf., e.g., Bruyn, 1963; Riesman and Watson, 1964). As Kai Erikson (1970, p. 337) puts it:

Any individual in a research setting brings with him from the different corners of his mind a potential for distortion and bias—inclinations that are related to his own private life and experience, inclinations related to his social class position and ethnic background. . . .

This bias also occurs in questioning, though in more complex form. Observation does not depend upon the ability or willingness of the subjects to report, but questioning does. The respondent is an intervening reporter who can add his own misperceptions to those of the researcher (cf. Hyman et al., 1954; Phillips, 1972).

The *second* decision confronting the observer—the way he establishes his presence at the scene—can to a certain extent govern the control effect. At one extreme, like Whyte or Gans [Part I], he may openly let his subjects know they are being observed. He may reason that the control effect will not be excessive or that it will eventually wear off (see, e.g., Deutsch, 1949). Or he may enter incognito, as Humphreys did, assuming some plausible role that the system affords. Such concealment was the intent in the study by *Sullivan, Queen, and Patrick,* in which the observer was trained for nine months in preparation for the role of enlistee. At the other extreme, and perhaps reducing control effect to a minimum, the researcher may conceal his presence altogether. Goldberg, Kiesler, and Collins [Part IV] do not divulge their true purpose to the subject, but ostensibly engage him in an interview while the experimenter is actually observing from behind a screen. In some instances the observer is entirely replaced by hidden microphones or other recording devices, as in the "blind bugging" of jury deliberations (cited in Webb et al., 1966, p. 150).

The *third* decision faced by the observer, though somewhat different in character from the first two, continually impresses itself upon the reader in these selections: How often can he depend solely on observation? The answer appears to be, rarely. In nearly all the selections in this part, the researcher not only watches and listens, but also interviews and talks with his respondents. The last two excerpts demonstrate reliance upon available data as well—*Goffman* upon the ideas and findings of others, as documented in his numerous footnotes, and *Dalton*[1] on company records of diverse kinds. Even Bales [Part I], prototypical among sociologists relying on observation, resorts to occasional questioning in order to learn how group members feel about each other or about the performance of the group. And Blau (1954, pp. 530-531), finding that unconcealed participants could not uncover certain deviant practices in a public employment agency through either observation or questioning, resorted to the official record of these transactions. These and many other studies underscore the emphasis in our Introduction on the importance of supplementing observation with other sources of data, since the sociologist's concern is seldom restricted to current and overt behavior alone.

Some Methodological Implications

In view of the depth of understanding and the veristic detail attainable, assessments of observation tend to be enthusiastic.[2] However, apart from the inherent insufficiency of observation when unsupported by questioning or available data, such assessments must acknowledge that the observer's role poses two dangers with which the researcher must grapple. First, there are countless *ethical* issues.[3] Questions arise over concealed observation; see, for example, the protest by Coser (1959) on the study by Sullivan, Queen and Patrick, or the controversy over jury bugging previously mentioned. Other issues arise over the observation of private or deviant behavior; see, for example, the numerous attacks on the study by Humphreys (e.g., Von Hoffman, 1970). Many ethical dilemmas are matters of conscience not only for the individual researcher—who must weigh both the potential harm to subjects and the potential value of new knowledge to be gleaned—but for the profession as well. While they hardly provide ready solutions for such issues, official codes of ethics published by both the American Sociological Association and the American Psychological Association can serve as guides.

Second, the observer encounters dangers of *invalidity;* he may be misled by what he erroneously takes as fact. Webb et al. (1966) have devoted an entire book to the threats of control effects (or, in their terms, "reactive" effects), and to a host of "unobtrusive" procedures, such as the hidden observation approach (p. 170), designed to meet these threats. A long literature is devoted to the companion problem of biased viewpoint effect,[4] leading to Merton's dictum (1972, p. 41) that much sociological understanding "requires a theoretical and technical competence which . . . transcends one's status as Insider or Outsider." While the "insider's" experiential knowledge of a group, situation, or status may often be required, the sociologist must also apprehend "the conditions and often complex processes in which people are caught up without much awareness of what is going on."

In practice, researchers attempt in various ways to cope with threats to validity. One means is for each single study to probe in depth for as much understanding as possible; e.g., Florence Kluckhohn (1940), as a participant observer in a Spanish village in New Mexico, reports her efforts to overcome the contaminants of age (by attending high school to learn the language) and of sexual identity (by working in a trading post). Another means of meeting this threat is to offset the biases and control effects of particular studies through widespread replication, retesting under varying conditions, and use of many different observers—possibilities that will be explored further as applied to observation in Part VI of this book.

NOTES

1. Among the earlier ethnographic studies of organizations, see Roethlisberger and Dickson (1939); Caudill (1958).
2. For a famous spoof on a pure ethnographic approach, see Miner (1956).
3. The many instances and commentaries on these issues include Vidich, Bensman, and Stein (1964); Erikson (1967); Roth (1962); Ruebhausen and Brim (1965).
4. Compare Toby's (1955) provocative formulation of the threat to the validity of personal experience: in waiting to catch a bus in a given direction, one may often draw fallacious inferences from the observation that more buses are going the *wrong* way.

10

KURT LANG AND GLADYS ENGEL LANG

THE UNIQUE PERSPECTIVE
OF TELEVISION AND ITS
EFFECT: A PILOT STUDY

By taking MacArthur Day in Chicago, as it was experienced by
millions of spectators and video viewers, we have attempted to study
an event transmitted over video. The basis of this report is the
contrast between the actually recorded experience of participant
observers on the scene, on the one hand, and the picture which a
video viewer received by way of the television screen, and the way in
which the event was interpreted, magnified, and took on added
significance, on the other. The contrast between these two perspectives from which the larger social environment can be viewed and
"known," forms the starting point for the assessment of a particular
effect of television in structuring public events. . . .

Thirty-one participant observers took part in the study. They were
spatially distributed to allow for the maximum coverage of all the
important phases of the day's activities, i.e., no important vantage
point of spectatorship was neglected. Since the events were tem-
porally distributed, many observers took more than one station, so
that coverage was actually based on more than 31 perspectives. Thus
the sampling error inherent in individual participant observation or
unplanned mass-observation was greatly reduced. Observers could
witness the arrival at Midway Airport and still arrive in the Loop area
long before the scheduled time for the parade. Reports were received
from 43 points of observation.

Volunteers received instruction sheets which drew their attention

Reprinted in part with permission from *American Sociological Review* 18 (February 1953):
3-12.

to principles of observation and details to be carefully recorded. Among these was the directive to take careful note of any activity indicating possible influences of the televising of the event upon the behavior of spectators, e.g., actions specifically addressed to the cameras, indications that events were staged with an eye towards transmission over television, and the like. . . .

Detailed Illustration of Contrast. The Bridge ceremony provides an illustration of the contrast between the two perspectives. Seven observers witnessed this ceremony from the crowd.

TV perspective: In the words of the announcer, the Bridge ceremony marked "one of the high spots, if not the high spot of the occasion this after-noon. . . . The parade is now reaching its climax at this point."

The announcer, still focusing on MacArthur and the other participating persons, took the opportunity to review the ceremony about to take place. . . . The camera followed and the announcer described the ceremony in detail. . . . The camera focused directly on the General, showing a close-up. . . . There were no shots of the crowd during this period. But the announcer filled in. "A great cheer goes up at the Bataan Bridge, where the General has just placed a wreath in honor of the American boys who died at Bataan and Corregidor. You have heard the speech . . . the General is now walking back . . . the General now enters his car. This is the focal point where all the newsreels . . . frankly, in 25 years of covering the news, we have never seen as many newsreels gathered at one spot. One, two, three, four, five, six. At least eight cars with newsreels rigged on top of them, taking a picture that will be carried over the entire world, over the Chicagoland area by the combined network of these TV stations of Chicago, which have combined for this great occasion and for the solemn occasion which you have just witnessed."

During this scene there were sufficient close-ups for the viewer to gain a definite reaction, positive or negative, to the proceedings. He could see the General's facial expressions and what appeared to be momentary confusion. He could watch the activities of the Gold Star mothers in relation to MacArthur and define this as he wished—as inappropriate for the bereaved moment or as understandable in the light of the occasion. Taking the cue from the announcer, the entire scene could be viewed as rushed. Whether or not, in line with the official interpretation, the TV viewer saw the occasion as *solemn*, it can be assumed that he expected that the participant on the scene was, in fact, experiencing the occasion in the same way as he.

Actually, this is the way what was meant to be a solemn occasion was experienced by those attending, and which constitutes the crowd perspective. The dedication ceremony aroused little of the sentiment it might have elicited under other conditions. According to Observer 31, "People on our corner could not see the dedication ceremony very well, and consequently after he had passed immediately in front of us, there was uncertainty as to what was going on. As soon as word had come down that he had gone down to his car, the crowd dispersed." Observer 8 could not quite see the ceremony from where he was located on Wacker Drive, slightly east of the bridge. Condensed descriptions of two witnesses illustrate the confusion which surrounded the actual wreath-laying ceremony (three other similar descriptions are omitted here).

It was difficult to see any of them. MacArthur moved swiftly up the steps and immediately shook hands with people on the platform waiting to greet him. There was some cheering when he mounted the platform. He walked north on the platform and did not reappear until some minutes later. In the meantime the crowd was so noisy that it was impossible to understand what was being broadcast from the loud-speakers. Cheering was spotty and intermittent, and there was much talk about Mrs. MacArthur and Arthur . . . (Observer 2).

Those who were not on boxes did not see MacArthur. They did not see Mrs. MacArthur, but only her back. MacArthur went up on the platform, as we were informed by those on boxes, and soon we heard some sound over the loudspeakers. Several cars were standing in the street with their motors running. . . . Some shouted to the cars to shut their motors off, but the people in the cars did not care or did not hear. . . . The people in our area continued to push forward trying to hear. When people from other areas began to come and walk past us to go toward the train, the people in our area shrugged their shoulders. "Well, I guess it's all over. That noise must have been the speech." One of the three men who had stood there for an hour or more, because it was such a good spot, complained, "This turned out to be a lousy spot. I should have gone home. I bet my wife saw it much better over television" (Observer 30).

Regardless of good intentions on the part of planners and despite any recognition of the solemn purpose of the occasion by individuals in the crowd, the solemnity of the occasion was destroyed, if for no other reason, because officials in the parade were so intent upon the time-schedule and cameramen so intent upon recording the solemn dedication for the TV audience and for posterity that the witnesses could not see or hear the ceremony, or feel "solemn" or communicate a mood of solemnity. A crowd of confused spectators, cheated in their hopes of seeing a legendary hero in the flesh, was left unsatisfied.

Reciprocal Effects. There is some direct evidence regarding the way in which television imposed its own peculiar perspective on the event. In one case an observer on the scene could watch both what was going on and what was being televised.

It was possible for me to view the scene (at Soldiers Field) both naturally and through the lens of the television camera. It was obvious that the camera presented quite a different picture from the one received otherwise. The camera followed the General's car and caught that part of the crowd immediately opposite the car and about 15 rows above it. Thus it caught that part of the crowd that was cheering, giving the impression of a solid mass of wildly cheering people. It did not show the large sections of empty stands, nor did it show that people stopped cheering as soon as the car passed them (Observer 13).

In much the same way, the television viewer received the impression of wildly cheering and enthusiastic crowds before the parade. The camera selected shots of the noisy and waving audience, but in this case, the television camera itself created the incident. The cheering, waving, and shouting was often largely a response to the aiming of the camera. The crowd was thrilled to be on television, and many attempted to make themselves apparent to acquaintances who might be watching. But even beyond that, an event important enough to warrant the most widespread pooling of television facilities in Chicago video history, acquired in its own right some magnitude and significance. Casual conversation continually showed that being on television was among the greatest thrills of the day. . . .

Other Indices of the Discrepancy. In order to provide a further objective check on the discrepancies between observer impressions and the event as it was interpreted by those who witnessed it over television, a number of spot checks on the reported amount of participation were undertaken. Transportation statistics, counts in offices, and the volume of sales reported by vendors provided such indices.

The results substantiate the above finding. The city and suburban lines showed a very slight increase over their normal loads. To some extent the paltry 50,000 increase in inbound traffic on the street cars and elevated trains might even have been due to rerouting. The suburban lines had their evening rush hour moved up into the early afternoon—before the parade had begun.

Checks at luncheonettes, restaurants, and parking areas indicated no unusual crowding. Samplings in offices disclosed only a minor interest in the parade. Hawkers, perhaps the most sensitive judges of enthusiasm, called the parade a "puzzler" and displayed unsold wares. . . .

KURT LANG AND GLADYS ENGEL LANG

Conclusion

It has been claimed for television that it brings the truth directly into the home: the "camera does not lie." Analysis of the above data shows that this assumed reportorial accuracy is far from automatic. Every camera selects, and thereby leaves the unseen part of the subject open to suggestion and inference. The gaps are usually filled in by a commentator. In addition the process directs action and attention to itself.

Examination of a public event by mass observation and by television revealed considerable discrepancy between these two experiences. The contrast in perspectives points to three items whose relevance in structuring a televised event can be inferred from an analysis of the television content:

1. technological bias, i.e., the necessarily arbitrary sequence of telecasting events and their structure in terms of foreground and background, which at the same time contains the choices on the part of the television personnel as to what is important;
2. structuring of an event by an announcer, whose commentary is needed to tie together the shifts from camera to camera, from vista to close-up, helping the spectator to gain the stable orientation from one particular perspective;
3. reciprocal effects, which modify the event itself by staging it in a way to make it more suitable for telecasting and creating among the actors the consciousness of acting for a larger audience.

11

LAUD HUMPHREYS

TEAROOM TRADE: IMPERSONAL SEX IN PUBLIC PLACES

At shortly after five o'clock on a weekday evening, four men enter a public restroom in the city park. One wears a well-tailored business suit; another wears tennis shoes, shorts, and teeshirt; the third man is still clad in the khaki uniform of his filling station; the last, a salesman, has loosened his tie and left his sports coat in the car. What has caused these men to leave the company of other homeward-bound communters on the freeway? What common interest brings these men, with their divergent backgrounds, to this public facility?

They have come here not for the obvious reason, but in a search for "instant sex." Many men—married and unmarried, those with heterosexual identities and those whose self-image is a homosexual one—seek such impersonal sex, shunning involvement, desiring kicks without commitment. Whatever reasons—social, physiological, or psychological—might be postulated for this search, the phenomenon of impersonal sex persists as a widespread but rarely studied form of human interaction.

There are several settings for this type of deviant activity—the balconies of movie theaters, automobiles, behind bushes—but few offer the advantages for these men that public restrooms provide. "Tearooms," as these facilities are called in the language of the homosexual subculture, have several characteristics that make them

Reprinted in part from Laud Humphreys, *Tearoom Trade: Impersonal Sex in Public Places* (Chicago: Aldine Publishing Company, 1970), pp. 23-24, 27-28, 37-38, 59-65; also as reprinted in *Trans-action* (January 1970), pp. 11-25.

126

attractive as locales for sexual encounters without involvement. . . . They are accessible, easily recognized by the initiate, and provide little public visibility. Tearooms thus offer the advantages of both public and private settings. They are available and recognizable enough to attract a large volume of potential sexual partners, providing an opportunity for rapid action with a variety of men. When added to the relative privacy of these settings, such features enhance the impersonality of the sheltered interaction. . . .

For one who wishes to participate in (or study) such activity, the primary consideration is finding where the action is. . . . I became able to identify the more popular tearooms by observing certain physical evidence, the most obvious of which is the location of the facility. During the warm seasons, those restrooms that are isolated from other park facilities, such as administration buildings, shops, tennis courts, playgrounds, and picnic areas, are the more popular for deviant activity. The most active tearooms studied were all isolated from recreational areas, cut off by drives or lakes from baseball diamonds and picnic tables. . . .

WHAT THEY WANT, WHEN THEY WANT IT

The availability of facilities they can recognize attracts a great number of men who wish, for whatever reason, to engage in impersonal homoerotic activity. Simple observation is enough to guide these participants, the researcher, and, perhaps, the police to active tearooms. It is much more difficult to make an accurate appraisal of the proportion of the male population who engage in such activity over a representative length of time. Even with good sampling procedures, a large staff of assistants would be needed to make the observations necessary for an adequate census of this mobile population. . . .

Participants assure me that it is not uncommon in tearooms for one man to fellate as many as ten others in a day. I have personally watched a fellator take on three men in succession in a half hour of observation. One respondent, who has cooperated with the researcher in a number of taped interviews, claims to average three men each day during the busy season.

I have seen some waiting turn for this type of service. Leaving one such scene on a warm September Saturday, I remarked to a man who left close behind me: "Kind of crowded in there, isn't it?" "Hell, yes," he answered, "It's getting so you have to take a number and wait in line in these places!"

There are many who frequent the same facility repeatedly. Men will come to be known as regular, even daily, participants, stopping off at the same tearoom on the way to or from work. One physician in his late fifties was so punctual in his appearance at a particular restroom that I began to look forward to our daily chats. This robust, affable respondent said he had stopped at this tearoom every evening of the week (except Wednesday, his day off) for years "for a blow-job." Another respondent, a salesman whose schedule is flexible, may "make the scene" more than once a day—usually at his favorite men's room. At the time of our formal interview, this man claimed to have had four orgasms in the past 24 hours.

According to participants I have interviewed, those who are looking for impersonal sex in tearooms are relatively certain of finding the sort of partner they want. . . .

You go into the tearoom. You can pick up some really nice things in there. Again, it is a matter of sex real quick; and, if you like this kind, fine—you've got it. You get one and he is done; and, before long, you've got another one.

. . . and when they want it:

Well, I go there; and you can always find someone to suck your cock, morning, noon, or night. I know lots of guys who stop by there on their way to work—and all during the day.

It is this sort of volume and variety that keeps the tearooms viable as market places of the one-night-stand variety. . . .

SHELTERING SILENCE

There is another aspect of the tearoom encounters that is crucial. I refer to the silence of the interaction.

Throughout most homosexual encounters in public restrooms, nothing is spoken. One may spend many hours in these buildings and witness dozens of sexual acts without hearing a word. Of 50 encounters on which I made extensive notes, only in 15 was any word spoken. Two were encounters in which I sought to ease the strain of legitimizing myself as lookout by saying, "You go ahead—I'll watch." Four were whispered remarks between sexual partners, such as, "Not so hard!" or "Thanks." One was an exchange of greetings between friends.

The other eight verbal exchanges were in full voice and more extensive, but they reflected an attendant circumstance that was exceptional. When a group of us were locked in a restroom and attacked by several youths, we spoke for defense and out of fear. This event ruptured the reserve among us and resulted in a series of conversations among those who shared this adventure for several days afterward. Gradually, this sudden unity subsided, and the encounters drifted back into silence.

Barring such unusual events, an occasionally whispered "thanks" at the conclusion of the act constitutes the bulk of even whispered communication. At first, I presumed that speech was avoided for fear of incrimination. The excuse that intentions have been misunderstood is much weaker when those proposals are expressed in words rather than signaled by body movements. As research progressed, however, it became evident that the privacy of silent interaction accomplishes much more than mere defense against exposure to a hostile world. Even when a careful lookout is maintaining the boundaries of an encounter against intrusion, the sexual participants tend to be silent. The mechanism of silence goes beyond satisfying the demand for privacy. Like all other characteristics of the tearoom setting, it serves to guarantee anonymity, to assure the impersonality of the sexual liaison. . . .

Only a public place, such as a park restroom, could provide the lack of personal involvement in sex that certain men desire. The setting fosters the necessary turnover in participants by its accessibility and visibility to the "right" men. In these public settings, too, there exists a sort of democracy that is endemic to impersonal sex. Men of all racial, social, educational, and physical characteristics meet in these places for sexual union. With the lack of involvement, personal perferences tend to be minimized. . . .

Patterns of Collective Action

The nature of sexual activity presents two severe problems for those who desire impersonal one-night-stands. In the first place, except for masturbation, sex necessitates collective action; and all collective action requires communication. Mutually understood signals must be conveyed, intentions expressed, and the action sustained by reciprocal encouragement. Under normal circumstances, such communication is ritualized in those patterns of word and movement we call courtship and love-making. Verbal agreements are reached and intentions conveyed. Even when deception is involved in such exchanges, as it often is, self-revelation and commitment are likely by-products of courtship rituals. In the search for impersonal, anonymous sex, however, these ordinary patterns of collective action must be avoided.

A second problem arises from the cultural conditioning of Western man. For him, sex is invested with personal meanings: interpersonal relationship, romantic love, and an endless catalogue of sentiments. Sex without "love" meets with such general condemnation that the essential ritual of courtship is almost obscured in rococo accretions that assure those involved that a respectable level of romantic intent has been reached. Normal preludes to sexual action thus encourage the very commitment and exposure that the tearoom participant wishes to avoid. Since ordinary ways reveal and involve, special ritual is needed for the impersonal sex of public restrooms.

Both the appeal and the danger of ephemeral sex are increased because the partners are usually strangers to one another. The propositioning of strangers for either heterosexual or homosexual acts is dangerous and exciting—so much so that it is made possible only by concerted action, which progresses in stages of increasing mutuality. The special ritual of tearooms, then, must be both noncoercive and noncommital.

APPROACHING

The steps, phases, or general moves I have observed in tearoom games all involve somatic motion. As silence is one of the rules of these encounters, the strategies of the players require some sort of physical movement: a gesture with the hands, motions of the eyes, manipulation and erection of the penis, a movement of the head, a change in stance, or a transfer from one place to another.

The approach to the place of encounter, although not a step within the game, resembles moves of the latter sort. Although occurring outside the interaction membrane, the approach may affect the action inside. An automobile may circle the area a time or two, finally stopping in front of the facility. In what I estimate to be about a third of the cases, the driver will park a moderate distance away from the facility—sometimes as far as 200 feet to the side or in back, to avoid having his car associated with the tearoom.

Unless hurried (or interested in some particular person entering, or already inside, the facility), the man will usually wait in his auto for five minutes or longer. While waiting, he looks the situation over: Are there police cars near? Does he recognize any of the other autos? Does another person waiting look like a desirable partner? He may read a newspaper and listen to the radio, or even get out and wipe his windshield, invariably looking up when another car approaches. The purpose here is to look as natural as possible in this setting, while taking the opportunity to "cruise" other prospective players as they drive slowly by.

Sometimes he will go into the restroom on the heels of a person he has been watching. Should he find the occupant of another auto interesting, he may decide to enter as a signal for the other man to follow. If no one else approaches or leaves, he may enter to see what is going on inside. Some will wait in their autos for as long as an hour, until they see a desirable prospect approaching or sense that the time is right for entry.

From the viewpoint of those already in the restroom, the action of the man outside may communicate a great deal about his availability for the game. Straights do not wait; they stop, enter, urinate, and leave. A man who remains in his car while a number of others come and go—then starts for the facility as soon as a relatively handsome, young fellow approaches—may be revealing both his preferences and his unwillingness to engage in action with anyone "substandard." . . .

POSITIONING

Once inside the interaction membrane, the participant has his opportunity to cruise those already there. He will have only the brief time of his passage across the room for sizing-up the situation. Once he has positioned himself at the urinal or in a stall, he has already begun his first move of the game. Even the decision as to which urinal he will use is a tactical consideration. If either of the end fixtures is occupied, which is often the case, an entering party who takes his position at the center of the three urinals is "coming on too strong." This is apt to be the "forward" sort of player who wants both possible views. Should both ends be occupied, it is never considered fair for a new arrival to take the middle. He might interrupt someone else's play. For reasons other than courtesy, however, the skilled player will occupy one of the end urinals because it leaves him more room to maneuver in the forthcoming plays.

If the new participant stands close to the fixture, so that his front side may not easily be seen, and gazes downward, it is assumed by the players that he is straight. By not allowing his penis to be seen by others, he has precluded his involvement in action at the urinals. This strategy, followed by an early departure from the premises, is all that those who wish to "play it straight" need to know about the tearoom game. . . .

A man who knows the rules and wishes to play, however, will stand comfortably back from the urinal, allowing his gaze to shift from side to side or to the ceiling. At this point, he may notice a man in the nearest stall peer over the edge at him. The next step is for the man in the stall (or someone else in the room) to move to the urinal at the opposite end, being careful to leave a "safe" distance between himself and the other player. . . .

SIGNALING

. . . Every move in the . . . encounter is not only a means of bettering one's physical position in relation to other participants but also a means of communication.

Whereas, for most insertees, positioning is vital for informing others of their intentions, about half of the eventual insertors convey such information in the signaling phase. The primary strategy employed by the latter is playing with one's penis in what may be called "casual masturbation."

> *Respondent*: The thing he [the potential insertee] is watching for is "handling," to see whether or not the guy is going to play with himself. He's going to pretend like he is masturbating, and this is the signal right there. . . .
> *Interviewer*: So the sign of willingness to play is playing with oneself or masturbation?
> *Respondent*: Pseudomasturbation.

The willing player (especially if he intends to be an insertor) steps back a few inches from the urinal, so that his penis may be viewed easily. He then begins to stroke it or play with the head of the organ. As soon as another man at the urinals observes this signal, he will also begin autoerotic manipulation. Usually, erection may be observed after less than a minute of such stimulation.

The eyes now come into play. The prospective partner will look intently at the other's organ, occasionally breaking his stare only to fix directly upon the eyes of the other. "This mutual glance between persons, in distinction from the simple sight or observation of the

other, signifies a wholly new and unique union between them."
(Georg Simmel) . . .

Through all of this, it is important to remember that showing an
erection is, for the insertor, the one essential and invariable means of
indicating a willingness to play. No one will be "groped" or
otherwise involved in the directly sexual play of the tearooms unless
he displays this sign. This touches on the rule of not forcing one's
intentions on another, and I have observed no exceptions to its use.
On the basis of extensive and systematic observation, I doubt the
veracity of any person (detective or otherwise) who claims to have
been "molested" in such a setting without first having "given his
consent" by showing an erection. Conversely, anyone familiar with
this strategy may become involved in the action merely by following
it. He need not be otherwise skilled to play the game. . . .

Occasionally, there is no need for the parties to exchange signals at
this stage of the game. Others in the room may signal for a waiting
person to enter the stall of an insertee. There may have been
conversation outside the facility—or acquaintance with a player—
which precludes the necessity of any such communication. . . .

The Sociologist as Voyeur

The methods employed in this study of men who engage in restroom
sex are the outgrowth of three ethical assumptions: First, I do not
believe the social scientist should ever ignore or avoid an area of
research simply because it is difficult or socially sensitive. Second, he
should approach any aspect of human behavior with those means
that least distort the observed phenomena. Third, he must protect
respondents from harm—regardless of what such protection may cost
the researcher.

Because the majority of arrests on homosexual charges in the
United States result from encounters in public restrooms, I felt this
form of sexual behavior to provide a legitimate, even essential,
topic for sociological investigation. In our society the social control forces, not the criminologist determine, what the latter shall
study.

Following this decision, the question is one of choosing research
methods which permit the investigator to achieve maximum fidelity

to the world he is studying. I believe ethnographic methods are the only truly empirical ones for the social scientist. . . .

PREPARING FOR THE FIELD

As an ethnographer, my first task was to acquaint myself with the homosexual subculture. Because of my pastoral experience, I was no total stranger to those circles. While a seminarian, I was employed for two years in a parish that was known in the homosexual world as Chicago's "queen parish"—a place to which the homosexuals could turn for counsel, understanding priests, good music, and worship with an aesthetic emphasis. I soon came to know the gay parishioners and to speak their language. . . .

This particular part of my education was supplemented in the summer of 1953, when I spent three months in clinical training at the State University of Iowa's psychiatric hospital. . . . From 1955 to 1965, I served parishes in Oklahoma, Colorado, and Kansas, twice serving as Episcopal campus chaplain on a part-time basis. Because I was considered "wise" and did not attempt to "reform" them, hundreds of homosexuals of all sorts and conditions came to me during those years for counselling. Having joined me in counselling parishioners over the coffee pot for many a night, my wife provided much understanding assistance in this area of my ministry.

The problem, at the beginning of my research, was threefold: to become acquainted with the sociological literature on sexual deviance; to gain entry to a deviant subculture in a strange city where I no longer had pastoral, and only part-time priestly, duties; and to begin to listen to sexual deviants with a scientist's rather than a pastor's ear.

PASSING AS DEVIANT

Like any deviant group, homosexuals have developed defenses against outsiders: secrecy about their true identity, symoblic gestures and the use of the eyes for communication, unwillingness to expose the whereabouts of their meeting places, extraordinary caution with strangers, and admission to certain places only in the company of a recognized person. Shorn of pastoral contacts and unwilling to use professional credentials, I had to enter the subculture as would any newcomer and to make contact with respondents under the guise of being another gay guy.

Such entry is not difficult to accomplish. Almost any taxi driver can tell a customer where to find a gay bar. A guide to such gathering places may be purchased for five dollars. The real problem is not one of making contact with the subculture but of making the contact "stick." . . .

. . . When human behavior is being examined, systematic observation is essential; so I had to become a participant-observer of furtive, felonious acts. . . .

The very fear and suspicion encountered in the restrooms produces a participant role, the sexuality of which is optional. This is the role of the lookout ("watchqueen" in the argot), a man who is situated at the door or windows from which he may observe the means of access to the restroom. When someone approaches, he coughs. He nods when the coast is clear or if he recognizes an entering party as a regular.

The lookouts fall into three main types. The most common of these are the "waiters," men who are waiting for someone with whom they have made an appointment or whom they expect to find at this spot, for a particular type of "trick," or for a chance to get in on the action. The others are the masturbaters, who engage in autoerotic behavior (either overtly or beneath their clothing) while observing sexual acts, and the voyeurs, who appear to derive sexual stimulation and pleasure from watching the others. . . .

In terms of appearances, I assumed the role of the voyeur—a role superbly suited for sociologists and the only lookout role that is not overtly sexual. . . . Before being alerted to the role of lookout by a cooperating respondent, I tried first the role of the straight and then that of the waiter. As the former, I disrupted the action and frustrated my research. As the latter—glancing at my watch and pacing nervously from window to door to peer out—I could not stay long without being invited to enter the action and could only make furtive observation of the encounters. As it was, the waiter and voyeur roles are subject to blurring and I was often mistaken for the former.

By serving as a voyeur-lookout, I was able to move around the room at will, from window to window, and to observe all that went on without alarming my respondents or otherwise disturbing the action. I found this role much more amenable and profitable than the limited roles assumed in the earlier stages of research. . . .

. . . After developing a systematic observation sheet, I recorded 50 of these encounters (involving 53 sexual acts) in great detail. These records were compared with another 30 made by a cooperating respondent who was himself a sexual participant. . . .

Although primarily interested in the stigmatized behavior, I also wanted to know about the men who take such risks for a few moments of impersonal sex. I was able to engage a number of participants in conversation outside the restrooms; and, eventually, by revealing the purpose of my study to them, I gained a dozen respondents who contributed hundreds of hours of interview time. This sample I knew to be biased in favor of the more outgoing and better educated of the tearoom population.

To overcome this bias, I cut short a number of my observations of encounters and hurried to my automobile. There, with the help of a tape recorder, I noted a brief description of each participant, his sexual role in the encounter just observed, his license number, and a brief description of his car. I varied such records from park to park and to correspond with previously observed changes in volume at various times of the day. This provided me with a time-and-place-representative sample of 134 participants. With attrition, chiefly of those who had changed address or who drove rented cars, and the addition of two persons who walked to the tearooms, I ended up with a sample of 100 men, each of whom I had actually observed engaging in fellatio. . . .

Identification of the sample was made by using the automobile license registers of the states in which my respondents lived. Fortunately, friendly policemen gave me access to the license registers, without asking to see the numbers or becoming too inquisitive about the type of "market research" in which I was engaged. These registers provided the names and addresses of those in the sample, as well as the brand name and year of the automobiles thus registered. The make of the car, as recorded in the registers, was checked against my transcribed description of each car. In the two cases where these descriptions were contradictory, the numbers were rejected from the sample. Names and addresses were then checked in the directories of the metropolitan area, from which volumes I also acquired marital and occupational data for most of the sample. . . .

At this stage, my third ethical concern impinged. I already knew that many of my respondents were married and that all were in a highly discreditable position and fearful of discovery. How could I approach these covert deviants for interviews? By passing as deviant, I had observed their sexual behavior without disturbing it.

Now, I was faced with interviewing these men (often in the presence of their wives) without destroying them. Fortunately, I held another research job which placed me in the position of preparing the interview schedule for a social health survey of a random selection of male subjects throughout the community. With permission from the survey's directors, I could add my sample to the larger group (thus enhancing their anonymity) and interview them as part of the social health survey.

To overcome the danger of having a subject recognize me as a watchqueen, I changed my hair style, attire, and automobile. At the risk of losing more transient respondents, I waited a year between the sample gathering and the interviews, during which time I took notes on their homes and neighborhoods and acquired data on them from the city and county directories.

Having randomized the sample, I completed 50 interviews with tearoom participants and added another 50 interviews from the social health survey sample. The latter control group was matched with the participants on the bases of marital status, race, job classification, and area of residence.

This study, then, results from a confluence of strategies: systematic, firsthand observation, in-depth interviews with available respondents, the use of archival data, and structured interviews of a representative sample and a matched control group. At each level of research, I applied those measures which provided maximum protection for research subjects and the truest measurement of persons and behavior observed. . . .

12

MORTIMER A. SULLIVAN, JR., STUART A. QUEEN, AND
RALPH C. PATRICK, JR.

PARTICIPANT OBSERVATION AS EMPLOYED IN THE STUDY OF A MILITARY TRAINING PROGRAM

Until recently the Air Force included in its research and development planning an extensive social science program. This program, itself part of a larger and more elaborate organization devoted to the Air Force's personnel and training requirements, utilized in its studies classical experimental design, polling, the interview, and, occasionally, observation and the ethnographic or survey approach. There existed, however, certain aspects of the Air Force training situation which apparently could not adequately be understood through the use of these techniques. In particular, certain officers wished to gain a better notion of how basic and technical training were lived, understood, and felt by new airmen. Hence, after a year of preliminary study, a plan was drawn up and approved for the utilization of a participant-observer.

The general purpose of the study was to gain insight into the motivations and attitudes of personnel (in training) as reflected in both their military and social behavior. . . . Participant observation was therefore adopted for a pilot study in order to identify first, problems viewed by enlistees during basic and technical training, and second, new areas for research by other methods.

To accomplish this purpose it was decided that a research officer should "enlist" as a basic trainee. He would be a fullfledged member

Reprinted in part with permission from *American Sociological Review* 23 (December 1958): 660-667.

of the group under study, his identity, mission, and role as a researcher unknown to every one (except the investigators), even to his own commanding officer. This then became one of the few cases of real participant observation.

There were literally thousands of problems to overcome, not only in deciding how the study would be conducted, but also in determining how the participant-observer would be guided in his work, the things to be looked for or recorded if observed, the form reports should take, and how the data would be used after the study was completed. There were also less obvious difficulties arising from the mechanics involved and, of course, the problem of preparation for the role to be played by the participant-observer himself.

It was assumed that the recruit airman, having been drafted, enters the service with a structure of attitudes favorable to the service, or at least neutral to the Air Force and his place in it. There was evidence from previous research that during his service the airman's attitudes change, frequently turning against the Air Force. Thus the research problem posed was: What are the processes through which the recruit airman's attitudes toward the service and his place within it change, resulting often in behavior which is, from the organizational point of view, deviant?

The assumptions and frame of reference guiding the research were derived from general social science theory. The first guiding assumption was that membership in the American social system provides the airman with many predispositions toward nonconforming behavior in the armed forces, as well as predispositions toward conformity. Second, we anticipated that there would be found patterns of behavior which might be called a subculture of the Air Force. We expected that this culture would include "unofficial" patterns different from the "official" expectations contained in the formal rules and regulations of the service, and that the recruit airman would acquire both the "unofficial" and the "official" patterns of the subculture. Thirdly, we expected to find an "informal" social organization in addition to the formal organization imposed by Air Force Regulations. The recruit airman would be "socialized," presumably, during his training into the "informal" as well as the "formal" structure of the service. Finally, we hypothesized that certain aspects of the "unofficial" culture and the "informal" social structure of the Air Force would tend to increase the tendencies to nonconforming behavior already present in the airman. The method of participation-observation would, we believed, be especially useful in revealing these patterns of "unofficial" culture and "informal" social structure which contribute to behavior which is, from the standpoint of the official Air Force, deviant.

Preparation for the Study

The preliminary arrangements for the "enlistment" of the observer and the recording and transporting of data were well taken care of by high ranking Air Force personnel. The provost marshal of the command for which the study was undertaken worked closely with those primarily concerned in providing the needed support and information, and the Air Force's social science agency which guided the study made available a capable member of its organization, a civilian sociologist, to oversee and coordinate the research.

Once the participant-observer was in the field the reporting burden fell primarily upon three men: the observer himself, and a sociologist and anthropologist who were available at a nearby university. The sociologist, in addition to research in urban culture, had conducted field work in the Cumberland mountains and undertaken a combination of research and administration in jails and prisons of California. The anthropologist had field experience among the Havasupai Indians and in a study of a South Carolina community. These men had been members of the Air Force in earlier days. . . . The participant-observer, who had not undergone basic training before, was a 26-year-old first lieutenant with undergraduate work in psychology and a year of graduate training. At the time of the study he was assigned as a research psychologist with the Air Force's personnel and training research organization. The personal compatability of the members of the "team" and their ability to realign their approaches to the problem were of major importance to the successful outcome of the study. The fact that each "team member" provided a distinctive perspective on the findings improved the chances of identifying useful data and interpreting them in ways that might be of value both to social scientists and to the Air Force. However, it decreased the probability that results could be fitted easily into any closed system or established school of thought.

Extensive requirements had to be met in order to make the study possible, including "enlistment," processing, assignment, and, finally, "discharge" of the participant-observer. Since the observer was to "enlist" under an assumed name, even his "existence" had to be verified. Such problems would probably have been insuperable were it not for the cooperation of key personnel in the highly structured military establishment.

The plan agreed upon was to have the participant-observer "enlist" in a northern city, undergo his first four weeks of basic training at an Air Force Base in the South, and attend a technical training school (an overall time of four months). During the period in which the observer was in basic training, the problem of reporting was most difficult. Every minute of the trainee's waking time being allocated, it was necessary for hours to be taken from sleeping in order to write reports. Of equal importance, the observer's contacts with his associates were limited to a few visits by the Air Force's civilian sociologist and correspondence with the other team members. As a consequence, the observer was never certain whether his reports were adequate or whether he was "getting across" what he was observing.

Once the observer arrived at his technical training base he could meet with the other two team members. During the week, the observer took whatever notes he could, consolidating them each evening. On those weekends when he was able to leave the base, he transcribed his notes onto a dictating machine. Thereafter, he would meet, usually for eight to ten hours, with the other team members. Then the three researchers would discuss the preceding report, first as to what it meant itself, then as to how it fit into the overall picture as viewed at that time. Sometimes it was found that significant patterns of behavior could be agreed upon; at other times it was necessary to realign "team" thinking.

The team was very important to the participant-observer because it enabled him to keep the purpose of the study in sight. Aspects of the reports which were vague or which the observer mistakenly took for granted sometimes were cleared up during the weekend "conferences." At the same time, however, the conferences were difficult for the observer, because of the minor trauma experienced when he returned to the airman role.

In addition to the other team members, the provost marshal, and the Air Force's civilian sociologist, there were many individuals who contributed to the study. After the participant-observer left the South and arrived at the technical training base, he was told that an additional person had been informed of his presence and of his mission, a young chaplain who had had enlisted service in World War II and whose primary duty, in addition to ministerial responsibilities, was counseling newly arrived trainees. The chaplain contributed to the investigation not only through his familiarity with the training situation, but also by his personal interest in the problems of the observer. While the observer came to rely heavily upon the team for professional guidance whenever they met, he also depended upon the chaplain as his sole contact between meetings with the other team members.

The creation of a "new personality" for the observer was of some importance to the study. It would have been entirely possible for him to have "enlisted" and undergone training without disguising his name, age, or education. On the other hand, it appeared advantageous to provide the observer with an identity through which he might achieve a maximum of rapport with other trainees—most of whom, it was known, were under 20 years old and few of whom had any college education. Furthermore, a two-day meeting between the observer and William Foote Whyte and one of his "corner boys" emphasized the value of prior knowledge of those who were to be observed.

For nine months before the beginning of the field study itself, the observer was coached in the ways of the adolescent subculture. A young airman was told the requirements of the study and given the job of creating a "new personality" for the observer. Dress, speech, and mannerism, as well as interests, attitudes, and general appearance were "corrected" by the observer's enthusiastic coach. On one occasion, the observer thought he had succeeded in meeting the requirements when he was told, "You look real tough, hey." But the coach quickly added, "You ain't supposed to look tough. You're supposed to look like you're *trying* to be tough, but you ain't supposed to be." So successful was the airman's tutoring that when the time for "enlistment" arrived, the recruiting sergeant (who did not know of the study) suggested that the observer not be accepted by the Air Force because by all appearances he was a juvenile delinquent. To make the observer's role further convincing, it was decided that his age would be reported as being 19 instead of 26. To accomplish this appearance, the observer underwent minor surgery and lost 35 pounds.

There was also the problem of providing the observer with an acceptable "cover" story. Here again, the "coach" was relied upon to suggest significant items which would help convince not only the other trainees but also the training personnel that the observer was genuine. The suggestions of the coach were painstakingly followed (even to the extent of using the name "Tom" which he said fit the observer). The following biographical "facts" were seemingly accepted and responded to by the other trainees. "Tom" was from a lower middle class, but potentially mobile, family. As a result of an automobile accident, in which Tom was driving, his father, a laborer who had started college but encountered "bad breaks," was killed. This left Tom's mother to support him (an only child). Tom wanted to quit high school but his mother persuaded him to get his diploma and tried to induce him to go to college. During an argument over this issue, Tom left home and went to Northern City from which he enlisted in the Air Force. Again the coach's advice was convincing. During an interview in the early stages of training, an Air Force neuro-psychologist identified the observer as having mild anxiety over "killing" his father, and suggested that he be reclassified.

In deliberately cultivating a second self the research observer was engaged in something superficially like intelligence work or espionage. But there was a very important difference in goal for, in this case, it was a general understanding of a significant subculture, the processes of its development and transmission to new recruits, and its effect on the official training program. It was not the indictment of anybody or the immediate change of anyone's behavior. In fact, the data were so safeguarded that they could not lead to disciplinary action against any of the men under study. Neither was the objective a general indictment or defense of the Air Force. It was simply to gather a body of previously unavailable information and to interpret it in a way that might be helpful both to the military and to social scientists.

A very important aspect of preparation for the field study, was the training of the observer for the job of reporting. On the one hand, there was very little detailed material on participant-observer reporting and, on the other, the observer had had no experience in field study. The former problem was considerably resolved by the meetings with Professor Whyte, but the latter required many weeks of coordinated effort by the sociologist and anthropologist members of the team and the Air Force's civilian sociologist.

Conduct of the Study

As the study progressed, the observer felt that he had been well prepared for his job. Since there was a lag of only one week between the dictation of a report and discussion of it by the team, the observer could take quick advantage of comments, suggestions, and questions, all of which reassured the observer and lessened his uncertainty as to the adequacy of his reporting. The Air Force's civilian sociologist sat in with the team during several of its discussions and provided information on the progress of other aspects of the study.

The first month was the most hectic for the observer. Anyone familiar with military basic training will understand the extent to which the observer and his fellow airmen were caught up in a swirl of regimented activity. Whereas the observer had just undergone a nine-month "prenatal" period of preparation for his new "life," the Air Force instructors undertook to assure him that he was "not a civilian any more . . . but in the Air Force." On the first day, the observer, in an attempt to demonstrate the "new personality" which he had worked so hard to develop, intentionally appeared to defy an order of an instructor. A short time later, the instructor told his men, "I have handled many hundreds of enlistees and I know my job. I have already spotted some of you that I'm going to have trouble with."

At first, when the training was roughest or when he was spoken to gruffly by an instructor, the observer attempted to reassure himself that he was really an Air Force officer. He even would say to himself, "If these people knew what my *real* rank was they'd certainly act differently toward me." Interestingly, this attitude was apparently shared by another trainee who told the observer, "Back home I was a big shot." It wasn't long, however, before the observer realized that it made no difference who he *really was* as long as those around him *thought* he was Tom, and that there was little consolation in "pretending" that he was anybody else. Just as the other trainees were legally bound by the training situation, so the participant-observer considered himself morally bound and he felt that there was little difference between their respective positions. With the passage of time, the observer "forgot" about his old self; there was only the ever-present note taking to remind him that he was not just another trainee. His role in the barracks brought him so closely in contact with the men and their problems that he sometimes lost perspective. Here, again, the team was important in reassuring the observer and helping him regain his objectivity.

Perhaps the most interesting phenomenon to the participant-observer was the case with which he was able to carry out his role with the other trainees. The men not only accepted him and his cover story, but identified many aspects of his past as being similar to their own lives. The observer shared the sorrows and hopes of the other trainees and felt compelled to do his best out of loyalty to them. When the others learned of "tricks" by which to pass inspections or to give the appearance of doing a job which they had actually not done, the observer joined in and suffered no guilt for doing what he, as an officer, knew was "wrong." The observer is convinced that his complete integration into the trainees' subculture was essential for understanding and conveying the attitudes and problems which he reported. However, he also attaches importance to the professional guidance given by the other team members and the counsel and reassurance which they and the chaplain offered.

When the field study was completed, everyone who had been reading the reports felt that the effort had been successful; but this feeling had to be identified and codified. The reports were typed with a three-inch margin so that the sociologist and anthropologist could make comments and point out significant items. This somewhat simplified the task of compiling key items, but it did not solve it. There remained the difficult job of reviewing each of the more than 600 pages and listing those items which the team members thought most significant.

During the field study itself, the sociologist and anthropologist prepared memoranda pointing out critical aspects of the training environment with which they assumed their report would be concerned. This made it possible to develop categories or items which were believed to be sufficiently general (and significant) for consideration. Nevertheless, the three team members were faced with a mass of narrative and descriptive material, concrete, rich in detail, and vivid in language. For many weeks the team went over the items one by one. Because of their different training and experience and the unique requirements of this study, they found it necessary to develop a common language (common not only to them, but also to the people whose comments and views were expressed in the study).

When it was agreed that the significant items had been identified, the sociologist and anthropologist prepared summaries of the seven stages into which they had dividied the field study. The summaries were then sent to the Air Force sociologist who, together with the participant-observer, used them as the basis of their final report.

As indicated above, the "team" was able to identify many reoccurring items in the reports. Some of these were behavior patterns of trainees and instructors, others were attitudes toward military life. . . . A brief general statement of the findings should be of value at this time.

Some of the Findings

As had been anticipated the trainees' images of the Air Force and of themselves changed in the course of their experiences. In the strange world of basic training the men looked to their instructors, exclusively at first, for leadership and explanations of their day-by-day activities. Then, as the training took shape, as the trainees saw themselves becoming airmen, as they began to understand the structure of their environment, they learned how to meet the multitude of requirements with which they were faced. There then began an unending search for shortcuts, methods by which one job could be done more quickly so as to allow more time for doing a second, third, and fourth. In seeking shortcuts, the trainees learned that some things were never checked up on even though they were officially required, and others did not have to be done as long as the appearance of doing them was demonstrated. There were instances when it seemed that "the Air Force" *expected* the trainees to indulge in these "patterned evasions," and one who had learned the "trick" behind the requirement did not need to feel any guilt.

While in basic training patterned evasion was used almost exclusively as a means for keeping up with all the tasks required in the short time allowed, this was not the only benefit it could provide. After the trainees reached their technical training base, but before they were actually able to begin school (a period of about four weeks during which they were assigned to a "holding" squadron), one flight was able to make use of numerous evasions in order to win the highly competitive honor of best flight in the squadron, and with this honor went privileges. Although winning the title of "honor flight" required the men to outwork the other flights, the "outworking" also involved a certain amount of "outfoxing."

The trainees were naturally disappointed at having to wait several weeks after reaching their technical training base before actually starting school, and at having to perform a great deal of "KP" during that time, but they were probably more discouraged at finding that they were not yet members of the "real Air Force." Even after receiving their first stripe, the feeling that they were still basic trainees persisted. Once in technical school, the patterned evasions upon which they had come to depend had to be abandoned in many instances because the added requirement of attending classes made it necessary for the squadrons to function differently. There were still many of the original requirements in effect, but it was almost impossible to know which ones were "important" and which ones were not. Since the men were in what seemed to be an unstructured and fluctuating situation, they began to slip in meeting requirements. This resulted in periodic crackdowns, which themselves led to the renewed use of patterned evasions—this time, however, not for the purpose of winning "honor flight" or solely as a means of allowing time to get everything done (as in basic training), but rather as a technique for providing the men with more leisure time. They felt that their job was to do their best in technical school and that any time which they could save from their squadron (housekeeping) duties should be theirs to enjoy.

Certain men seemed to be able to cope with this problem better than others by virtue of their ability to separate the "testable" requirements from the "untestable" ones and to anticipate the crackdowns. Those who appeared to have rigid personalities never seemed to be able to structure the situation, nor to realize when they were spending their time on tasks which were never recognized. Such airmen, because of their inability to perceive subtle differences between situations, were most likely to get into trouble with both the official Air Force and the unofficial peer groups. The more adaptive airmen noticed that inspecting officers looked for certain things and not for others.

At four times during the field study, the men in the participant-observer's organizations were given a questionnaire which contained 37 items intended to reflect the subjects' attitudes toward aspects of their training and their image of the Air Force. The responses to these items, although often mysterious in themselves, were almost entirely explainable in terms of the field study reports. Significant increases were found in favorable responses given after the initial phase of basic training as compared with favorable responses given to the same items at the beginning of enlistment. While only an "educated guess" would suggest that this was due to the airmen's belief that "the worst was over," the field study demonstrated it. The highly consistent drop in favorable responses after technical training, as compared to responses before it, would probably have been unaccountable but for the mass of information which was available to describe the events of that period. The questionnaire, although inconclusive by itself, was of value to the study insofar as it confirmed in quantitative terms some of the findings of participant-observation research.

Significance of the Study

Of course, a study of this type cannot, by itself, guarantee representativeness of samples nor afford rigorous testing of hypotheses. Its function seems to us to be that of supplementing other research procedures, turning up new leads for questioning, observation, and interpretation. The method of participant observation was adopted in this case only after responsible Air Force personnel believed they had obtained about all they could from general observation, questionnaires, and formal interviews. In addition, they suspected that airmen, like other human beings, could and did maintain "false fronts," often deceiving officers, researchers, and perhaps themselves. Here seemed to be a new approach that might probe beneath the surface in a revealing way. Now that the study has been completed, both responsible Air Force personnel and we ourselves believe that significant results were obtained.

Obviously no other study could duplicate our procedures in complete detail. But something of the sort could profitably be done, we believe, in the study of institutions such as prisons and hospitals. We suspect that heretofore most would-be participant-observers have been early "spotted" by the objects of study and thereby prevented from entering fully into the life of the group in question. This study has at least demonstrated that thoroughgoing participant-observation is very difficult, but not impossible.

148

THE UNDERLIFE OF A PUBLIC INSTITUTION: A STUDY OF WAYS OF MAKING OUT IN A MENTAL HOSPITAL

My immediate object in doing field work at [Central Hospital, a mental institution of somewhat over 7000 inmates] was to try to learn about the social world of the hospital inmate, as this world is subjectively experienced by him. I started out in the role of an assistant to the athletic director, when pressed avowing to be a student of recreation and community life, and I passed the day with patients, avoiding sociable contact with the staff and the carrying of a key. I did not sleep in the wards, and the top hospital management knew what my aims were.

It was then and still is my belief that any group of persons—prisoners, primitives, pilots, or patients—develop a life of their own that becomes meaningful, reasonable, and normal once you get close to it, and that a good way to learn about any of these worlds is to submit oneself in the company of the members to the daily round of petty contingencies to which they are subject.

The limits, of both my method and my application of it, are obvious: I did not allow myself to be committed even nominally, and had I done so my range of movements and roles, and hence my data, would have been restricted even more than they were. Desiring to obtain ethnographic detail regarding selected aspects of patient social

Reprinted in part from Erving Goffman, *Asylums* (Chicago: Aldine Publishing Company, 1961), pp. ix-x, 188-189, 199, 203, 206-219.

life, I did not employ usual kinds of measurements and controls. I assumed that the role and time required to gather statistical evidence for a few statements would preclude my gathering data on the tissue and fabric of patient life. My method has other limits, too. The world view of a group functions to sustain its members and expectedly provides them with a self-justifying definition of their own situation and a prejudiced view of nonmembers, in this case, doctors, nurses, attendants, and relatives. To describe the patient's situation faithfully is necessarily to present a partisan view. (For this last bias I partly excuse myself by arguing that the imbalance is at least on the right side of the scale, since almost all professional literature on mental patients is written from the point of view of the psychiatrist, and he, socially speaking, is on the other side). Further, I want to warn that my view is probably too much that of a middle-class male; perhaps I suffered vicariously about conditions that lower-class patients handled with little pain. Finally, unlike some patients, I came to the hospital with no great respect for the discipline of psychiatry nor for agencies content with its current practice. . . .

. . . Every organization . . . involves a discipline of activity, but our interest here is that at some level every organization also involves a discipline of being—an obligation to be of a given character and to dwell in a given world. And my object here is to examine a special kind of absenteeism, a defaulting not from prescribed activity but from prescribed being.

. . . When an individual cooperatively contributes required activity to an organization and under required conditions—in our society with the support of institutionalized standards of welfare, with the drive supplied through incentives and joint values, and with the promptings of designated penalties—he is transformed into a cooperator; he becomes the "normal," "programmed," or built-in member. He gives and gets in an appropriate spirit what has been systematically planned for, whether this entails much or little of himself. In short, he finds that he is officially asked to be no more and no less than he is prepared to be, and is obliged to dwell in a world that is in fact congenial to him. I shall speak in these circumstances of the individual having a *primary adjustment* to the organization and overlook the fact that it would be just as reasonable to speak of the organization having a primary adjustment to him.

I have constructed this clumsy term in order to get to a second one, namely, *secondary adjustments*, defining these as any habitual arrangement by which a member of an organization employs unauthorized means, or obtains unauthorized ends, or both, thus getting around the organization's assumptions as to what he should do and get and hence what he should be. Secondary adjustments represent ways in which the individual stands apart from the role and the self that were taken for granted for him by the institution. . . .

An interest in the actual place in which secondary adjustments are practiced and in the drawing region from which practitioners come shifts the focus of attention from the individual and his act to collective matters. In terms of a formal organization as a social establishment, the corresponding shift would be from an individual's secondary adjustment to the full set of such adjustments that all the members of the organization severally and collectively sustain. These practices together comprise what can be called the *underlife* of the institution, being to a social establishment what an underword is to a city. . . .

All of the conditions that are likely to promote active underlife are present in one institution that is receiving considerable attention today: the mental hospital. In what follows I want to consider some of the main themes that occur in the secondary adjustments I recorded in a year's participant observation study of patient life in a public mental hospital of over 7000 patients, hereafter called "Central Hospital."

Institutions like mental hospitals are of the "total" kind, in the sense that the inmate lives all the aspects of his life on the premises in the close company of others who are similarly cut off from the wider world. These institutions tend to contain two broad and quite differently situated categories of participants, staff and inmates, and it is convenient to consider the secondary adjustments of the two categories separately. . . . I turn now to consider the sources of materials that patients employ in their secondary adjustments.

I

The first thing to note is the prevalence of *make-do's*. In every social establishment participants use available artifacts in a manner and for an end not officially intended, thereby modifying the conditions of life programmed for these individuals. A physical reworking of the artifact may be involved, or merely an illegitimate context of use, in either case providing homely illustrations of the Robinson Crusoe theme. Obvious examples come from prisons, where, for example, a knife may be hammered from a spoon, drawing ink extracted from the pages of *Life*[1] magazine, exercise books used to write betting slips,[2] and cigarettes lit by a number of means—sparking an electric-light outlet,[3] a homemade tinderbox,[4] or a match slit into quarters.[5] While this transformation process underlies many complex practices, it can be most clearly seen where the practitioner is not involved with others (except in learning and teaching the technique), he alone consuming what he just produced.

In Central Hospital many simple make-do's were tacitly tolerated. For example, inmates widely used free-standing radiators to dry personal clothing that they had washed, on their own, in the bathroom sink thus performing a private laundry cycle that was officially only the institution's concern. On hard-bench wards, patients sometimes carried around rolled-up newspapers to place between their necks and the wooden benches when lying down. Rolled-up coats and towels were used in the same way. Patients with experience in other imprisoning institutions employed an even more effective artifact in this context, a shoe.[6] In transferring from one ward to another, patients would sometimes carry their belongings in a pillow slip knotted at the top, a practice which is semiofficial in some jails.[7] The few aging patients fortunate enough to have a private sleeping room would sometimes leave a towel underneath their room washstand, transforming the stand into a reading desk and the towel into a rug to protect their feet from the cold floor. Older patients who were disinclined or unable to move around sometimes employed strategies to avoid the task of going to the toilet: on the ward, the hot steam radiator could be urinated on without leaving too many long-lasting signs; during twice-weekly shaving visits to the basement barber shop, the bin reserved for used towels was used for a urinal when the attendants were not looking. Back-ward patients of all ages sometimes carried around paper drinking cups to serve as portable spittoons and ashtrays, since attendants were sometimes more concerned about keeping their floors clean than they were in suppressing spitting or smoking. . . .

In total institutions make-do's tend to be focused in particular areas. One area is that of personal grooming—the fabrication of devices to facilitate presenting oneself to others in a seemly guise. For example, nuns are said to have placed a black apron behind a window pane to create a mirror—a mirror being a means of self-examination, correction, and approval ordinarily denied the sisterhood.[8] In Central Hospital, toilet paper was sometimes "organized"; neatly torn, folded, and carried on one's person, it was apologetically used as Kleenex by some fastidious patients. So, too, during the hot summer months a few male patients cut and tailored their hospital-issue khaki pants into neat-appearing summer shorts.

II

The simple make-do's I have cited are characterized by the fact that to employ them one need have very little involvement in and orientation to the official world of the establishment. I consider now a set of practices that imply somewhat more aliveness to the legitimated world of the institution. Here the spirit of the legitimate activity may be maintained but is carried past the point to which it was meant to go; we have an extension and elaboration of existing sources of legitimate satisfactions, or the exploitation of a whole routine of official activity for private ends. I shall speak here of "working" the system.

Perhaps the most elementary way of working the system in Central Hospital was exhibited by those patients on back wards who went on sick call or declined to comply with ward discipline in order, apparently, to trap the attendant or physician into taking notice of them and engaging them in social interactions, however disciplinarian. . . .

In order to work a system effectively, one must have an intimate knowledge of it;[9] it was easy to see this kind of knowledge put to work in the hospital. For example, it was widely known by parole patients that at the end of charitable shows at the theater hall cigarettes or candy would probably be given out at the door, as the patient audience filed out. Bored by some of these shows, some patients would come a few minutes before closing time in order to file out with the others; still others would manage to get back into the line several times and make the whole occasion more than ordinarily worth-while. Staff were of course aware of these practices, and latecomers to some of the hospital-wide patient dances were locked out, the assumption being that they timed their arrival so as to be able to eat and run. The Jewish Welfare women apparently served brunch after the weekly morning service and one patient claimed that "by coming at the right time you can get the lunch and miss the service." Another patient, alive to the little-known fact that the hospital had a team of seamstresses to keep clothes in repair, would take his own clothes there and get shirts and pants tailored to a good fit, showing his gratitude by a package or two of cigarettes or a small sum of money. . . .

The possibility of working the system was one that a few patients excelled in exploiting, leading to individual feats that could hardly be called customary secondary adjustments. On a service with two convalescent wards, one locked and one open, one patient claimed he arranged a transfer from the locked ward to the open one because the cloth on the pool table in the open ward was in superior condition; another patient claimed to have arranged a transfer in the other direction because the locked ward was "more sociable," some of its members being forced to remain on it. Another patient, with town parole, would periodically get excused from his hospital job and be given carfare to ride into town to look for work; he claimed that once in town he would settle down for the afternoon in a movie.

I would like to add that patients with experience in other situations of deprivation, patients who were in some sense con-wise, often showed very rapidly that they knew how to work the system. For example, one inmate, with prior experience in Lexington, on his first morning in the hospital had rolled himself a supply of roll-your-owns, obtained polish and done two pairs of his shoes, uncovered which fellow inmate had a large cache of detective stories, organized himself a supply of coffee by means of instant coffee and the hot-water tap, and found himself a place in the group psychotherapy session, sitting up close and waiting quietly for a few minutes before beginning to build up what was to be an active role. It is understandable, then, why an attendant claimed that "it takes no more than three days and you can tell if a man's off the street."

The means of working the system that I have so far mentioned are ones that profit only the actor himself or the persons he is closely related to. Practices designed with corporate interests in mind are found in many total institutions,[10] but collective means of working the system seem not too common in mental hospitals. . . .

In considering the process of "working the system," one must inevitably consider the ways in which hospitalization itself was worked. For example, both the staff and inmates sometimes claimed that some patients came into the hospital to dodge family and work responsibilities,[11] or to obtain free some major medical and dental work, or to avoid a criminal charge.[12] I cannot speak for the validity of these claims. There were also cases of patients with town parole who claimed they used the hospital as a tank to sober up in after weekend drinking episodes, this function being apparently facilitated by the claimed value of tranqualizers as a treatment for acute hangovers. And there were other town parolees who could accept below-subsistence pay for part-time civilian work, ensuring their own competitive position on the basis of free hospital food and lodging[13]. . . .

One of the interesting means by which a few patients worked the hospital system had to do with sociable association with outsiders. Concern for interaction with outsiders seemed to be related to the caste-like position of patients in the hospital and to myths associated with the stigma label of insanity. Although some patients claimed they could not feel comfortable with someone not a patient, other patients, exhibiting the opposite side of the same coin, felt that it was intrinsically healthier to associate with nonpatients and, in addition, a recommendation of some kind. Also, outsiders were less likely to be as offensive as staff members about patient status; outsiders did not know how lowly the position of patient was. Finally, a few patients claimed to be very tired of talking about their incarceration and their case with fellow patients and looked to conversation with outsiders as a means of forgetting about the culture of the patient.[14] Association with outsiders could confirm a sense of not being a mental patient. Understandably, therefore, on the grounds and in the recreation building some "passing" was effected, serving as an important source of assurance that one was really indistinguishable from the sane and that the sane themselves were really not very smart.

There were several strategic points in the hospital social system where association with outsiders was possible. Some of the adolescent female children of the resident doctors participated as sociable equals in the small circle of paroled male patients and student nurses who dominated the hospital tennis court.[15] During and after games this group would lounge on the nearby grass, engage in horseplay, and in general maintain a nonhospital tone. Similarly, on evenings when outside charitable organizations ran a dance, bringing some young females with them, one or two male patients affiliated themselves with these women, apparently obtaining from them a nonhospital response. So, too, on the admission ward where student nurses were spending their period of psychiatric training, some young male patients regularly played cards and other games with them, during which a dating, not a nursing, ethos was maintained. And during the "higher" therapies such as psychodrama or group therapy, visiting professionals would often sit in to observe the latest methods; these persons, too, provided patients with a source of interaction with normals. Finally, patients on the all-star hospital baseball team, when playing against teams from the environing community, were able to enjoy the special camaraderie that develops between opposing teams in a game and that separates both teams off from the spectators. . . .

NOTES

1. Holley Cantine and Dachine Ranier, eds., *Prison Etiquette* (Bearsville, N.J.: Retort Press, 1950), p. 42.
2. Frank Norman, *Bang to Rights* (London: Secker and Warburg, 1958), p. 90.
3. *Ibid.*, p. 92.
4. George Dendrickson and Frederick Thomas, *The Truth About Dartmoor* (London: Gollancz, 1954), p. 172.
5. *Ibid.*, pp. 172-73.
6. Compare the naval equivalent (Herman Melville, *White Jacket* [New York: Grove Press, n.d.] p. 189): " . . . the hard, unyielding, and ponderous man-of-war and Navy regulation tarpaulin hat which, when new, is stiff enough to sit upon, and indeed, in lieu of his thumb, sometimes serves the common sailor for a bench."
7. For a British example, see Dendrickson and Thomas, *op. cit.*, p. 66.
8. Kathryn Hulme, *The Nun's Story* (London: Muller, 1956), p. 33. Norman, *op. cit.*, p. 87, states that during Christmas-day relaxation of discipline at the British prison, Camp Hill, homosexuals made their faces up with white tooth powder and reddened their lips with dye obtained by wetting the covers of books.
9. Knowledge of a guard's routine figures in many fictional escape stories. Desperation and knowledge of routines are also linked in real experience as Eugene Kogon, *The Theory and Practice of Hell* (New York: Berkeley Publishing Corp., n.d.) p. 180, illustrates in discussing the response of Buchenwald prisoners to reduction and withdrawal of rations: " . . . *When an inmate had died in the tents, the fact was concealed and the dead man was dragged or carried by one or*

two men to the bread issue point, where the ration was issued to the 'helpers.' The body was then simply dumped anywhere in the roll-call area."

10. For example, Kogon, *op. cit.*, p. 137: "*In every concentration camp where the political prisoners attained any degree of ascendancy, they turned the prisoner hospital, scene of fearful SS horrors that it was, into a rescue station for countless prisoners. Not only were patients actually cured wherever possible; healthy prisoners, in danger of being killed or shipped to a death camp, were smuggled on the sick list to put them beyond the clutches of the SS. In special cases, where there was no other way out, men in danger were nominally permitted to 'die,' living on under the names of prisoners who had actually died.*"

11. In one service in the hospital there were a considerable number of male patients who entered at a time when jobs were scarce and, being somewhat cut off from the flow of events outside, still believed that the "deal" they were getting on the inside was a good one. As one suggested upon receiving his free dessert, "You don't get apple pie like this on the outside for twenty-five cents, you don't." Here the apathy and quest for a safe berth, characteristic of the depression years, could still be studied, preserved in institutional amber.

12. For a lower-class male who already has the stigma of having been in a mental hospital and who is restricted to the kind of job in which length of work experience or seniority is of small significance, coming into a mental hospital where he knows the ropes and has friends among the attendants is no great deprivation. It was claimed that a few of these expatients carried a card attesting to their medical history; when picked up by police, on whatever charge, they produced their medical card, thereby influencing their disposition. Patients I knew, however, claimed that, except for a murder charge, hospitalization was in general a poor way to beat a rap: prisons provide determinate sentences, the possibility of earning a little money, and, increasingly, good TV facilities. I felt, however, that this line ought really to be considered as part of antistaff morale, except in those hospitals, such as Central, which had a specially walled-in building for the "criminally insane."

13. In militant psychiatric doctrine, as suggested, these motives for exploiting hospitalization can be interpreted as symptomatic of a "real" need for psychiatric treatment.

14. All of these themes may of course be traced in any stigmatized group. Ironically, patients, in saying, "We're just different from normal people, that's all," do not appreciate, just as other "normal deviants" do not, that there are few sentiments so stereotyped, predictable, and "normal" in any stigmatized grouping.

15. Socially speaking, no female patient "made it" with this group. Incidentally, children of resident doctors were the only nonpatient category I found that did not evince obvious caste distance from patients; why I do not know.

14

MELVILLE DALTON

CONFLICTS BETWEEN STAFF AND LINE MANAGERIAL OFFICERS

In its concentration on union-management relations, industrial sociology has tended to neglect the study of processes inside the ranks of industrial management. Obviously the doors to this research area are more closely guarded than the entry to industrial processes through the avenue of production workers, but an industrial sociology worthy of the name must sooner or later extend its inquiries to include the activities of all industrial personnel.

The present paper is the result of an attempt to study processes among industrial managers. It is specifically a report on the functioning interaction between the two major vertical groupings of industrial management: (1) the *staff* organization, the functions of which are research and advisory; and (2) the *line* organization, which has exclusive authority over production processes.... In practice there is often much conflict between industrial staff and line organizations and in varying degrees the members of these organizations oppose each other.

The aim of this paper is, therefore, to present and analyze data dealing with staff-line tensions.

Data were drawn from three industrial plants in which the writer had been either a participating member of one or both of the groups or was intimate with reliable informants among the officers who were. [These plants were in related industries and ranged in size from

Reprinted in part with permission from *American Sociological Review* 15 (June 1950): 342-351.

4500 to 20,000 employees, with the managerial groups numbering from 200 to nearly 1000.

Approached sociologically, relations among members of management in the plants could be viewed as a general conflict system caused and perpetuated chiefly by: (1) power struggles in the organization stemming in the main from competition among departments to maintain low operating cost; (2) drives by numerous members to increase their status in the hierarchy; (3) conflict between union and management; and (4) the staff-line friction which is the subject of this paper. This milieu of tensions was not only unaccounted for by the blueprint organizations of the plants, but was often contradictory to, and even destructive of, the organizations' formal aims. All members of management, especially in the middle and lower ranks, were caught up in this conflict system. Even though they might wish to escape, the obligation of at least appearing to carry out formal functions compelled individuals to take sides in order to protect themselves against the aggressions of others. And the intensity of the conflict was aggravated by the fact that it was formally unacceptable and had to be hidden.

For analytical convenience, staff-line friction may be examined apart from the reciprocal effects of the general conflict system. Regarded in this way, the data indicated that three conditions were basic to staff-line struggles: (1) the conspicuous ambition and "individualistic" behavior among staff officers; (2) the complication arising from staff efforts to justify its existence and get acceptance of its contributions; and, related to point two, (3) the fact that incumbency of the higher staff offices was dependent on line approval. The significance of [the first of] these conditions [is] discussed in [this excerpt].

Mobile Behavior of Staff Personnel

As a group, staff personnel in the three plants were markedly ambitious, restless, and individualistic. There was much concern to win rapid promotion, to make the "right impressions," and to receive individual recognition. Data showed that the desire among staff members for personal distinctions often overrode their sentiments of group consciousness and caused intrastaff tensions.

159

The relatively high turnover of staff personnel quite possibly reflected the dissatisfactions and frustrations of members over inability to achieve the distinction and status they hoped for. (Turnover was determined by dividing the average number of employees for a given year, in line or staff, into the accessions or separations, whichever was the smaller.) Several factors appeared to be of importance in this restlessness of staff personnel. Among these were age and social differences between line and staff officers, structural differences in the hierarchy of the two groups, and the staff group's lack of authority over production.

With respect to age, the staff officers were significantly younger than line officers. (Complete age data were available in one of the larger plants.) This would account to some extent for their restlessness. Being presumably less well-established in life in terms of material accumulations, occupational status, and security, while having greater expectations . . . and more energy, as well as more life ahead in which to make new starts elsewhere if necessary, the staff groups were understandably more dynamic and driving.

Age-conflict was also significant in staff-line antagonisms. The incident . . . of the young staff officer seeking to get direct acceptance by the line of his contribution failed in part—judging from the strong sentiments later expressed by the line superintendent—because of an age antipathy. The older line officers disliked receiving what they regarded as instruction from men so much younger than themselves, and staff personnel clearly were conscious of this attitude among line officers. In staff-line meetings staff officers frequently had their ideas slighted or even treated with amusement by line incumbents. Whether such treatment was warranted or not, the effects were disillusioning to the younger, less experienced staff officers. Often selected by the organization because of their outstanding academic records, they had entered industry with the belief that they had much to contribute, and that their efforts would win early recognition and rapid advancement. Certainly they had no thought that their contributions would be in any degree unwelcome. This naiveté was apparently due to lack of earlier firsthand experience in industry (or acquaintance with those who had such experience), and to omission of realistic instruction in the social sciences from their academic training. The unsophisticated staff officer's initial contacts with the shifting, covert, expedient arrangements between members of staff and line usually gave him a severe

160

shock. He had entered industry prepared to engage in logical, well-formulated relations with members of the managerial hierarchy, and to carry out precise, methodical functions for which his training had equipped him. Now he learned that: (1) his freedom to function was snared in a web of informal commitments; (2) his academic specialty (on which he leaned for support in his new position) was often not relevant for carrying out his formal assignments; and that (3) the important thing to do was to learn who the informally powerful line officers were and what ideas they would welcome which at the same time would be acceptable to his superiors.

Usually the staff officer's reaction to these conditions is to look elsewhere for a job or make an accommodation in the direction of protecting himself and finding a niche where he can make his existence in the plant tolerable and safe. . . .

Behavior in the plants indicated that line and staff personnel belonged to different social status groups and that line and staff antipathies were at least in part related to these social distinctions. For example, with respect to the item of formal education, the staff group stood on a higher level than members of the line. . . .

The social antipathies of the two groups and the status concern of staff officers were indicated by the behavior of each toward the established practice of dining together in the cafeterias reserved for management in the two larger plants. Theoretically, all managerial officers upward from the level of general foremen in the line, and general supervisors in the staff, were eligible to eat in these cafeterias. However, in practice the mere taking of one of these offices did not automatically assure the incumbent the privilege of eating in the cafeteria. One had first to be invited to "join the association." Staff officers were very eager to "get in" and did considerable fantasying on the impressions, with respect to dress and behavior, that were believed essential for an invitation. One such staff officer, a cost supervisor, dropped the following remarks:

> There seems to be a committee that passes on you. I've had my application in for three years, but no soap. Harry [his superior] had his in for over three years before he made it. You have to have something, because if a man who's in moves up to another position the man who replaces him doesn't get it because of the position—and he might not get it at all. I think I'm about due.

Many line officers who were officially members of the association avoided the cafeteria, however, and had to be *ordered* by the assistant plant manager to attend. One of these officers made the following statement, which expressed more pointedly the many similar spontaneous utterances of resentment and dislike made by other line officers:

> There's a lot of good discussion in the cafeteria. I'd like to get in on more of it but I don't like to go there—sometimes I have to go. Most of the white collar people [staff officers] that eat there are stuck-up. I've been introduced three times to Svendsen [engineer], yet when I meet him he pretends to not even know me. When he meets me on the street he always manages to be looking someplace else. G—d—such people as that! They don't go in the cafeteria to eat and relax while they talk over their problems. They go in there to look around and see how somebody is dressed or to talk over the hot party they had last night. Well, that kind of damn stuff don't go with me. I haven't any time to put on airs and make out I'm something that I'm not. . . .

Summary

Research in three industrial plants showed conflict between the managerial staff and line groups that hindered the attainment of organizational goals. Privately expressed attitudes among some of the higher line executives revealed their hope that greater control of staff groups could be achieved, or that the groups might be eliminated and their functions taken over in great part by carefully selected and highly remunerated lower-line officers. On their side, staff members wanted more recognition and a greater voice in control of the plants.

All of the various functioning groups of the plants were caught up in a general conflict system; but apart from the effects of involvement in this complex, the struggles between line and staff organizations were attributable mainly to: (1) functional differences between the two groups; (2) differentials in the ages, formal education, potential occupational ceilings, and status group affiliations of members of the two groups (the staff officers being younger, having more education but lower occupational potential, and forming a prestige-oriented group with distinctive dress and recreational tastes); (3) need of the staff groups to justify their existence; (4) fear in the line that staff bodies by their expansion, and well-financed research activities, would undermine line authority; and (5) the fact that aspirants to higher staff offices could gain promotion only through approval of influential line executives.

If further research should prove that staff-line behavior of the character presented here is widespread in industry, and *if* top management should realize how such behavior affects its cost and production goals—and be concerned to improve the condition—then remedial measures could be considered. For example, a corrective approach might move in the direction of: (1) creating a separate body whose sole function would be the coordination of staff and line effort; (2) increasing the gradations of awards and promotions in staff organizations (without increase of staff personnel); (3) granting of more nearly equal pay to staff officers, but with increased responsibility (without authority over line processes or personnel) for the practical working of their projects; (4) requiring that staff personnel have a minimum supervisory experience and have shared repeatedly in successful collaborative staff-line projects before transferring to the line; (5) steps by top management to remove the fear of veiled personal reprisal felt by officers in most levels of both staff and line hierarchies (This fear—rising from a disbelief in the possibility of bureaucratic impersonality—is probably the greatest obstacle to communication inside the ranks of management); (6) more emphasis in colleges and universities on realistic instruction in the social sciences for students preparing for industrial careers.

PART IV

Systematic Control

over the Observed Action

INTRODUCTION

It is not always the aim of the sociological observer [as was often the case in Part III] to prevent his data-gathering operations from controlling or changing the natural dynamic processes of the people or groups under study. He may deliberately build "systematic controls" into the research design. Indeed, the potential for strategically introducing a variety of controls constitutes a major strength of observation, as an investigative procedure occurring simultaneously with the action under scrutiny.

The studies in Part IV illustrate two uses of systematic controls: general manipulation of clusters of potentially explanatory variables in order to examine the "effects" on other variables, and, more specificially, directing the action along lines of the observer's interest (reducing irrelevancies of the "dross rate," as Webb et al., 1966, pp. 133-134 and elsewhere, would put it). Against such assets must be set the inevitable caveats: *any* intrusion by an observer—whether he aims to avoid control or to use it systematically—can produce undesired, unsystematic, unmeasurable "control effects." And such intrusion may compound the ethical problems discussed in Part III.

Systematic control can be introduced into a research design to varying degrees and in diverse forms. The widely used method instituted by Bales [Part 1] illustrates three of these forms, thereby pointing to some of the strengths and weaknesses involved (cf., e.g., the discussion by Swanson, 1951). First, Bales establishes a special *setting* (in this instance a small-groups laboratory) for the action he is observing, thus facilitating his access to people for study, but at the same time casting doubt on the naturalness of behavior in artificial surroundings.

Second, Bales himself puts together the *groups* he will observe, regulating their size and composition but at the same time losing information about some of the norms and expectations that would govern behavior in established groups. Third, Bales focuses activity on a standardized *task*, thus heightening the opportunity to discover uniformities in system processes, but again risking reactive effects of artificiality.

The first three studies in this part hint at the many permutations and combinations of design features involved in controlling just these three aspects: the setting, the task, and the number and kinds of people observed (cf. Weick, 1968). *Strodtbeck's* observation of interaction over revealed differences controls the task, but not the setting (he took his sound truck into the Arizona-New Mexico desert) or the make-up of the groups (who were in large part Navaho, Texan, and Mormon husband-wife pairs). In this case, controlling the task serves to focus the action on the variables of interest (talking time in relation to decision winning in instances in which husband and wife had disagreed).

Hartshorne and May, in their classic studies in deceit, worked with school children in their regular classrooms, but contrived a series of tasks to allow varied opportunities to cheat. In the brief excerpt, for example, these researchers gave children the opportunity to change their original answers surreptitiously as they graded their own papers. The research demonstrates the success of this control device in developing highly calibrated measures of dishonesty, the character trait under scrutiny.

The study by *Sampson and Brandon*, which controls setting and task in the Bales tradition, also exemplifies a widely used device for controlling group composition—the inclusion of confederates or "stooges." Here the confederate, instructed in each case to assume either a deviant or a nondeviant ideological stance, is used as a means of manipulating a key independent variable in order to disclose the consequences for group interaction. Similarly, Asch (1952; 1956) instructs confederates to give wrong answers to a test as a means of controlling the group pressure toward conformity exerted upon naive members; normal people gain secret admission to psychiatric hospitals to see whether or not they are discovered to be sane (Rosenhan, 1973); or Franzen (1950) sends a confederate as a "customer" to report his "symptoms" to a sample of pharmacists, in order to learn whether they themselves would prescribe or would refer the customer to a physician. (In fact, the confederate returned with large shopping bags filled with purchases of drugs recommended by the pharmacists.)

These examples thus show how selected aspects of the design (group composition, setting, or task) may each be independently controlled in line with particular research objectives. The two remaining excerpts in this part are drawn from the long list of studies which manipulate the independent variable as a presumed "casual" factor of central concern. (As early as the eighteenth century the French government made detailed observations of citizen reactions to planted rumors regarding taxes and military recruitment—Lécuyer and Oberschall, 1968, p. 38.) At the microlevel, *Goldberg, Kiesler, and Collins* manipulate the distance in seating between interviewer and subject and then observe how this distance relates to the amount of time the subject looks directly into the interviewer's eyes.[1] At the community level, *Miller*, reflecting the current rash of designs for evaluating planned social interventions, uses observation of "behavior sequences" in adolescent gangs as one means of gauging the impact, over a three-year period, of an elaborate program for delinquency control (the "causal" factor).

Some Methodological Implications

These selections clearly indicate that varied systematic controls are in common use, and appear to be largely unconstrained by other aspects of the research design [as in Parts II and III]. What further variations or improvements seem indicated? At least two avenues are open through consideration of the ideal experimental design—a design clearly implicated but rarely approximated in most of the observational research we have been examining.

The first avenue for improvement lies in *randomizing* the effects of extraneous variables in order to focus on the explanatory variables of interest. The experiment, as the optimal design for interpreting change in causal terms, requires not only systematic manipulation of the experimental factor, but also random assignment of this factor to experimental and control samples. Randomization is required because the researcher can never be sure that he has recognized and held constant *all* the associated confounding factors.

Goldberg, Kiesler, and Collins do use random numbers to determine the distance between interviewer and subject[2] (their experimental factor) in each particular trial. By contrast, Miller makes no attempt at randomization despite the precedent set by Powers (1949) some two decades earlier, as he uses a control sample only with data drawn from court appearance statistics, not from observation. Hence Miller's behavior sequences lend credence to Donald Campbell's contention that, for sundry administrative and ethical reasons, "most ameliorative programs end up with no interpretable evaluation" (Campbell, 1969, p. 409). For situations not amenable to randomization, Campbell recommends alternative quasi experiments.[3]

A second means of improvement suggested by the experimental model consists of *minimizing control effect* unwittingly produced by the intentional introduction of systematic controls. Of course, every explicit manipulation of the action under study (e.g., contrivance of the setting, introduction of stooges) tends to evoke unintended as well as intended reactions (cf. Orne, 1962; Leik, 1965). Yet the wary researcher can diminish the likelihood of unintended ones. For example, the children in the Hartshorne and May studies, because they were unaware of their contrived experimental task, may have performed more naturally than the aware subjects used by Strodtbeck or by Bales [Part I]. Similarly, Milgram's "lost-letter technique," whereby letters addressed to various organizations are scattered about a city to learn which types of letters will be returned, suggests an ingenious approach to the unobtrusive study of community political orientations (Milgram, Mann, and Harter, 1965). In particular, Rosenthal's (1966, pp. 158 ff.) demonstration that the experimenter's expectancy can influence the behavior of animal, as well as human, subjects alerts us once again to the need for double-blind experiments (used by the Vienna Medical Society at least as early as 1844), in which the possibility of control effect is reduced because neither the subjects nor the experimenter know the subjects' experimental condition (Rosenthal, 1966, pp. 367 ff.).

Still unsettled and unsolved are many ethical dilemmas that often thwart classical experimentation, as well as other forms of controlled observation. Campbell (1969) points to several means of handling one such dilemma—that of withholding a presumed benefit from a randomly chosen control group. In many situations, he suggests, the random assignment may be justified as a democratic allocation of an initially scarce resource (such as the Salk vaccine), or as a pilot stage of innovation (a trial program which, if it works, can then become more widely used). Yet, numerous experiments not involving allocation of scarce resources have incited ethical controversy—as in attempts to induce subjects to violate their values, such as Milgram's experimental studies (1965a; 1965b) of obedience to authority in administering pain; or in deceiving people about their status as participants in an experiment, such as the double-blind use of placebos in experimental trials of oral contraceptives conducted in a birth control clinic (as widely discussed in the public press in the early 1970s). Thus, the researcher's deliberate and systematic control of the action under study can only intensify the salience of his ethical responsibility for undesirable and unintended consequences of the research.

NOTES

1. Among several other small-group studies of spatial arrangements as related to communication, leadership, task, eye contact, and so on, see Bavelas, (1951); Sommer (1961; 1965). The social-psychological literature is replete with experiments, of course; see, as one example, Bandura et al. (1963). See also the detailed discussion in Weick, (1968).

2. No attention is paid here and in many similar designs to the issue of representativeness, which we shall discuss in Part VI. For example, are these Yale students, who are randomly assigned for experimental purposes, representative of some definable population (e.g., college students)? Campbell (1957) defines the distinction as between internal validity, ("Did in fact the experimental stimulus make some significant difference in this specific instance?") and external validity ("To what populations, settings, and variables can this effect be generalized?").

3. Such quasi experiments are discussed in detail in Campbell and Stanley (1963). An example is the "time-series design," which consists of "a periodic measurement process on some group or individual and the introduction of an experimental change into this time series of measurements" (p. 37).

15

FRED L. STRODTBECK

HUSBAND-WIFE INTERACTION
OVER REVEALED DIFFERENCES

Background

During 1948-49 the writer observed a series of groups engaged in decision making. An effort was made to determine some of the correlates of differential ability to persuade others in accordance with the actor's desires. In one instance, four mathematics students were requested to recommend jointly the best of three possible solutions to particular problems. While these students were in the process of developing consensus they were asked to record privately the alternative they personally favored. Thus, the experimenter was provided with a continuous means of relating a type of private opinion to public behavior. The experimentation indicated that the ultimate decision could be most accurately predicted by simply weighting the privately predetermined opinion of each participant by the total time he had spoken during the experimental interaction. This finding was duplicated in various groups who worked at the task of jointly selecting the best move in a chess problem. . . .

We recognized that we had up to this time worked with *ad hoc* groups which had no group structure at the beginning of the observation period and no expectation of participating with one another at a later time. The problems they had considered were delimited and specific; the nature of their arguments and responses was highly structured. On the basis of this analysis, we were led to consider experimentation with groups whose members approached

Reprinted in part with permission from *American Sociological Review* 16 (August 1951): 468-473.

the opposite extreme of broad common interests, daily contact, and permanence—so-called primary groups.

Among the various types of primary groups that might profitably be studied, husband-wife dyads were selected because of the ease of replication of these units. Each couple was asked to pick three reference families with whom they were well acquainted. The husband and wife were then separated and requested to designate which of the three reference families most satisfactorily fulfilled a series of 26 conditions such as: Which family has the happiest children? Which family is the most religious? Which family is most ambitious? After both husband and wife had individually marked their choices they were requested to reconcile their differences and indicate a final "best" choice from the standpoint of their family. For the first ten couples studied, this pooling took place with the experimenter out of the room and under conditions such that the couple did not know they were being observed or having their voices recorded. Their lack of knowledge of the observation was ascertained after the session, at which time their permission to use the material in a scientific inquiry was obtained. The anticipated experimental difficulties—(a) producing "polite" interaction because of the intrusion of the experimenter, and (b) structuring the task to such a degree that the mode of interaction would be highly determined—were judged to have been satisfactorily avoided.

. . . It was found that women won 47 of the contested decisions and men, 36. In six of the eight cases in which there was a difference both in number of decisions-won and in talking-time, the spouse who talked most won the majority of the decisions. At this time there was no basis for appraising whether the women had won slightly more decisions because they had known more about the types of information under discussion, or whether the decision winning represented, as we had hoped, the operation of structured power relations in an area in which both participants were equally informed. The observed margin by which the women exceeded the men was not significant—a result which might have been much more valuable if we had predicted it in terms of independent knowledge of the equalitarian characteristics of the married veteran couples used in the sample. In short, further application was necessary to determine whether the technique was a valid method of indicating in any more general sense the balance of power between participants.

A field study was designed to throw further light on this problem.

Three communities were selected which presumably differed in terms of the degree to which the wife was favored by the cultural phrasing of power. The communities were at the same time sufficiently small to increase greatly the probability that both spouses would be adequately, if not equally, informed concerning the behavior of the reference couples. The technique as described above was applied to ten couples from each of these cultures. It was proposed that the conformity of the experimental results with the a priori cultural expectations be taken as a crude measure of the validity with which the technique reflected power differences.

Description of Cultures

The cultures which were selected for study [as part of the larger Harvard Comparative Study of Values Project] are geographically adjacent communities in the Arizona-New Mexico area. Briefly described, the groups are Navaho Indians; dry farmers from Texas who have recently homesteaded in the area; and early settlers who utilize a dam operated under the supervision of the Mormon church. . . .

The favored position of the Navaho woman in contrast to the Mormon woman was judged in terms of economic, religious, and kinship considerations to be quite unequivocal. Between Texan and Mormon women there is less difference, but in terms of holding church office and the present possession of productive land and semiprofessional jobs, the women in the Texan community appear to be more favored than the Mormon women. On the basis of this analysis it was predicted that Navaho women would win the highest percentage of the decisions and the Mormon women the smallest.

Experimental Procedure

The area under study had no electrification, and since it was impractical to attempt to bring the subjects to an observation room, the field sessions of the experimental procedure were recorded by portable sound equipment powered from a truck. Although the subjects were separated from the experimenter and other persons, they knew that their voices were being recorded. The task was explained to the Navahos by an interpreter. An appropriate picture was presented for each question and underneath the illustration there were pockets representing the three reference couples. The Navaho would place his marker in the pocket which represented the couple of his choice. In those instances in which there had been a difference between the choice of the man and wife, the illustration was presented again to the two of them with their markers in separate pockets. They were requested to combine their markers in the position which best represented their joint opinion. Some questions were changed somewhat by translation into Navaho: for example, the question "Which family is the most religious?" became "Which family follows the 'Navaho Way' best?" It was not felt that these changes would significantly modify the results here presented. These recording were transcribed and, in the case of the Navaho, translated into English.

The written protocols were analyzed to determine the number of acts used by each participant and the distribution of these acts in terms of [Bales'] interaction process categories. This information plus knowledge of the number of decisions won by each participant provides the basis for the analysis presented below.

Findings

We present in Table 15-1 the sum of the decisions won by the husbands and wives in each of the three cultures. The appropriate null hypothesis is compounded of two elements: (a) the proposition that the Mormon wives win an equal or greater number of decisions than their husbands ($p = .007$); and (b) the proposition that Navaho husbands win an equal or greater number of decisions than the wives ($p = .16$). Since the combined probability associated with these two propositions is less than .01, we reject the null hypothesis and conclude that we were able to predict the balance of decision winning from our study of the comparative social and cultural organization of the groups from which our sample was drawn.

TABLE 15-1.

Decisions Won, by Spouse and Culture

CULTURE	NUMBER OF COUPLES	DECISIONS WON BY	
		HUSBAND	WIFE
Navaho	10	34	46
Texan	10	39	33
Mormon	10	42	29

Having to this limited degree established the validity of the technique, we are encouraged to inquire further into elements of behavior in the small group situation which are linked with decision winning. Our earlier experience had indicated a very strong relationship between decision winning or leadership and talking-time in *ad hoc* groups of four persons. In the present instance two-person primary groups are involved. From a broader study of the rank characteristics of participants in groups ranging in size from two to ten persons it is known that differentiation in speaking time in two-person groups is relatively less than it is in larger groups, hence it is probable that the relation between speaking-time and decision winning is less clearly defined in two-person than in larger groups. There was no compelling rationale for predicting the effects of the primary relationships upon "speaking and decision winning." By combining the ten cases observed at Cambridge with the 30 cases from the field and eliminating the six cases in which the decisions were split evenly, we obtain the thirty-four cases compared in Table 15-2. The null hypothesis of independence between talking most and winning may be rejected at the .05 but not the .01 level.

TABLE 15-2.

Decisions Won and Talking-Time for Thirty-Four Married Couples

SPOUSE WHO TALKED MOST	SPOUSE WHO WON MOST	
	HUSBAND	WIFE
Husband	14	5
Wife	5	10

To approach a more systematic description of the interaction characteristics of the spouse who talks most, we have selected the 24 cases in which there was a significant difference between the number of acts originated by the husband and the wife. We find that the most talking spouse tended more frequently to *ask questions*, carry out *opinion and analysis*, and make *rewarding remarks*. As Simmel suggested, in a dyad there can be no coalitions—the speaker does not have alternative audiences, so the "threat of withdrawal" is generally a more compelling adjustmental device in two-person than in larger groups. While we do not as yet have norms by group size for category usage on a common task, the unexpected finding in the present study that the most active participant is significantly high in question asking gives us further insight into how withdrawal is anticipated and prevented. The finding that the frequency of opinion and analysis acts is higher for the most talking person is in agreement with Bales' notion that acts of this type have a central generative function which results in their being heavily represented in the profile of the most talking person in groups of any size.

The categories which discriminate the profile of the least talking participants are, in order of magnitude, the following: simple *acts of agreement*, *aggressive acts* designed to deflate the other actor's status, and simple *disagreements*. Taken together, these characteristics suggest the passive agreeing person who from time to time becomes frustrated and aggresses. . . .

Summary

The essence of the revealed difference technique here described consists of: (a) requesting subjects who have shared experiences to make individual evaluations of them; and then (b) requesting the subjects to reconcile any differences in interpretations which may have occurred. It has been shown that the disposition of these reconciled decisions is related both to power elements in the larger social and cultural organization and amount of participation in the small group situation. It is believed that other couples as well as parent-child, foreman-worker, and similar relationships may be profitably studied with the technique, since it appears not only to reveal the balance of power, but also to produce a sample of interaction in which modes and techniques of influence can be studied by methods of content and process analysis.

STUDIES IN DECEIT

The Scope and Method of the Inquiry

[Our studies] are concerned with devising tests and techniques for measuring deceptive behavior. The general procedure has been to place the child in a situation in which deceit may be practiced and record his conduct. . . . [These] studies have resulted in the development of a large battery of deception tests, of which 22 use ordinary classroom situations, four use an athletic contest, two are in parties, and one is work done at home. There are also two lying tests and two stealing tests. These situations are intended as samples of the sort which it would be necessary to use if a complete picture of a person's tendencies to deceive were to be compiled. . . .

Some 11,000 children of ages 8 to 16 have been subjected to parts (and in a few cases to nearly all) of our test situations. . . .

[Using correlation procedures], we find that one form of deceit or another is definitely associated with such facts as dullness, retardation, school grade, emotional instability, socio-economic handicaps, cultural limitations, certain national, racial, and religious groupings, suggestibility of a certain type, frequency of attendance at motion pictures, and poor deportment at school.

Deception runs in families in about the same way as intelligence, eye color, or height. This does not prove of course that deception is inherited, but only that certain things are found together. Deception also goes by gangs and classrooms. A pupil resembles his friends in his tendency to deceive.

Reprinted in part from H. Hartshorne and M. A. May, *Studies in the Nature of Character*, Vol. I. *Studies in Deceit* (New York: The Macmillan Company, 1938), pp. 14-15, 47-48, 51-52, 65-66, 110, 116, 377, 387-390, 407-408.

Where relations between teachers and pupils are characterized by an atmosphere of cooperation and good-will, there is less deception, and to this effect the general morale of the school and classroom also contributes. On the other hand, attendance at Sunday school or membership in at least two organizations which aim to teach honesty does not seem to change behavior in this regard, and in some instances there is evidence that it makes children less rather than more honest.

Honesty appears to be a congeries of specialized acts which are closely tied up with particular features of the situation in which deception is a possibility, and is apparently not greatly dependent on any general ideal or trait of honesty. Motives for cheating, lying, and stealing are highly complex, and are specialized just as are the acts of deception. The most common extraneous motive is the desire to do well in class.

Methods Used by the Inquiry for Measuring Deception

. . . In setting up our techniques we tried to satisfy as many as possible of the requirements which should be met by tests of this type. We have formulated these in ten criteria. . . .

1. The test situation should be as far as possible a natural situation. It should also be a controlled situation. The response should as far as possible be natural even when directed.

2. The test situation and the response should be of such a nature as to allow all subjects equal opportunity to exhibit the behavior which is being tested. That is, there should be nothing about the test itself which would prevent anyone who desired to deceive from so doing; on the other hand, there should be nothing about it to trick an honest subject into an act he would repudiate if he were aware of its import.

3. No test should subject the child to any moral strain beyond that to which he is subjected in the natural course of his actual life situations.

4. The test should not put the subject and the examiner in false social relations to one another. The examiner should guard against being deceptive himself in order to test the subject.

5. The test should have "low visibility"; that is, it should be of such a nature as not to arouse the suspicions of the subject. This is one of the fundamental difficulties in all such testing since the entire purpose of the test cannot be announced in advance. This criterion is all the more difficult to meet when coupled with criterion number four, for the examiner must keep

secret one aspect of his purpose and at the same time be honest with the subjects.

6. The activity demanded of the subject in taking the test should have real values for him whether he is aware of these values or not.

7. The test should be of such a nature as not to be spoiled by publicity.

8. If tests are to be used in statistical studies they should be group tests. They should also be easy to administer and should be mechanically scored. They should be short enough to be given in single school periods.

9. The test results should be clear and unambiguous. It should be obvious from the results whether the subject did or did not exhibit the behavior in question. The evidence should be such as would be accepted in a court of law.

10. The scores should be quantitative, showing the amount as well as the fact of deception. Each test therefore should be flexible enough to include within its scope wide ranges of deceptive tendency....

[Example of One Method of Measuring Cheating]

[One] rather common form of classroom deceptiveness occurs when the pupil makes illegitimate use of a key or answer sheet either in doing his work or in the scoring of his own test paper. This is one type of behavior which we have been most successful in testing....

Any sort of test is given, preferably the short answer type. The papers are collected and taken to the office, where a duplicate is made of each paper. Great care is taken to be certain that an exact record is made of what the pupil actually did on the test. At a later session of the class the papers are returned and each child is given a key, or answer sheet, and is asked to score his own paper. The self-scored papers are then compared with the duplicates and all changes are recorded. Deception consists in illegitimately increasing one's score by copying answers from the key....

[In a double testing technique] the pupils are tested twice. On one occasion there is strict supervision and no opportunity to deceive is given. On the other occasion the conditions are such as to permit deception: the barriers are let down, and the only resistance to the tendency to cheat is in the individual's own habits and attitudes. The difference between the scores made on the two occasions is roughly a measure of the tendency to deceive. Cheating consists in either copying answers from the key or in changing answers to match the key....

[Before applying such procedures] in order to try out and

standardize our method of administration, we set up a preliminary experiment. The variables we consciously attempted to control were the teacher, the examiner, the behavior of the examiner in the room, the opportunity offered to be dishonest, the motive under which the pupil was operating, and the type of test material used. . . . Profiting by our first experience, we revised our testing technique. [For example,] we omitted all attempts to motivate cheating by repeating a formula. A colorless routine statement was adopted: "We are going to have some tests today. When the papers are passed out they will be fully explained. Be sure you have a sharpened pencil."

The Specific Nature of Conduct and Attitudes

Strictly speaking, what we measure by our techniques is not conduct but tendency or attitude, for we remove the external barriers which ordinarily prevent the full expression of the tendency and permit the individual to go as far as he wishes to in the direction of dishonest performance. . . . The tendency to copy answers from answer sheets and substitute them for one's own work, for example, exists in a measurable quantity peculiar to the individual. Whatever may be the motives which combine to make him use the answer sheet, they operate to overcome just so much resistance and no more, and this resistance can be arranged to begin with just no resistance at all and move up by measured steps to the point where no one will overcome it in order to cheat. The scheme used was roughly as follows:

We first arranged a test so that it would be very troublesome and risky to cheat on it. The answers to the questions were made by drawing a line in ink around the correct answer. In order to cheat, a pupil had to erase this mark made in ink and draw another. At the other end of the scale was a spelling test the answers to which were made by entering a check mark in lead pencil against a misspelled word. To cheat, all one had to do was to add more check marks or erase and change those already made. In between were procedures requiring varying amounts of time and trouble in order to make one's paper appear like the answer sheet. In order to be absolutely sure of every change made, we gave the test in school and then took it to the office and had an exact copy made of each paper. Then we returned to the school and asked the pupils to score their own papers by referring to the keys we provided. We then compared their papers as they now appeared with what they were before the scoring had been done. In this way every bit of deception was recorded.

By figuring the percentage of cases that cheated at each level of difficulty we were able to give a numerical value to the amount of resistance that had to be overcome at each level of difficulty. We found that practically all who cheated at any one level cheated also at each lower level, and that all the one-cheaters cheated at the lowest level, the two-cheaters at the two lowest levels, etc. In other words, we had a scale for measuring the amount of the tendency to cheat. The extent to which this scale actually worked is shown in Figure 16-1. The steps on the scale are represented by the darkness of the shaded bands, each one of which stands for one of the tests. The length of a band represents the number of cases cheating at that level. If the scale had been perfect, there would have been no gaps in it. As it is, 89 percent of the gaps are filled; *i.e.*, the scale is 89 percent perfect. . . .

On the chart, the arrows represent the direction in which the cheating drive is operating, and, as was suggested before, the darkness of the shaded blocks represents the varying resistances to be overcome if cheating is to be accomplished. Forty-eight cases . . . did not overcome even the least resistance, but six overcame even the heaviest resistance and all six also cheated on all the tests with less resistance.

The significance of this for our present discussion is that, although other types of cheating may probably each be scaled in the same way, when the types are intermingled the results *do not* scale. That is, if we put together a series of speed tests, those cheating on the one requiring the most trouble to cheat will also cheat on the rest. But if we attempt to combine all techniques in one scale, . . . whether in classroom or out, the results do not scale, *i.e.*, the drives are specific and are a function of the situation and the mode of deception for which the situation calls.

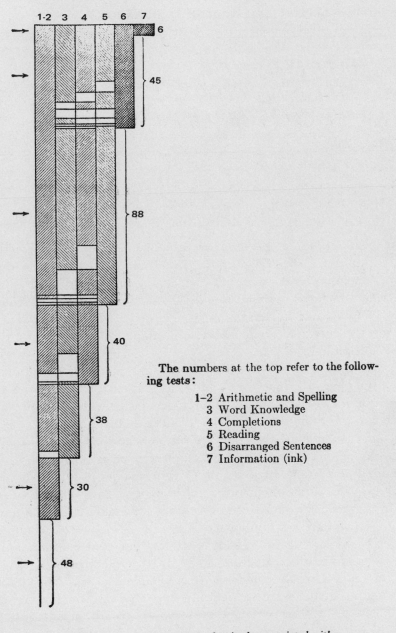

The numbers at the top refer to the following tests:

1-2 Arithmetic and Spelling
3 Word Knowledge
4 Completions
5 Reading
6 Disarranged Sentences
7 Information (ink)

FIGURE 16-1. *The scaling of attitudes associated with one form of deception.*

17

EDWARD E. SAMPSON AND ARLENE C. BRANDON

THE EFFECTS OF ROLE
AND OPINION DEVIATION
ON SMALL GROUP BEHAVIOR

When two or more persons come together in an interactive relationship for a specific purpose, the course and nature of their interaction importantly depends on their definitions of their situation, which includes themselves and the other participants. Although many factors enter to determine the particular definition given to any specific interactive encounter, this paper focuses on the two factors of opinion and role.

. . . We shall assume that one important attribute of another person (O) that influences one's (P's) definition of a situation is O's belief, opinion, or attitude. . . . Other persons provide an important source for the definition of social reality; thus we are attentive to their opinions and beliefs, compare our conceptions of reality with theirs, and modify ours or theirs when discrepancies exist.

Another important attribute of O which serves as a basis for P's definition of a situation involves those expectations central to O's role in a particular social structure: e.g., the university community. . . . As we have conceptualized it, *role* may include expectations for one's opinions, beliefs, and attitudes, but is a broader, more inclusive concept than *opinion*. That is, role refers to a particular position in a social structure (e.g., student), and the entire *constellation* of behavior-and-opinion expectations coincident with that position. In this sense, therefore, we feel it meaningful to

Reprinted in part with permission from *Sociometry* 27 (September 1964): 261-281.

conceive of *role* and *opinion* as two qualitatively distinct concepts which will be separately considered throughout this paper. . . .

[We suggest] that two foci for P's definition of his interactive encounters with O involve P's perception of O's opinion relative to his own and P's perception of O's actual behavior relative to his expected behavior. Encounters with an opinion deviate and a role or expectancy deviate are seen as a source of problems for the course and nature of P's interaction with O. The opinion deviate presents a problem for P's efforts to attain a consensually valid sense of social reality. The role deviate presents a problem for P's efforts to establish a stable interactive situation, in which his own behavior is dependent on his expectations for O's behavior. . . . A solution to the dilemma created by the opinion deviate involves the use of influence-oriented communications with the purpose of changing the opinion deviate into an opinion conformant. . . . The solution to the dilemma created by the role deviate involves either increasing communications towards the deviate in an effort to bring his behavior into line with P's expectations or decreasing communication to the deviate, thereby isolating oneself from further confrontations with him. . . .

Methods

In order to establish the conditions which would permit us to test the above formulation, . . . *ad hoc* groups of five members, one of whom was a paid assistant, were convened to discuss what was purported to be the case history of a Negro juvenile delinquent, James Amthor Johnson. The subjects were female students at the University of California, Berkeley, and were recruited both from introductory psychology classes and from campus dormitories. The paid assistant was a senior in the School of Education, carefully trained for the two roles she was required to play.

Establishing Role Deviation and Role Conformity. We established O as a role deviate within the broad context of a more liberal University setting, by assuming that the expected role behavior for a student at the University of California, Berkeley, would involve a general attitude of liberalism on various racial and religious issues. O could therefore deviate from this assumed background by presenting herself as a bigot rather than a liberal. That is, most students at the University of California at Berkeley tend to look upon themselves as rather liberal and as generally supporting causes in line with liberal points of view on racial issues. Thus, encountering someone who was a "student-bigot" would be incongruent with their expectations for the behavior of the typical Cal student.

When all the subjects had arrived for their scheduled experimental session—including O who was usually the third to arrive—they were given a contrived explanation for the experiment: they were told that this experiment was designed to investigate empathic ability. Each was informed that she would be asked to predict how members of the group would behave under specific circumstances. Ostensibly to facilitate these later predictions, the experimenter would conduct an interview with each person in turn so that, "you may get to know one another better."

O's prepared and carefully rehearsed answers to the experimenter's list of questions permitted us to create two disparate roles, one of which conformed to the general expectations of student behavior and one of which deviated from these expectations. We refer to these roles as *role B,* the bigot, and *role L,* the liberal. In *role B,* O was instructed to give answers which would suggest to the others that she had rather narrowly defined, negative feelings towards minority groups, especially Negroes. She introduced herself as coming from a neighborhood into which many Negro families had moved, threatening her family financially through loss of property values and threatening her personally by providing a "dangerous" atmosphere in which to live. In response to further probing by the experimenter, she hesitantly volunteered further information about her prejudices, including her present feelings of uneasiness when Negro students were in her classes or in her apartment house. During this portion of the interview, she showed signs of tension, presumably because she realized that her views were different from the others in the group: e.g., she doodled on a piece of scratch paper, making long, heavy strokes covering the entire paper, while looking down at the floor. She never communicated a very rational basis for her bigoted feelings, but rather gave the impression that for some irrational reason she disliked Negroes, did not want to associate with them, and was opposed to giving them equal rights and opportunities.

By contrast, in *role L,* O was instructed to be a little more extreme in her liberalism than most of the others. Within the context of the interview she mentioned her membership in CORE, the American Civil Liberties Union, and a somewhat liberal campus political organization. She not only espoused liberal points of view with respect to the racial issue, but indicated that she was an active participant in activities designed to alleviate discriminatory practices.

The experimenter began the interview by asking each girl her name, age, year in school, etc. In order to stress the importance of each person's attending to the answers, they were then required to make a simple alternative choice prediction about one other subject, being corrected by the other when she was incorrect. The experimenter than reemphasized the difficulty of making accurate predictions about each other unless they had assimilated the information available from the interview. They were then told that the case history which they were to discuss later involved a Negro juvenile delinquent; thus many of the interview questions would center about the general topic of discrimination and prejudice. The experimenter then began the main body of the interview asking such questions as, "What was your neighborhood like? What was your school like?" The confederate was always first to be questioned, thereby making it more realistic for her to express a bigoted attitude openly.

At the conclusion of the entire interview procedure, a copy of the case history was given to each subject. Each was requested to read it over carefully and then to record on a seven-point scale her position with respect to the proposed treatment for the delinquent. Position #1 advocated love and care for the delinquent. (Love, kindness, and friendship are all that are necessary to make James a better kid. If he can be placed in a more agreeable environment, a warm, friendly foster home, for example, his troubles will clear up.) Position #7 advocated a more punitive handling of the case. (E.g., there's very little you can do with a kid like this but put him in a very severe disciplinary environment. Only by punishing him strongly can we change his behavior.) The positions between these two extremes were variants on this theme of love vs. punishment. After recording her own position on this scale, each subject was requested to write down her prediction for each of the others in her group.

If we had successfully created two distinct roles with two contrasting sets of expectations for O's behavior, we would expect that in *role B*, the subjects would attribute a more punitive attitude to O (e.g., closer to 7 on the scale) than in *role L*, in which they would see O's attitude as being more closely aligned with their own.

In comparing these predictions of O's position, we find the expected results: An average rating of 2.4 is obtained when O is playing *role L* and 5.4 in *role B* ($p < .001$).

Manipulation of the O-P Opinion Discrepancy. We assumed that our sample of college students would tend to express a liberal point of view with respect to the treatment of the delinquent: i.e., they would adopt an attitude position somewhere between #2 and #4 on the seven-point scale. Working on this assumption, we were able to instruct O to adopt a position which was either similar to that of the subjects' (position #3: "He should be sent into an environment where providing James with warmth and affection will be emphasized slightly more than punishing him, but discipline and punishment will be frequent if his behavior warrants it"), or widely discrepant from theirs (e.g., #7).

That our assumption with respect to the subjects' own position was correct is demonstrated by an examination of the mean position taken by them in the experimental conditions. These means range from 2.6 to 3.0, as we predicted.

Design of the Experiment. The preceding experimental manipulation of O's role and O's opinion produced a 2 x 2 experimental design:

	OPINION CONFORMANT	OPINION DEVIANT
Role Deviant	I	II
Role Conformant	III	IV

Eighty females were divided into five groups of four each (plus O, making a group size of five), in each experimental condition. The same female experimenter was used throughout the experiment.

This experimental design permits us to test our hypotheses by an analysis of variance technique. In this analysis, the main effect of opinion provides a test of the . . . model which predicts that greater communication will be directed towards the opinion deviate as compared with the opinion conformant. The main effect of role provides a test of the . . . model which suggests that the role deviate as compared with the role conformant will provide an interactional problem for the group. Whether the solution to this problem will involve increased influence-oriented communication or a withdrawal response is assumed to be a function of the nature of the deviation.

The role deviate we have created presents a life-style kind of deviation which is rather diffuse and is a pervasive, potentially unmodifiable characteristic of the individual. Since the group discussion was introduced as another means available to the girls for learning about one another in order to make later empathic predictions, there was no external pressure from the experimenter to achieve group consensus on the discussion material Thus the likely response to this deviate should be withdrawal from interaction rather than influence-oriented communication directed towards changing the deviate. . . .

Measurements. The dependent variables were measured by questionnaires administered at the conclusion of the experiment and by ongoing observations of the group interaction using Bales' category system. A single, trained observer recorded the entire interaction during the 20-minute group discussion.

Results

The results of the analyses of variance are grouped into four major sections based upon the particular set of dependent variables under consideration: (1) effects on the communication directed to O; [and three sections excluded from this excerpt] (2) effects on P's perception of O; (3) effects on P's attraction to O; (4) effects on P's attraction to the group.

I. Communication to O. In his original discussion of the effects of opinion deviance on the communication within a group, Schachter suggested a curvilinear relationship. [Stanley Schachter, "Deviation, Rejection and Communication," *Journal of Abnormal and Social-Psychology* 46 (September 1951): 190-207.] As time progressed in the discussion, the unwavering opinion deviate clarified his deviance to the rest of the group, and as he did, he received more communication form the other group members. A point was reached, however, when it became obvious that his deviation would continue and further communication attempting to sway his opinion would be fruitless. At this point, the communication directed towards him decreased.

These considerations suggested that the communication data be analyzed by time periods. To this end, we divided the total

20-minute discussion period into thirds and analyzed the percentage of communication directed towards O in each third. This provides us with a two-way analysis of variance with repeated measurements on the same subjects. . . . For each analysis, the dependent variable is the percentage of all communication within the group directed towards O.

. . . The total percentage of communication directed to O, summed over all Bales' categories, and the curves based on these data are summarized in . . . Figure 17-1. Both the main effects of role and of opinion are statistically significant ($p < .01$). The direction of the difference in mean percentages shows that the subjects direct more of their communication towards the role conformant than the role deviant, but more towards the opinion deviant than the opinion conformant.

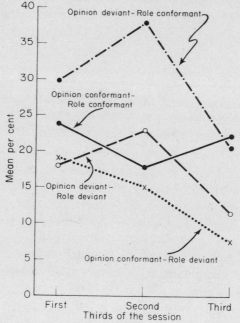

FIGURE 17-1. *Mean percent of total units directed to O in each third of the session.*

That the opinion deviate receives a greater amount of communication than the opinion conformant is consistent with the original findings of Schachter. . . . The reduction in communication towards the role deviate [suggests that] the subjects reduce their communication as an attempt to avoid further confrontations or encounters with the deviant, confrontations which we assume they perceive would be tensionful and embarrassing for both themselves and her.

That there is no significant interaction effect suggests that the strength of the more pervasive role deviation was greater than that of the specific incongruity created by O's acting in a manner inconsistent with expectations, i.e., by stating a specific opinion on the case history which was not consistent with the role she portrayed.

Although the overall effects of time (i.e., the third of the interaction period in which the communication occurred) are not significant, inspection of Figure 17-1 indicates some interesting trends. For example, in both conditions of opinion deviance (II and IV), the overall trend is the same: the communication directed towards the opinion deviate increases up to a point, but then rapidly decreases. This pattern follows that originally suggested by Schachter. By comparison, the pattern with respect to the remaining two experimental conditions is rather different. In Condition I, in which O was a role deviate whose specific opinion was unexpectedly the same as the subjects', communication shows a steady decrease over time. It is as if there are two reasons for not talking further to this individual: she already has an opinion similar to that of the group's, so there is no need to influence her here; and she is a role deviate with whom they would prefer to avoid further confrontations.

The initial decrease in communication in Condition III in which O is a role and opinion conformant fits the general predictions: there is no need to change this individual in any way, nor is there any need to withdraw from further confrontation with the individual. Thus there is a subsequent rise in communication, which seems to hinge less upon an attempted influence model than from a model in which one would expect greater communication between persons sharing many similarities: e.g., role and opinion. . . .

. . . Analyses detailing the volume and type of communication [using Bales categories] towards O in our four experimental conditions . . . indicate: (1) greater overall communication; (2) less communication expressing solidarity; (3) more communication expressing hostility; and (4) more communication seeking information, directed towards the opinion deviate as compared with the opinion conformant.

A second consistent set of findings . . . indicates that there are: (1) greater overall communication; (2) more expression of hostility;

and (3) more information-giving communication to the role conformant than to the role deviant. These findings indicate a relatively strong withdrawal from further interactions with the role deviant. . . .

Discussion

In this experiment we were able to study the effects of two kinds of deviation upon small group behavior. The first kind involved a discrepancy of opinion between one person and a group of persons who shared an opinion on an issue of social reality. The second involved a discrepancy of role between one person and a group of persons who generally shared the same role in the larger context of a liberal university. The responses of the group to these two kinds of deviation, although similar in some respects (e.g., some self-report measures of perceiving the deviate to be uncomfortable and dissatisfied), most markedly differed with respect to the communications directed towards O. Whereas the subjects increased their communications towards the opinion deviate in order to modify her behavior, they decreased their communications towards the role deviate in order to avoid further confronting and being confronted by her.

These findings with respect to communications appear consistent with the interpretation that the more pervasive, potentially unmodifiable behavior which characterizes the role deviate more easily permits the subjects to withdraw from interaction than does the more specific, potentially modifiable behavior of the opinion deviate.

If we may assume that one function served by communication between persons involved attempted influence, our data suggest that our subjects were in good touch with reality: they communicated to the person who could be changed and ignored the person who could not be changed.

On the other hand, if we may assume that the communication between persons also serves an *enlightenment* function such that one may learn further about another without attempting in any direct way to modify that person, our data suggest that our subjects were out of touch with this aspect of reality. They did not care to be further enlightened about the student-bigot, how she felt, why she felt that way, etc. Rather, they preferred to avoid further mutually embarrassing encounters. The potential age of enlightenment gave way to the upsurge of an age of anxiety and interpersonal embarrassment. . . .

18

GORDON N. GOLDBERG, CHARLES A. KIESLER, AND
BARRY E. COLLINS

VISUAL BEHAVIOR AND FACE-TO-FACE DISTANCE DURING INTERACTION

... The present paper reports [an] examination of the effect of interaction distance on visual behavior. ...

Method

SUBJECTS AND PROCEDURE

Thirty-seven Yale College men required to participate in psychological experiments as part of their course work served as subjects. Each was run individually in a small room.

Base period. The first five or six minutes of the experimental session served as a base period during which conditions were identical for each subject. The subject and the experimenter sat on opposite sides of a three-foot-square table at an interaction distance of about four-and-a-half feet. Immediately behind the experimenter was a wall with a one-way window, and through this window, over the experimenter's shoulder, the person who later interviewed the subject observed the subject's visual behavior.

During the base period, the experimenter first presented a cover story for the experiment, informing the subject he was in the control condition of a study on interviewing methods, and then asked for some "background information" on matters such as the subject's age

Reprinted in part with permission from *Sociometry* 32 (March 1969): 43-53.

and home town. While presenting the cover story, the experimenter gazed at the subject's eyes only during the last few words of each independent clause. While obtaining the background information, the experimenter read each question from a sheet of paper, looked up at the end of the question, gazed steadily at the subject's eyes while the subject replied, and then looked back at the paper to record the answer. . . .

After obtaining the background information, the experimenter explained that a Yale junior psychology major he had hired would conduct the interview itself, while he, the experimenter, handled the tape-recording equipment in the rooms behind the one-way windows. The experimenter then excused himself.

Unstructured conversation. A few seconds after the experimenter left the room, the interviewer entered, introduced himself, sat down in the chair vacated by the experimenter, and initiated a casual conversation with the subject. The conversation was not structured in any way, and the interviewer's visual and verbal behavior were not programmed. The interviewer simply played the role of a Yale junior psychology major, which had actually been his status three years before.

Test period. While the subject and interviewer conversed, the experimenter consulted a random number table to determine the condition to which the subject was assigned. After three minutes of conversation, the experimenter knocked on the wall of the room. Two knocks indicated the close condition, three knocks the far condition. "That's the signal that the tape-recording equipment is ready," the interviewer responded. He then asked the subject to move to one end of a table two-and-a-half feet wide and six feet long, while he himself moved to the opposite end. In the close condition, the interviewer and the subject sat the short way across this table; in the far condition, they sat the long way across the table. In both conditions, the interviewer pulled his chair up tight against the table and asked the subject to do the same. "We experimented," he said, "and found that this is the best set-up for the microphone." There was no reference to distance in this explanation. If the subject leaned back in his chair during the interview, the interviewer immediately reminded him to sit up tight against the table. An interaction distance of either two-and-a-half feet or six feet was thus established and maintained during the interview, but the distance was not called to the subject's attention.

In both conditions, the subject and the interviewer were seated directly across from each other, with a microphone between them and the reflecting side of a one-way window a foot behind the interviewer. The subject's view in the mirror in both conditions was similar—that of the bare wall behind him.

The interviewer read the interview questions from a notebook which he held so that the subject could not see its pages. Each question inquired only whether most Yale undergraduates approved or disapproved of a certain action, policy, or person, so that the answers required were very short. The interviewer looked up from the notebook to the subject's eyes at the end of each question and gazed steadily at the subject's eyes while the subject replied. The interviewer repeated each answer, ostensibly to increase the chance the answer would be understood when the tape was played back, but actually to provide some interaction approximating that of a normal conversation. While repeating the answers, the interviewer gazed steadily at the subject's eyes.

During the interview, the experimenter observed the subject's visual behavior from behind the one-way window located just behind the interviewer. Measurements were taken over three three-minute intervals separated by 35-second gaps.

Thirty-five seconds after the third three-minute interval, the experimenter knocked on the wall of the room. The interviewer responded by saying to the subject, "That's the signal that time's up." He then shook hands and left the room.

Questionnaire. The experimenter immediately returned and asked the subject to fill out a questionnaire concerned with the subject's "impressions" of the interviewer. The experimenter stressed the importance of obtaining honest answers to the questionnaire items and promised the subject that the interviewer would not see the questionnaire.

MEASUREMENT OF VISUAL BEHAVIOR

[In measuring] the subject's visual behavior, . . . a single observer operated both instruments employed. The observer attempted to discriminate glances which the subject directed at the eyes of his coactor from glances which the subject directed elsewhere. Each time the subject seemed to begin a glance at the coactor's eyes, the observer started a cumulative stopwatch and advanced a hand-held counter. Each time the subject seemed to shift his gaze away from the coactor's eyes, the observer stopped the watch and advanced the counter again. Thus the total amount of time the subject was judged to have spent in gazing at the coactor's eyes and twice the number of discrete glances he seemed to have used could be read from the instruments at the end of the measurement period.

RELIABILITIES

The reliabilities of these measurement techniques were estimated only for the far condition. The experimenter and the interviewer both took measurements on a person playing the role of a subject who sat the long way across the table from the interviewer. Observations were made over eight three-minute intervals, and with this N of eight a correlation of .99 was obtained both for readings on the watches and for readings on the counters. These figures accord with other reports of the high reliability with which visual behavior can be judged.

CELL Ns AND MISSING DATA

Nineteen subjects were run in the close condition and 18 in the far condition. Because of equipment failure, observations for the first three-minute interval of the test period were not obtained for two subjects at the closer distance and one subject at the greater distance.

Results

COMPARABILITY OF THE DISTANCE CONDITIONS

Evidence was available to rule out the confounding of interaction distance by four variables which could have influenced subjects' visual behavior: (a) None of the 16 questionnaire items intended as measures of subjects' evaluations of the interviewer was answered differentially (largest $t_{35} = 1.91$, $p > .05$) [two-tailed tests used throughout], and there was no difference between conditions in scores on either factor identified in the factor analysis of these items ($t < 1$ for both). Hence differential attraction to the interviewer cannot plausibly explain any effect of interaction distance. (b) The number of questions asked by the interviewer did not differ at the two distances ($t = 1.23$), a finding which provides evidence that subjects' answers did not vary systematically in length. Thus the tendency for subjects to look more often at the eyes of a coactor while listening to him than while speaking to him cannot plausibly account for any effect of interaction distance. (c) Answers to the Likert-type questionnaire item "How comfortable did the interviewer make you feel during the interview?" did not differ in the two conditions ($t<1$). This finding suggests that the subject's task, as intended, did obviate differential disruption of the subject's thought by the interviewer and differential expectation of disapproval from the interviewer.

PERCENT TIME GAZING

As Fig. 18-1 shows, subjects sitting six feet from the interviewer were judged to spend about 60 percent of each three-minute interval of the test period gazing at the interviewer's eyes, while subjects sitting two-and-a-half feet from him were judged to spend about 40 percent of the time gazing at his eyes. A repeated-measures analysis of variance using only the 17 subjects in each condition with complete data revealed a strong effect for interaction distance ($F_{1/32} = 15.06$, $p < .001$) but no tendency for scores to change over the three intervals of the test period ($F_{2/64} = 1.46$) and no interaction between distance and intervals ($F_{2/64} < 1$).

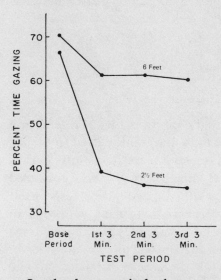

FIGURE 18-1. *Average percent time gazing during the base period and during the three intervals of the test period for subjects who sat at the 2½-foot distance during the test period and for subjects who sat at the 6-foot distance during the test period.*

In the base period, there was a much smaller difference between the means for the two groups of subjects in the proportion of time they were judged to spend gazing at the eyes of the interviewer, and this difference was not significant ($t = 1.25$).

RATE OF GLANCING

A repeated-measures analysis of variance performed on the judged rate of glancing, using only the 17 subjects in each condition with complete data, revealed no significant effects (largest $F = 2.33$). The difference between the two groups during the base period was not significant ($t_{35} = 1.55$, $p > .10$), and analyses of covariance using the base-period rate as covariate showed no significant effects ($F_{1/34} = 0.19$, 3.24, 0.01 for the three intervals of the test period, respectively; $p > .05$ in each case). The mean rate score for subjects in the two conditions during the base period and during the three intervals of the test period varied between 9.5 and 11.5 glances per minute, with the average for subjects in the close condition higher at each point. . . .

Discussion

INTERACTION DISTANCE AND VISUAL BEHAVIOR

The difference in visual behavior observed at different interaction distances in [an earlier] study was also found in the present experiment. At a closer interaction distance, subjects were judged to spend less time gazing at the eyes of the person they were interacting with.

Several factors which might have confounded the distance manipulation and produced this difference in visual behavior have already been considered, and evidence which rules out their influence has been presented. But a problem involving differential validity of the observations must still be discussed. Informal testing comparing the two distance conditions indicated that glances at the interviewer's eyes were less easily discriminated from glances at other parts of his face in the far condition. Thus if subjects gazed at parts of the interviewer's face other than his eyes to an appreciable extent in the far condition, the experimenter might have included enough more false positives in his measures of visual behavior in this condition to account for its greater percentage scores. Informal observation and questioning, however, suggest that a person interacting with a stranger rarely lets his gaze wander over the stranger's face, especially in a task-oriented setting like the one in the present study, and especially when the person and the stranger are directly facing each other, as in the present study. Some evidence for this proposition lies in the extreme infrequency with which the experimenter observed glances at parts of the interviewer's face other than his eyes in the close condition, where the locus of fixation could be identified fairly accurately. Thus this final alternative explanation of the data appears predicated on an unlikely state of affairs, and the present experiment would seem a fairly adequate demonstration that interaction distance influences visual behavior.

Unfortunately, though, the present experiment is no more than such a demonstration. It is not a test of any theoretical interpretation of the data, and it does not enable one to sort among various theoretical ideas which could account for the data in terms of underlying variables. Argyle and Dean's theory of "intimacy," it should be noted, "accounts for" these data only by redescribing them in terms of the construct "intimacy." The theory is not a testable statement of underlying variables. . . .

19

WALTER B. MILLER

THE IMPACT OF A "TOTAL-COMMUNITY" DELINQUENCY CONTROL PROJECT

The Midcity Project:
Methods and Client Population

The Midcity Project conducted a delinquency control program in a lower class district of Boston between the years 1954 and 1957. A major objective of the Project was to inhibit or reduce the amount of illegal activity engaged in by resident adolescents. . . .

Between June 1954 and May 1957, seven profect field workers (five men, two women) maintained contact with approximately 400 youngsters between the ages of 12 and 21, comprising the membership of some 21 corner gangs. Seven of these, totaling 205 members, were subjected to intensive attention. Workers contacted their groups on an average of 3.5 times a week; contact periods averaged about 5 or 6 hours; total duration of contact ranged from 10 to 34 months. Four of the intensive service groups were white males (Catholic, largely Irish, some Italians and Canadian French); one was Negro male, one white female, and one Negro female. All groups "hung out" in contiguous neighborhoods of a single district of Midcity—a fairly typical lower class "inner-city" community. . . .

ACTION METHODS WITH CORNER GANGS

The methods used by Project workers encompassed a wide range of techniques and entailed work on many levels with many kinds of

Reprinted with permission from *Social Problems* 10 (Fall 1962): 168-191.

groups, agencies and organizations. Workers conceptualized the process of working with the groups as a series of sequential phases, on the model of individual psychotherapy. Three major phases were delineated—roughly, relationship establishment, behavior modification, and termination. . . .

Phase I: Contact and relationship establishment. During this phase workers sought out and located resident corner gangs and established an acceptable role-identity. . . . A major objective in gaining entree to the groups was to establish what workers called a "relationship." . . .

Phase II: Behavior modification via mutual activity involvement. . . . Workers engaged in a wide variety of activities with and in behalf of their groups. The bulk of these activities, however, centered around three major kinds of effort: (1) organizing groups and using these as the basis of involvement in organized activities; (2) serving as intermediary between group members and adult institutions; (3) utilizing techniques of direct influence. . . .

Phase III: Termination. Since the Project was set up on a three-year "demonstration" basis, the date of final contact was known well in advance. Due largely to the influence of psychodynamic concepts, workers were very much concerned about the possibly harmful effects of "termination," and formulated careful and extensive plans for effecting disengagement from their groups. . . . What, then, was the impact of these efforts on delinquent behavior?

THE IMPACT OF PROJECT EFFORTS

The Midcity Project was originally instituted in response to a community perception that uncontrolled gang violence was rampant in Midcity. Once the furor attending its inception had abated, the Project was reconceptualized as a "demonstration" project in community delinquency control. This meant that in addition to setting up methods for effecting changes in its client population, the Project also assumed responsibility for testing the efficacy of these methods. The task of evaluating project effectiveness was assigned to a social science research staff which operated in conjunction with the action program. Since the major effort of the Project was its work with gangs, the evaluative aspect of the research design focused on the gang program, and took as a major concern the impact of group-directed methods on the behavior of target gangs. . . .

The principal question of the evaluative research was phrased as follows: *Was there a significant measurable inhibition of law-violating or morally-disapproved behavior as a consequence of Project efforts?* . . .

Following sections will report three separate measures of change in patterns of violative behavior. These are: 1) Disapproved forms of customary behavior; 2) Illegal behavior; 3) Court appearance rates. These three sets of measures represent different methods of analysis, different orders of specificity, and were derived from different sources. The implications of this for achieved results will be discussed later.

Trends in Disapproved Behavior

A central form of "violative" behavior is that which violates specific legal statutes (e.g., theft, armed assault). Also important, however, is behavior which violates "moral" norms or ethical standards. . . . In addressing the question—"Did the Project bring about a decrease in morally-violative behavior?", at least four sets of moral codes are of relevance—those of middle class adults, of middle class adolescents, of lower class adults, and of lower class adolescents. While there are large areas of concordance among these sets, there are also important areas of noncorrespondence. The method employed in this area was as follows:

A major source of data for Project research was a large population of "behavior sequences" engaged in by group members during the study period. These were derived from a variety of sources, the principal source being the detailed descriptive daily field reports of the workers. All recorded behavioral events involving group members were extracted from the records and typed on separate data cards. These cards were coded, and filed in chronological order under 65 separate categories of behavior such as drinking behavior, sexual behavior, and theft. A total of 100,000 behavior sequences was recorded, coded, and filed.

Fourteen of the 65 behavior categories were selected for the purpose of analyzing trends in immoral behavior. These were: theft, assault, drinking, sex, mating, work, education, religion, and involvement with courts, police, corrections, social welfare, family, and other gangs. Seventy-five thousand behavioral sequences were included under these 14 categories.

201

A separate set of evaluative standards, based primarily on the workers' own values, was developed for each of the 14 areas. The workers as individuals were essentially oriented to the value system of middle class adults, but due largely to their training in social work, they espoused an "easier" or more permissive version of these standards. In addition, as a result of their experiences in the lower class community, their standards had been further modified to accommodate in some degree those of the adolescent gangs. The workers' standards thus comprised an easier baseline against which to measure change since they were considerably less rigid than those which would be applied by most middle class adults.

Listings were drawn up for each of the 14 areas which designated as "approved" or "disapproved" about 25 specific forms of behavior per area. A distinction was made between "actions" (behavioral events observed to occur) and "sentiments" (attitudes or intentions). Designations were based on three kinds of information: evaluative statements made by the workers concerning particular areas of behavior; attitudes or actions workers had supported or opposed in actual situations; and an attitude questionnaire administered to each worker. Preliminary listings were submitted to the workers to see if the items did in fact reflect the evaluative standards they felt themselves to espouse; there was high agreement with the listings; in a few instances of disagreement modifications were made.

A total of 14,471 actions and sentiments were categorized as "approved," "disapproved," or "evaluatively-neutral." While these data made possible detailed and extensive analysis of differential patterns of behavior change in various areas and on different levels, the primary question for the most general purposes of impact measurement was phrased as: "Was there a significant reduction in the relative frequency of *disapproved actions* during the period of worker contact?" With some qualifications, the answer was "No."

Each worker's term of contact was divided into three equal phases, and the relative frequency of disapproved actions during the first and third phase was compared. During the full study period, the 205 members of the seven intensive analysis groups engaged in 4518 approved or disapproved actions. During the initial phase, 785 of 1604 actions (48.9 percent) were disapproved; during the final phase, 613 of 1364 (44.9 percent)—a reduction of only 4 percent. . . .

Trends in Illegal Acts

The central question to be asked of a delinquency control program is: "Does it control delinquency?" One direct way of approaching this question is to focus on that "target" population most directly exposed to program action methods and ask: "Was there a decrease in the frequency of crimes committed by the target population during the period of the program?" Under most circumstances this is difficult to answer, owing to the necessity of relying on records collected by police, courts, or other "official" agencies. The drawbacks of utilizing official incidence statistics as a measure of the actual occurrence of criminal behavior have frequently been pointed out; among these is the very complex process of selectivity which governs the conversion of committed crimes into official statistics; many crimes are never officially detected; many of those detected do not result in an official arrest; many arrests do not eventuate in court action, and so on. . . .

The Midcity Project was able to a large extent to overcome this difficulty by the nature of its base data. Because of their intimate daily association with gang members, workers were in a position both to observe crimes directly, and to receive reports of crimes shortly after they occurred. The great majority of these never appeared in official records.

The research question in the area of illegal behavior was phrased: "Was there a significant decrease in the frequency of statute violations committed by Project group members during the period of worker contact?" As in the case of disapproved actions, the answer was, with some qualifications, "No." Methods and results were as follows:

Every statute-violating act committed by a Project group member during the course of the contact period was recorded on an individual record form. While the bulk of recorded acts were derived from the workers' field reports, information was obtained from all available sources, including official records. Very few of the crimes recorded by official agencies were not also recorded by the Project; many of the crimes recorded by the Project did not appear in official records. During the course of the Project, a total of 1005 legally violative acts was recorded for members of the seven intensive analysis groups. Eighty-three percent of the 205 Project group members had committed at least one illegal act; 90 percent of the 150 males had been so involved. These figures alone show that the Project did not prevent crime, and there had been no expectation that it would. But did it "control" or "inhibit" crime?

Offenses were classified under 11 categories: theft, assault, alcohol violations, sex offenses, trespassing, disorderly conduct, truancy, vandalism, gambling violations, and "other" (e.g., strewing tacks on street, killing cats). Each worker's term of contact was divided into three equal phases, and the frequency of offenses during the initial and final phase was compared.

Seven hundred and fifty-two of the 1005 offenses were committed during the initial and final phases. Of these, 394 occurred during the initial phase, and 358 during the final—a reduction of 9.1 percent. Considering males only, however, 614 male crimes accounting for 81.6 percent of all offenses showed an *increase* of 1.3 percent between initial and final phases. . . . The modest decrease shown by the total sample was accounted for largely by the girls and by minor offenses; major offenses by boys, in contrast, increased in frequency during the course of the Project, and major offenses by younger boys increased most of all.

Trends in Court Appearances

The third major index to Project impact was based on court appearance statistics. The principal research question in this area was phrased: "Did the Project effect any decrease in the frequency with which Project group members appeared in court in connection with crimes?" The use of court appearance data made it possible to amplify and strengthen the measurement of impact in three major ways. (1) It permitted a considerable time-extension. Previous sections describe trends which occurred during the actual period of worker contact. Sound determination of impact makes it necessary to know how these "during" trends related to trends both preceding and following the contact period. . . . (2) The data were compiled by agencies which were essentially independent of the Project. Although the Project made every attempt to recognize, accommodate to, and correct for the possibility of in-project bias, exclusive reliance on data collected primarily by those in the employ of the Project would admit the possibility that the objectives or values of Project staff would in some way prejudice results. . . . (3) It made possible the application of time-trend measures to groups other than those taken by the Project as objects of change. The inclusion of a control population as part of the basic evaluative design was of vital importance. . . .

Looking at the period of worker contact as one phase within the overall period of adolescence, it would appear that the presence of the workers did not inhibit the frequency of court appearances, but that a dip in appearance frequency at age 18 and a drop in frequency after age 20 may have been related to the workers' efforts.

Comparison of project and control group trends. Extending the examination of offense trends from the during-contact period to "before" and "after" periods, while furnishing important additional information, also raised additional questions. Was it just coincidental that the 16 to 19 peak in court appearances occurred during the contact period—or could the presence of the workers have been in some way responsible? Was the sharp decline in frequency of appearances after age 20 a delayed action result of worker effort? To clarify these questions it was necessary to examine the court appearance experience of a control population—a set of corner gangs as similar as possible to Project gangs, but who had *not* been worked with by the Project. The indexes reported [on Project gangs—full data omitted from excerpt] have provided information as to whether significant change occurred, but have been inconclusive as to the all-important question of cause-and-effect (To what extent were observed trends related to the workers' efforts?). The use of a control population entailed certain risks—primarily the possibility that service and control populations might not be adequately matched in some respects—but the unique potency of the control method as a device for furnishing evidence in the vital area of "cause" outweighed these risks. . . .

The court appearance frequency curves for Project and Control groups are very similar. . . . The unusual degree of similarity between the court appearance curves of Project and Control groups constitutes the single most powerful piece of evidence on Project impact obtained by the research. The fact that a group of similar gangs not worked with by the Project showed an almost identical decrease in court appearance frequency between ages 20 and 23 removes any reasonable basis for attributing the post-20 decline of Project groups to worker efforts. Indeed, the high degree of overall similarity in court appearance experience between "served" and "unserved" groups makes it most difficult to claim that anything done by the Project had any significant influence on the likelihood of court appearance. . . .

Summary of "Impact" Findings

It is now possible to provide a definite answer to the principal evaluative research question: "Was there a significant measurable inhibition of law-violating or morally disapproved behavior as a consequence of Project efforts?" The answer, with little necessary qualification, is "No." All major measures of violative behavior— disapproved actions, illegal actions, during-contact court appearances, before-during-after appearances, and Project-Control group appearances—provide consistent support for a finding of "negligible impact." . . . The fact that the various measures of impact are mutually consistent increases confidence in the overall "negligible impact" finding. . . .

PART V

Measurement and Analysis

INTRODUCTION

The fact that data for a study are gathered by observation imposes few constraints on methods of handling, organizing, and presenting these data. Many of the foregoing studies examine concepts and interrelationships among them in a purely discursive or descriptive (in this sense, "unsystematic") fashion. Other studies handle the data by structured or highly specified procedures, employing "systematic" measurement and analysis. In such studies, measurement typically involves an explicit, organized plan for classifying and often quantifying the particular data at hand in terms of clearly defined concepts. Analysis by such techniques as correlation, regression, or cross-tabulation specifies systematically, rather than describing verbally, the degree to which, and the conditions under which, one concept or property varies with others.

Although widely accepted and rigorously utilized in survey research based on questioning, measurement and related forms of systematic analysis have been more narrowly applied in sociological observation. The studies in Part V are chosen to emphasize the point that systematic handling of the observed data is not at all incompatible with observation (see Weick, 1968). On the contrary, a wide range of systematic procedures is feasible, and the reader is challenged to weigh the potential advantages and disadvantages of each (cf., e.g., M. W. Riley, 1964, pp. 997-1001).

The distinction between verbal description and measurement is brought into sharp focus in *Roy's* blending of the two in his observations in a piecework machine shop (cf. Whyte's [Part I] interpolation of systematic procedures such as positional mapping). For ten months on the job as an operator, Roy kept a daily record of his feelings, thoughts, experiences, observations, and conversations with fellow workers. Much like Gans [Part I] or Goffman [Part III], Roy handles part of these data *unsystematically*—describing specific verbal inter-

207

changes—in order to tease out the varieties of output restrictions in the repertoire of the work group or to explicate the motivations of the workers. In the same study, but more in the style of Hartshorne and May [Part IV] or of Bales [Part I], Roy also uses his data systematically—cataloguing and counting, analyzing in detail his own hourly production record, and checking his record against the work of others—in order to estimate the nature and amount of time "wasted" by operatives.

An important point to consider in applying measurement and analysis to observation is whether the systematic procedures are developed before or after the data are gathered.[1] *Roth*, as a participant observer in a tuberculosis hospital, clearly decides in advance on his measures, which are simple frequency counts of the wearing of protective clothing by employees of varying status. *Rosen and D'Andrade*, who devise a complex set of tasks for examining the child's achievement motivation in the context of family interaction, also preplan their categories (which are a modification of those of Bales) and, like Roth, code the behavior *as* it is being observed. Use of a priori categories for the gathering of observed data has a long history, appearing as embryonic measuring devices in portions of Le Play's nineteenth-century monographs [Part VI], in the "sociography" of Tönnies (Lécuyer and Oberschall, 1968, p. 49), or in the more systematic recording of nursery school behavior by Dorothy Thomas and her associates (1929). This practice is most useful when the researcher starts with a clear conceptual model, permitting identification and precise definition of relevant variables. Although it saves time by reducing the mass of material assembled, the practice tends to set limits on the data to be collected by fixing the number and definition of categories, excluding unforeseen details, and inhibiting the introduction of potentially important new concepts that may emerge as the research proceeds.

Not all systematic studies are vulnerable in these ways, however, since procedures for measurement and analysis are sometimes devised or refined only *after* the data are in hand. In the investigation by *Daniel,* elaborate observations of ritual were made in 40 Negro churches before the written reports were used for classification and comparison on a nominal scale of ceremonial, emotional, and ideational elements. In the far more complex and quantitative studies by *Short, Tennyson, and Howard,* the original observations of delinquent gang members were not entirely unsystematic, but the researcher did begin with a long list of sixty-nine categories that were reduced to five through factor analysis once the resultant data were available. Aggregation of factor scores for the members of each gang yielded profiles on which types of gangs could be compared. The ex post facto development of instruments for measurement and analysis affords flexibility in the search for details from which new theoretical insights may be generated. While avoiding the constraints of systematization intrinsic to the data-gathering procedures, however, this alternative practice cannot insure consistent recording of all the relevant information—the coder of materials already in hand often regrets omission of details not deemed worthy of notice at the time of observation.[2]

Some Methodological Implications

These selections indicate a variety of research objectives for which the sociolgical observer may decide to handle the data systematically, rather than through verbal description. Moreover they give evidence that he does not *necessarily* sacrifice, through this decision, the rich detail of the initial observations. Further perusal of the studies also suggests that the decision is often independent of the other design decisions we have discussed earlier: not only the data-gathering alternatives [Part III], but also the nature of interpretation [Part II] and the degree of the researcher's control over the processes under study [Part IV].

Thus wider use in observational studies of systematic measurement and analysis seems predictable. Clear advantages inhere in the standardization and openness to inspection that permit scientific rigor and comparability of findings. Yet a crucial issue intrudes itself: Will systematization threaten the desired bond between concept and data (cf. Parsons, 1949, p. 5)? As it is, Cicourel (1964, p. 4) contends that "Sociology's theoretical concepts remain ambiguous and divorced from their measurement in research situations." And there are numerous complaints that concern for reliability too often overrides fundamental questions of the validity of measures (e.g., Webb et al., 1966, pp. 6-7). While some methodologists await measures (comparable to the thermometer) that have withstood tests of time and repeated usage, others look for empirical tests of the assumption that the observed data, as selected and used to measure a characteristic, correspond in some meaningful way to the sociologist's conception of this characteristic (M. W. Riley, 1963, pp. 351-352 and Unit 9). An early example is the set of observations designed by Hartshorne and May [Part IV] for the precise purpose of uncovering the nature of honesty.[3] Their success is evidenced by the finding that, because various types of cheating did not hang together in a single measure, honesty was not, as they had assumed, a unified concept. This study demonstrates the feasibility of designing sophisticated measures that cannot only provide systematic indexes, but can also help clarify concepts and probe for deeper understandings.

NOTES

1. Of course, successive studies often complement each other, as measuring devices designed in earlier studies are applied in later ones.

2. As an example of systematic analysis combined with recording "everything" (through synchronized reports of multiple observers), see Merei (1949).

3. Preceding, but similar to, the more advanced scaling techniques developed by Louis Guttman for use with data from questionnaires.

QUOTA RESTRICTION
AND GOLDBRICKING
IN A MACHINE SHOP

Even those sociologists who nurse a distaste for studies of industrial administration, either because the problems involved are "practical" or because they fear managerial bias, will recognize that study of restriction of industrial output may yield knowledge free of both taints. Systematic "soldiering" is group activity. One may learn about the "human group" by studying behavior on a production line as well as in an interracial discussion group. And, if someone should find the knowledge useful, even for making a little money, perhaps its scientific value will not be completely vitiated.

I here report and analyze observations of restriction made during 11 months of work as a radial-drill operator in the machine shop of a steel-processing plant in 1944 and 1945. For 10 months I kept a daily record of my feelings, thoughts, experiences, and observations, and of conversations with my fellow-workers. I noted down the data from memory at the end of each workday, only occasionally making surreptitious notes on the job. I recorded my own production openly in the shop. I did not reveal my research interests to either management or workers. I remained "one of the boys on the line," sharing the practices and confidences of my fellows and joining them in their ceaseless war with management, rather indifferently at first, but later wholeheartedly.

As a member of the work group, I had access to inside talk and activity. As a machine operator, I could put various operations under

Reprinted in part from *American Journal of Sociology* 57 (March 1952): 427-442.

the microscope. These were great advantages, for *restrictus vulgaris* is a wary little thing. He does not like to be studied. Where groups are so sensitive and so skilled in eluding observation, participation observation can be a sensitive detector of relevant facts and relations (although the participant-observer can spoil it all by overworking this method or by claiming that it is the sole means of scientific observation). I will limit this paper to the presentation of a few discriminations which break up the blanket term "restriction" into several kinds and to a rough measuring of these restrictions in the shop where I worked.

From November 9, 1944, to August 30, 1945, I worked 1850.5 hours. 1350.9 (73 percent) were "production-piecework" hours. The remaining 499.6 hours were taken up with time study, rework, and set-up. In 669.4 (49.6 percent) of the production-piecework hours, I "made out." That is, I produced enough pieces of work to "earn," at the piece rates for the kinds of work done, the 85-cent-per-hour "base rate" which we received for every hour spent on the job. I thus "earned" my 85 cents in about half the hours when there was opportunity—through completing more pieces—to earn more than that. Obversely, about half the time my "turn in" (work done and turned in) fell below the base-rate standard.

The Bimodal Pattern of Output

My hourly earnings on production piecework varied from $0.09 to $1.66, a range of $1.57. Table 20-1 shows that the spread of hourly earnings for the various jobs, or "operations" performed, was bimodal; this distribution suggests two major types of output behavior.

About one-half of my hours of piecework "earnings" fell on either side of the 85-cent-an-hour "day-rate" and "make-out" point, indicating 85 cents as an approximate median. However, this distribution by no means forms a bell-shaped curve, with 85 cents as a modal point. "Make-out" and "non-make-out" piecework hours form two almost separate distributions, with 74.1 percent of the 669.4 "make-out" hours concentrated in the $1.25-$1.34 interval, and 43.2 percent of the 681.5 "non-make-out" hours clustered in two adjacent intervals, $0.35-$0.54. . . .

TABLE 20-1.

*Production Piecework Hours Worked
by Ten-Cent Earning Intervals*

EARNINGS PER HOUR (IN CENTS)	HOURS WORKED	PER CENT
Unknown*	103.9	7.7
5-14	3.0	0.2
15-24	51.0	3.8
25-34	49.8	3.7
35-44	150.1	11.1
45-54	144.5	10.7
55-64	57.7	4.3
65-74	63.8	4.7
75-84	57.7	4.3
Total under 85 cents	681.5	50.4
85-94	51.2	3.8
95-104	19.5	1.5
105-114	17.9	1.3
115-124	83.0	6.1
125-134	496.3	36.7
165-174	1.5	0.1
Total 85 cents or more	669.4	49.6
Total	1,350.9	100.0

*All "unknown" hourly earnings fell below the base-rate level of 85 cents per hour.

That this bimodal pattern of hourly earnings for the ten-month period does not represent the joining of the "tails" of two temporal distributions—i.e., one for an initial learning period and the other showing completely different production behavior with the acquisition of skill—is indicated by a comparison of earning distributions for two periods of four and six months, respectively. In this comparison the period from November through February represents one level of skill; that from March through August, a higher level. Although the proportion of make-out hours for the second period was more than double that of the first and although concentration of make-out hours in modal earning intervals increased, the pattern was clearly bimodal in both periods. Both "levels of skill" show the same modal earning interval of $1.25-$1.34 for make-out hours. The modal earning interval for non-make-out hours advanced but one notch, from $0.35 to $0.44 to $0.45 to $0.54.

While I did not keep a complete record of the hourly earnings of my "day man" on the radial drill (I worked a "second" shift), I frequently jotted down his day's run. His figures were roughly correlative with my own. References to the diary will be made to show that I was not out of line with other operators in the shop.

The bimodal pattern was the rule of the shop. An outsider might believe that it reflects the struggle of workers with two kinds of jobs, hard and easy. He might then posit any number of reasons why the jobs fall into two piles rather than into one bell-shaped heap: some peculiarity of time-study men or some change of company policy. It would indeed be difficult so to set piece rates that it would be equally easy to "make out" on all kinds of work. But one sophisticated in shop ways and aware of all the devices of time-study men would hardly credit them with either the ability or the will to turn up "tight" and "loose" piece rates in other than a single bell-shaped distribution. He would not attribute the bimodal distortion of hourly earnings to anything so improbable as bimodal distribution of hard and easy jobs. It could be that the operators, ignoring finer distinctions in job timing, sort jobs into two bins, one for "gravy" jobs, the other for "stinkers."

Let us assume that the average of worker effort will be constant from job to job. Job A might be rated as 5 cents an hour "harder" than Job B. But Job A turns out to yield 75 cents an hour less than Job B instead of the expected 5 cents an hour less. One suspects that effort has not been constant. When an operator discovers that he can earn $1.00 an hour on Job B, he will then put forth extra effort and ingenuity to make it $1.25. When, however, he finds that he can earn only 95 cents an hour on Job A, he rejects that amount and drops to a level of effort that earns only 50 cents an hour and relies upon his 85-cent base-pay rate for "take home." Job B has therefore become the "gravy" job, and Job A the "stinker." Into the "stinker" bin goes A, along with 90-cent jobs, 85-cent jobs, and 60-cent jobs.

The pronounced dichotomy in the production behavior of the machine operator suggests that restriction might be classified into two major types, "quota restriction" and "goldbricking." The heavy concentration of hours at the $1.25-$1.34 level with no spilling-over to the next level makes "quota restriction" appear as a limitation of effort on "gravy" jobs in order not to exceed set maximums. It could also be inferred that "goldbricking" appears as a "holding-back," or failure to release effort, when a close approach to the quota seems unattainable.

214

DONALD ROY

Quota Restriction

It is "quota restriction" which has received the most attention. The Mayo researchers observed that the bank-wiring group at Western Electric limited output to a "quota" or "bogey." . . .

Mayo thus joins those who consider the economic man a fallacious conception. Now the operators in my shop made noises like economic men. . . . It might be inferred from their talk that they did not turn in excess earnings because they felt that to do so would result in piecework price cuts; hence the consequences would be either reduced earnings from the same amount of effort expended or increased effort to maintain the take-home level.

When I was hired, a personnel department clerk assured me that the radial-drill operators were averaging $1.25 an hour on piecework. He was using a liberal definition of the term "averaging." Since I had no previous machine-shop experience and since a machine would not be available for a few days, I was advised to spend some time watching Jack Starkey, a radial-drill man of high rank in seniority and skill.

One of Starkey's first questions was, "What have you been doing?" When I said I had worked in a Pacific Coast shipyard at a rate of pay over $1.00 an hour, Starkey exclaimed, "Then what are you doing in this place?" When I replied that averaging $1.25 an hour wasn't bad, he exploded:

"Averaging, you say! Averaging?"

"Yeah, on the average. I'm an average guy; so I ought to make my buck and a quarter. That is, after I get onto it."

"Don't you know," cried Starkey angrily, "that $1.25 an hour is the *most* we can make, even when we *can* make more! And most of the time we can't even make that! Have you ever worked on piecework before?"

"No."

"I can see that! Well, what do you suppose would happen if I turned in $1.25 an hour on these pump bodies?"

"Turned in? You mean if you actually did the work?"

"I mean if I actually did the work and turned it in!"

"They'd have to pay you, wouldn't they? Isn't that the agreement?"

"Yes! They'd pay me—once! Don't you know that if I turned in $1.50 an hour on these pump bodies tonight, the whole God-dammed Methods Department would be down here tomorrow? And they'd retime this job so quick it would make your head swim! And when they retimed it, they'd cut the price in half! And I'd be working for 85 cents an hour instead of $1.25!"

From this initial exposition of Starkey's to my last day at the plant I was subject to warnings and predictions concerning price cuts. Pressure was the heaviest from Joe Mucha, day man on my machine, who shared my job repertoire and kept a close eye on my production. On November 14, the day after my first attained quota, Mucha advised:

"Don't let it go over $1.25 an hour, or the time-study man will be right down here! And they don't waste time, either! They watch the records like a hawk! I got ahead, so I took it easy for a couple of hours." . . .

Jack Starkey defined the quota carefully but forcefully when I turned in $10.50 for one day, or $1.31 an hour. . . .

Jack warned me that the Methods Department could lower their prices on any job, old or new, by changing the fixture slightly, or changing the size of drill. . . .

Starkey's beliefs concerning techniques of price cutting were those of the shop. Leonard Bricker, an old-timer in the shop, and Willie, the stock-chaser, both affirmed that management, once bent on slashing a piecework price, would stop at nothing. . . .

The association of quota behavior with such expressions about price cutting does not prove a causal connection. Such a connection could be determined only by instituting changes in the work situation that would effect a substantial reduction of "price-cut fear" and by observing the results of such changes. . . .

"Waste Time" on Quota Restriction

Whatever its causes, such restriction resulted in appreciable losses of time in the shop. I have evidence of it from observation of the work behavior and talk of fellow-operators and from my own work behavior. Since ability to "make out" early was related to skill and experience, it was some time before I found enough time wasted on quota restriction to record. But I discovered early that other operators had time to burn.

One evening Ed Sokolsky, onetime second-shift operator on Jack Starkey's drill, commented on a job that Jack was running:

"That's gravy! I worked on those, and I could turn out nine an hour. I timed myself at six minutes."

DONALD ROY

I was surprised.

"At 35 cents apiece, that's over $3.00 an hour!"

"And I got ten hours," said Ed. "I used to make out in four hours and fool around the rest of the night."

If Sokolsky reported accurately, he was "wasting" six hours per day. . . .

My own first "spare time" came on November 18.

Today I made out with such ease on the pedestals that I had an hour to spare. To cover the hour I had to poke along on the last operation, taking twice as much time to do 43 pieces as I ordinarily would. . . .

I reached my peak in quota restriction on June 27, with but three and a half hours of productive work out of the eight.

An Estimate of the Degree of Quota Restriction Practiced

The amount of quota restriction practiced by operators on the drill line may be estimated from my own production behavior.

During the ten-month diary period I received approximately 75 different piecework jobs, some of which were assigned from two to six times, but the majority of which were assigned only once. On only 31 of the jobs did I ever make out.

Of the 31 make-out jobs, only 20 afforded quota earnings of $1.25 an hour or more. . . .

By extending effort past quota limits to find the earning possibilities of the jobs, I discovered that on 16 of the 20 quota jobs I could have earned more than $1.30 an hour; on 4 of the 20 I was unable to exceed $1.30 per hour. . . .

Table 20-2 lists the 20 jobs which showed potentialities of yielding hourly earnings in excess of $1.30. Waste time and loss in earnings is computed for each job according to maximum earnings indicated in each case by actual test and according to the number of hours devoted to each job. For instance, operation "pawls," which leads the list with 157.9 total hours worked, showed, by test, possibilities of earnings of $1.96 per hour. At potentialities of $1.96 per hour, over 36 percent of each hour is wasted when the operator holds his turn-in to $1.25 an hour. Total waste time in the 157.9 hours expended on the pawls could then be computed at 57.2 hours, or over a third of the time actually put in. Earnings might have been, at $1.96 per hour, $309.48, whereas, at the quota level of $1.25, they would have been but $197.38—a loss of $112.10.

Total waste time for the 20 jobs is seen to be 286 hours, or 36.4 percent of a total 786.5 hours actually put in on them. This represents a wastage of 2.9 hours on each 8-hour day put in, or a total loss of 35.75 days out of 98.3 actually worked. With potential earnings of $1,584.43 for the 98 days and with quota earnings at $983.18, the wage loss to the worker would be $601.25, or $6.12 per day, or 76½ cents per hour. . . .

In order to generalize for the drill line from observation of my own behavior, I would have to establish (1) that I was an "average" performer and (2) that my job repertoire was representative of those of other operators.

Of the men on the same shift doing my kind of work, four (McCann, Starkey, Koszyk, and Sokolsky) could turn out greater volume than I and were my betters in all-around skills. Seven were below me in these respects, of them only three (Smith, Rinky, and Dooley) worked long enough to be in the core of the group. I was about average in skill and in the work assigned me. . . .

Piecework Goldbricking

On "gravy jobs" the operators earned a quota, then knocked off. On "stinkers" they put forth only minimal effort; either they did not try to achieve a turn-in equal to the base-wage rate or they deliberately slowed down. . . .

The attitude basic to the goldbricking type of restriction was expressed succinctly thus: "They're not going to get much work out of me for this pay!"

Complaints about low piecework prices were chronic and universal in the shop. . . .

The Slowdown

Resentment against piecework prices that were considered too low to offer possibilities of quota earnings often resulted in deliberate

218

TABLE 20-2

Time and Earnings Losses on Operations with Potentialities of Yielding Hourly Earnings in Excess of $1.30 Per Hour

OPERATION TESTED	TOTAL HOURS WORKED	MAXIMUM (PER HOUR)	WASTE TIME (PER HOUR)	TOTAL WASTE TIME (IN HOURS)	POTENTIAL EARNINGS	EARNINGS AT $1.25	LOSS IN EARNINGS
Pawls	157.9	$1.96	0.3625	57.2	$ 309.48	$197.38	$112.10
Pedestals	120.5	1.71	0.2625	31.6	206.08	150.63	55.43
NT bases	111.0	2.55	0.5125	56.9	283.05	138.75	144.30
Con rods	94.4	2.33	0.4625	43.7	219.95	118.00	101.95
Sockets	75.8	1.76	0.2875	21.8	133.41	94.75	38.66
B. housings	46.0	1.96	0.3625	16.7	90.16	57.50	32.66
Pinholes	37.7	1.87	0.3250	12.3	70.50	47.13	23.37
Casings	28.5	2.03	0.3750	10.7	57.86	35.63	22.23
Gear parts	24.0	1.83	0.3000	7.2	43.92	30.00	13.92
Replacers	19.3	2.20	0.4375	8.4	42.46	24.13	18.33
Spyglasses	18.0	1.57	0.1875	3.4	28.26	22.50	5.76
R. sockets	14.9	1.48	0.1375	2.0	22.05	18.63	3.42
Move. jaw	9.6	1.99	0.3625	3.5	19.10	12.00	7.10
Ped. $8.90	7.0	2.12	0.4000	2.8	14.84	8.75	6.09
Spot J1728	6.7	1.91	0.3375	2.3	12.80	8.38	4.42
G. sockets	4.5	2.53	0.5000	2.3	11.39	5.63	5.76
Ped. $5	4.3	1.85	0.3250	1.4	7.96	5.38	2.58
CB hubs	4.1	1.65	0.2375	1.0	6.77	5.13	1.64
SD cups	1.5	1.89	0.3250	0.5	2.84	1.88	0.96
Bolts	0.8	1.96	0.3625	0.3	1.57	1.00	0.57
TOTAL	786.5			286.0	$1,584.43	$983.18	$601.25
	(98.3 days)			(35.75 days)			

attempts to produce at lower rates than mere "dogging it along" would bring. This kind of goldbricking was particularly noticeable on jobs that came relatively often and in large lots. Toward a short order of poor price that was assigned to his machine but once or twice a year, the operator's attitude was likely to be one of "I don't give a damn," and the result would be production below "standard." But toward a low-priced order assigned every month or two and in amounts that would take several shifts to a week to process, i.e., jobs that played a major part in the operator's repertoire, the attitude was likely to be, "Just for that, you'll get as little as I can turn out and still be operating this machine!" . . .

Summary and Conclusion

These appraisals of output limitation can be accepted only as suggestive of the amount of time wasted by operatives in piecework machine shops. Certainly, the "waste" is great.

I have indicated that the time "wasted" on my own quota restriction for a six-month period was 1.39 hours out of every 8. I was 83 percent "efficient" for the 469.6 quota piecework-hours put in, by my own standards of performance, and thus could have increased production by 21 percent by abandoning quota limitations. If my wastage of 2 hours a day on quota restriction during the last two months of employment is accepted as characteristic of the behavior of more seasoned operators, efficiency would be 75 percent, with immediate possibilities for a 33.3 percent increase in production on quota jobs.

Also, by experimenting with twenty jobs which represented 58 percent of the total piecework-hours put in during a ten-month period, and which offered earning possibilities beyond quota limits, I derived an estimate of "potential quota restriction" of 2.9 hours a day. This restriction represented an efficiency of 64 percent, with possibilities for a 57 percent increase in production.

Furthermore, from observations of the work behavior of fellow-operators, I was able to speculate with some objective evidence on the degree of slowdown goldbricking practiced on non-make-out piecework. It was pointed out that four drill operators had been restricting production at a rate of 3.5 "waste" hours out of 8, as indicated by the output achieved by one of the four men when he ceased goldbricking. Efficiency had been 56 percent, with immediate possibilities for a 78 percent production increase. Renunciation of goldbricking did not, in this particular case, mean fulfillment of possibilities, however, for the conversion was to quota restriction with stabilization at 75 percent efficiency. . . .

Since these appraisals were confined to the behavior of machine operators, the loss of time accountable to the sometimes remarkable restraint exercised by the "service" employees, such as stock-chasers, toolcrib attendants, and inspectors, was not considered. Likewise unmentioned were the various defections of shop supervisors. A more complete record might also include the "work" of members of management at higher levels, whose series of new rules, regulations, orders, and pronunciamentos designed for purposes of expediting production processes actually operated to reduce the effectiveness of the work force. . . .

JULIUS A. ROTH

RITUAL AND MAGIC
IN THE CONTROL
OF CONTAGION

Tuberculosis is a contagious disease. But just how contagious is it? In what ways and under what circumstances is it likely to be transmitted from one person to another? And what procedures are most effective for preventing its transmission? The answers to these questions are quite uncertain and TB specialists show considerable disagreement in the details of the manner in which they deal with these problems. These uncertainties leave the way open for ritualized procedures that often depend more on convenience and ease of administration than on rationally deduced probabilities. They also leave the way open for irrational practices that can properly be called "magic."

Protecting the Outside World

In one Veterans Administration hospital, occupational therapy products are routinely sterilized by exposure to ultra-violet light before being sent out. (Patients sometimes by-pass this procedure by giving their OT products to their visitors to take out.) Books are sometimes sterilized before being sent out, sometimes not. Other articles mailed by patients may or may not be sterilized depending largely upon whether or not the patient requests it. Letters are never

Reprinted in part with permission from *American Sociological Review* 22 (June 1957): 310-314.

sterilized. The inconsistency of these procedures is not lost on the workers. One volunteer worker held up a package she was mailing for a patient and said: "Now, I can mail this without sterilizing it, but if someone wants to send home some OT work, I have to sterilize it before I can mail it for him. It doesn't make any sense."

The fact that sterilization is carried out by volunteer workers under the direction of the Special Services Division is in itself an indication that it is regarded as an auxiliary rather than an essential activity of the hospital. . . .

Money regularly passes out of the hospital without sterilization. Patients give money to volunteer shoppers, the newsman, canteen, and postal workers. These people put the money into pocket, purse, or money box, and pass it on to others without raising any questions about the possibility of spreading the disease. Quite often money changes hands quickly after being taken from the patients. . . . The danger of transmitting tubercle bacilli by money is probably very slight, but it is certainly many times greater than the chance of spreading the disease through books and OT products, which spend at least a day or two in transit through the mails.

An even more striking example of inconsistency is shown in the policy toward visitors. Visitors are not required to wear any protective clothing, not even masks, and none of them ever do. The same is true of entertainers and members of service and veterans organizations who play games with the patients or bring them gifts. Some patients have positive sputum, so that a visitor probably runs a much greater risk of taking viable bacilli into his body than does the person who handles money, books, or OT products of a patient after a period of several hours or several days. However, TB hospitals have a tradition of permitting persons without protective clothing to visit patients, and to break such a tradition would almost certainly bring strong protests from patients and their families and would in any case be evaded by many people. . . .

In summary, the devices for protection against the spread of the disease outside the hospital are controlled largely by tradition, convenience, and adherence to legal technicalities rather than to rational estimates of the chances of transmission of tubercle bacilli. The limited efforts at preventing the transmission of the disease are concentrated chiefly in those areas where the chances of transmission are probably the least.

Rank and Protective Clothing

A number of procedures are designed to protect the employees and patients within the hospital from spreading TB. One method . . . is the use of protective clothing—masks, gowns, and hair coverings—which the hospital personnel are supposed to wear when they come into contact with the patients or their effects. However, this protective clothing is often not worn. There is a definite relationship between the degree to which it is worn and the rank of the employee.

I recorded the wearing of surgical cap, gown, and mask by the nursing personnel of a VA hospital when entering a patient's room over a four-day period. The results are shown in Table 21-1.

TABLE 21-1.
Wearing of Protective Clothing by Nursing Personnel in Veterans Administration Hospital

	TIMES ENTERED ROOM	PERCENTAGES WEARING		
		CAP	GOWN	MASK
Nurses	56	100	57	75
Attendants	200	100	72	90

More detailed records were made of the use of protective clothing when entering patients' rooms in a state hospital that had a more complex nursing hierarchy. The record was made on ten different days, plus additional days for doctors and professional nurses in order to increase their very small number. The records were made on three different wards with different sets of personnel and were always for complete days to avoid the selective influence of certain work shifts or kinds of ward duties. Results are given in Table 21-2. The two instances of a doctor wearing cap and mask on recorded days (Table 21-2) both involved the same doctor—an assistant surgeon on a temporary assignment. His successor does not wear protective clothing.

As both of these tables show, the use of protective clothing is inversely related to occupational status level. The people of higher rank seem to have the privilege of taking the greater risks, particularly in the case of masks. The cap and gown are intended in part to prevent the spread of the disease to others; the mask is almost exclusively for the protection of the wearer.

TABLE 21-2.

Wearing of Protective Clothing by Doctors and Nursing Personnel in State Hospital

	TIMES ENTERED ROOM	PERCENTAGES WEARING		
		CAP	GOWN	MASK
Doctors	47	5	0	5
Professional nurses	100	24	18	14
Practical nurses	121	86	45	46
Aides	142	94	80	72
Students	97	100	100	100

It might be argued that the lower-status employees should wear protective clothing relatively more often because they perform tasks which require more intimate contact with the patients and their effects. Thus, the aides and students do most of the work of collecting food trays and trash, making beds, washing furniture, picking up soiled towels. Certainly, this factor makes a difference, but it is not sufficient to account for the whole difference.

When we examine overlapping functions (those carried out by two or more levels of nursing personnel), differences, if any, are almost always in the direction of more frequent wearing of protective clothing by the lower-status employees. . . .

Why do persons with higher status wear protective clothing less often? For one thing, it is not considered necessary by people who know best. There is no good evidence that the systematic wearing of protective clothing makes any difference (even the person who planned and administered this program could cite no evidence showing its effectiveness) and people who know most about TB do not seem to consider it worth the trouble. Doctors, and to a lesser extent professional nurses, are, of course, most likely to recognize the probable futility of these procedures. The relative ignorance of the lower levels of ward employees makes it more likely that they will have doubts about whether it is safe to go without the protective clothing, especially on routine duties when they must enter patients' rooms repeatedly in a short interval. . . . Probably a more important factor is the likelihood that the employee can "get away with" a violation. A doctor need not worry about a "bawling out" for not protecting himself. A professional nurse might be criticized, but usually she is the highest authority on a ward. The chance of criticism increases down the scale. . . .

Magic and the Tubercle Bacillus

Gauze or paper masks are rather difficult to breathe through. To make breathing easier patients and employees sometimes pull down the mask until their nostrils have a clear space. This, of course, destroys the point of wearing the mask and the mask then takes on the status of a charm necklace.

We can also find examples of institutional magic. In the state hospital patients are required to wear masks when they go to the first floor for a hair cut or for an x-ray and when they go to the eighth floor to see the social worker or the patient services director. They do not have to wear masks (and never do) when they go to the first floor for occupational therapy, to visit with their families, to attend socials or church services, or to see a movie, nor when they go to the eighth floor to the library and to play bingo. An examination of these two lists shows that patients must wear masks when they go somewhere on "business," but not when they go somewhere for "pleasure," even though they use the same parts of the building and come into contact with hospital personnel in both cases. The rules suggest that the tubercle bacillus works only during business hours.

The ward employee tends to wear protective clothing when carrying out her duties, but not when "socializing" with the patients. I kept a record over a short period of time on several practical nurses on the 3:00 to 11:00 P.M. shift. Table 21-3 shows the contrasts in their use of protective clothing. The nurses' contact with the patients was more prolonged and more intimate while socializing than while carrying out their duties. The average time spent in the room during this recorded period was less than half a minute for taking care of a duty and about three minutes for socializing. While giving out medicine or taking temperatures or bringing in food trays the nurses have very little close contact with the patients. While socializing, they often stand close to the patients, lean on their beds and other furniture, and handle their newspapers and other belongings.

Logically, there is a greater need for the protective clothing—and especially the mask, which was hardly used at all—while socializing than while carrying out the routine duties.

TABLE 21-3.

Wearing of Protective Clothing by Practical Nurses When Carrying Out Duties and When "Socializing" With Patients

	TIMES ENTERED ROOM	PERCENTAGES WEARING		
		CAP	GOWN	MASK
Carrying out duties	39	97	75	80
"Socializing"	23	91	17	9

Apparently, these nurses believe they need protection only when working. They remark that the gown, and more especially the mask, is a barrier to friendly intercourse.

Man's Laws and Nature's Laws

. . . The practices surrounding contagion control in a TB hospital represent an effort to make man's laws approximate the laws of nature, and when nature's laws are not well understood, man's rules are likely to be more or less irrational and their observance vacillating and ritualistic.

THE PSYCHOSOCIAL ORIGINS
OF ACHIEVEMENT MOTIVATION

The purpose of this study is to examine the origins of achievement motivation (*n* Achievement) within the context of the individual's membership in two important groups: family and social class. Specifically, this paper explores, through the observation of family interaction, the relationship between achievement motivation and certain child-training practices, and the relationship between these practices and the parent's social class membership. . . .

Methodological. This study departed from two practices common in studies of the origins of *n* Achievement. The first practice is to derive data exclusively from ethnographic materials; the second, to obtain information through questionnaire-type interviews with mothers. Interviews and ethnographies can be valuable sources of information, but they are often contaminated by interviewer and respondent biases, particularly those of perceptual distortion, inadequate recall, and deliberate inaccuracies. There was a need for data derived from systematic observation of parent-child relations. It is not enough to know what parents *say* their child-rearing practices are; these statements should be checked against more objective data, preferably acquired under controlled experimental conditions, that would permit us to *see* what they do. In this study, experiments were employed which enabled a team of investigators to observe parent-child interaction in problem-solving situations that were standardized for all groups and required no special competence associated with age or sex.

Reprinted in part with permission from *Sociometry*, 22 (September 1958): 185-218.

An equally strong objection can be raised against the tendency to ignore the father's role in the development of the child's need to achieve. Apart from an earlier study of father-son power relations, no efforts had been made to determine the father's contribution to achievement and independence training—a surprising omission even granted the mother's importance in socializing the child in American society. Although we were not prepared to take a position on the nature of the role relationships between father, mother, and son with respect to this motive, we deliberately created experimental conditions which would enable us to observe the way in which the three members of the family interacted in a problem-solving situation. Finally, this study incorporated in one design the variables of group membership, child-training practices, and motivation, variables that heretofore had not been studied simultaneously. In so doing we hoped to establish the nexus among class membership, socialization practices, and achievement motivation.

Hypotheses

This study was designed to provide data that would permit testing two basic hypotheses.

1. Achievement motivation is a result of the following socialization practices: (a) *achievement training,* in which the parents set high goals for their son to attain, indicate that they have a high evaluation of his competence to do a task well, and impose standards of excellence upon tasks against which he is to compete, even in situations where such standards are not explicit; (b) *independence training,* in which the parents indicate to the child that they expect him to be *self-reliant,* while at the same time permit him relative *autonomy* in situations involving decision making where he is given both freedom of action and responsibility for success or failure; (c) *sanctions,* rewards and punishments employed by parents to ensure that their expectations are met and proper behavior is reinforced. Although each contributes to the development of achievement motivation, achievement training is more important than independence training. Neither are effective without supporting sanctions.

2. Differences in the mean level of achievement motivation between social classes is in part a function of the differential class

emphases upon independence and achievement training: middle-class parents are more likely than lower-class parents to stress self-relience, autonomy, and achievement in problem-solving situations, particularly those involving standards of excellence. They are more likely to recognize and reward evidences of achievement, as well as to be more sensitive of and punitive toward indications of failure.

Experimental Procedure

The subjects selected to provide data needed for the testing of these hypotheses about the origins of achievement motivation were 120 persons who made up 40 family groups composed of a father, mother, and their son, aged nine, ten, or eleven. The selection of the family groups began with testing the boy. Seven schools in three northeastern Connecticut towns were visited by the same field worker who administered a Thematic Apperception Test individually and privately to 140 boys, aged nine, ten, or eleven. As is customary in the TAT procedure, the subject was presented with a set of four ambiguous pictures and asked to tell a story about each. His imaginative responses were then scored according to a method developed by McClelland and his associates. . . . Subjects with scores of plus 2 to minus 4 (approximately the bottom quartile) were labeled as having low *n* Achievement, those with scores of plus 9 to plus 22 (approximately the top quartile) as having high *n* Achievement. Any boy with an I.Q. score below 98, with physical defects, whose parents were separated, or who had been raised during part of his life by persons or relatives other than his parents (e.g., grandparents) was eliminated from the sample.

Forty boys, matched by age, race, I.Q., and social class were chosen for further study. All were white, native born, and between nine and eleven years of age; the average was ten years. Half of the boys had high *n* Achievement scores, half had low scores. In each achievement motivation category, half of the boys were middle class, half were lower class. Their social class position was determined according to a modified version of the Hollingshead Index of Social Position which uses the occupation and education of the chief wage-earner—usually the father—as the principal criteria of status. . . .

It can be seen that the study was designed in such a way that the subjects fell into one of four cells, with the achievement motivation level of the boys and the class position of the parents as the classificatory variables. Within each cell there were ten families. This four-cell factorial design was constructed so as to facilitate the use of the analysis of variance technique in the statistical analysis of the data.

After the boy was selected, a letter was sent to his parents from the principal of the school asking their cooperation with the investigators. Later, appointments were made over the telephone to visit the families. Cooperation was very good; there were only two refusals. A pair of observers visited each family group, usually at night. There were two teams of observers, each composed of a man and woman. Both teams had been trained together to ensure adequate intra- and interteam reliability.

Once in the home, the observers explained that they were interested in studying the factors related to success in school and eventually to a career, and that the son was one of many boys selected from a cross section of the community. When rapport had been established, the parents and their son were placed at a table—usually in the kitchen—and it was explained that the boy was going to perform certain tasks.

EXPERIMENTAL TASKS

The observers wanted to create an experimental situation from which could be derived objective measures of the parents' response to their son as he engaged in achievement behavior. Tasks were devised which the boy could do and which would involve the parents in their son's task performance. The tasks were constructed so that the subjects were often faced with a choice of giving or refusing help. At times they were permitted to structure the situation according to their own norms; at other times the experimenters set the norms. In some situations they were faced with decision conflicts over various alternatives in the problem-solving process. The observation of the parents' behavior as their son engaged in these experimental tasks provided information about the demands the parents made upon him, the sanctions employed to enforce these demands, and the amount of independence the child had developed in relations with his parents. A category system, similar to the Bales system, was devised to permit scoring interaction between parents and son so that the amount and form of each subject's particpation could be examined. The investigators were able to learn from these interaction data how self-reliant the parents expected their son to be, how much autonomy they permitted him in decision-making situations, and what kind and amount of affect was generated in a problem-solving situation.

In creating the experimental tasks an effort was made to simulate two conditions normally present when boys are solving problems in the presence of their parents: (1) tasks were constructed to make the boys relatively dependent upon their parents for aid; and (2) the situation was arranged so that the parents either knew the solution to the problem or were in a position to do the task better than their son. In addition, tasks were created which tapped manual skills as well as intellectual capacities, although intelligence is a factor in any problem-solving situation. It was for this reason that the experimenters controlled for I.Q.

In one particular respect the experimental situation was deliberately made atypical. The investigators sought to get the parents involved in the experiment by deliberately building stress into the situation. It was hoped that these *stress experiments* would so involve the parents that they would abandon their protective "company behavior" and generate more authentic action in several hours then could be gained through casual observation over several days. This maneuver was generally successful, although it is impossible to evaluate how and in what way the nature of the experiments and the presence of observers affected the subjects. It is a basic assumption of this study that by studying present-time interaction in a controlled situation one can achieve a valid picture of the patterns of interaction between parents and child most likely to have occurred in the child's earlier years. It is recognized, however, that the conflicting evidence about changes in socialization practices as the child grows older leaves the wisdom of this assumption an open question.

Pretesting had shown that no single task would provide sufficient data to test all hypotheses. Hence, five tasks were constructed, each designed to attack the problem from a somewhat different angle and yet provide certain classes of data that could be scored across tasks. The five tasks used in this study are as follows:

1. *Block Stacking.* The boys were asked to build towers out of very irregularly shaped blocks. They were blindfolded and told to use only one hand in order to create a situation in which the boy was

relatively dependent upon his parents for help. His parents were told that this was a test of their son's ability to build things, and that they could *say* anything to their son but could not touch the blocks. A performance norm was set for the experiment by telling the parents that the average boy could build a tower of eight blocks; they were asked to write down privately their estimate of how high they thought their son could build his tower. The purposes of this experiment were: (a) to see how high were the parents' aspirations for and evaluations of their son, e.g., if they set their estimates at, above, or below the norm; (b) to see how self-reliant they expected or permitted their son to be, e.g., how much help they would give him.

There were three trials for this task. The first provided measures of parental evaluations and aspirations not affected by the boy's performance; the second and third trial estimates provided measures affected by the boy's performance. The procedure for the third trial differed from the first two in that the boy was told that he would be given a nickel for each block he stacked. Each member of the family was asked to estimate privately how high the boy should build his tower. No money would be given for blocks stacked higher than the estimate nor would the subject receive anything if the stack tumbled before he reached the estimate. Conservative estimates, hence, provided security but little opportunity for gain; high estimates involved more opportunity for gain but greater risk. The private estimates were then revealed to all and the family was asked to reach a group decision. In addition to securing objective measures of parental aspiration-evaluation levels, the observers scored the interaction between subjects, thus obtaining data as to the kind and amount of instructions the parents gave their son, the amount of help the son asked for or rejected, and the amount and kind of affect generated during the experiment.

2. *Anagrams.* In this task the boys were asked to make words of three letters or more out of six prescribed letters: G, H, K, N, O, R. The letters, which could be reused after each word was made, were printed on wooden blocks so that they could be manipulated. The parents were given three additional lettered blocks, T, U, and B, and a list of words that could be built with each new letter. They were informed that they could give the boy a new letter (in the sequence T, U, B) whenever they wished and could say anything to him, short of telling him what word to build. There was a ten-minute time limit

for this experiment. Since this is a familiar game, no efforts were made to explain the functions of the task.

The purposes of this experiment were: (a) to see how self-reliant the parents expected their son to be, e.g., how soon they would give him a new letter, how much and what kind of direction they would give him, if they would keep him working until he got all or most of the words on the list or "take him off the hook" when he got stuck; and (b) to obtain, by scoring interaction between the subjects, measures of the affect generated by the problem-solving process, e.g., the amount of tension shown by the subjects, the positive and negative remarks directed toward one another.

3. *Patterns.* In this experiment the parents were shown eight patterns, graduated in difficulty, that could be made with Kohs blocks. The subjects were informed that pattern 1 was easier to make than pattern 2, pattern 3 was more difficult than 2 but easier than 4, and so forth. The subjects were told that this was a test of the boy's ability to remember and reproduce patterns quickly and accurately. Each parent and boy was asked to select privately three patterns which the boy would be asked to make from memory after having seen the pattern for five seconds. All three patterns were chosen *before* the boy began the problem solving so that his performance in this task would not affect the choice of the patterns. Where there were differences of choice, as inevitably there were, the subjects were asked to discuss their differences and make a group decision. Insofar as possible the observers took a verbatim account of the decision-making process, scoring for three kinds of variables: (a) the number of acts each subject contributed to the decision-making process; (b) the number of times each individual initiated a decision; and (c) the number of times each subject was successful in having the group accept his decision or in seeing to it that a decision was made.

The purposes of this experiment were: (a) to obtain another measure of the parents' evaluations of and aspirations for the boy, e.g., whether they would pick easy or difficult tasks for him to do; (b) to get a measure of the autonomy permitted the boy, e.g., whether they would let him choose his own patterns or impose their choices upon him; and (c) to see how much help they would give him and what affect would be generated by the experiment.

4. *Ring Toss.* In this experiment each member of the group was asked to choose privately ten positions, from each of which the boy was to throw three rings at a peg. The distance from the peg was

delineated by a tape with one-foot graduations laid on the floor. The subjects were told that this was a test of discrimination and judgment and that after each set of three tosses they would be asked to make a judgment as to the best distance from which to make the next set of tosses. Group decisions were made as to where the boy should stand. The purposes of this experiment were: (a) to see whether the parents imposed standards of excellence upon a task for which no explicit standard had been set, e.g., whether the parents would treat this as a childish game or see it as a task which could and should be done well. Would they choose easy or difficult positions? (b) To determine how much autonomy they permitted their son, e.g., would they let him choose his own position?

5. *Hatrack.* The Maier Hatrack Problem was used in this experiment. The boy was given two sticks and a C-clamp and instructed to build a rack strong enough to hold a coat and hat. His parents were told that this was a test of the boy's ability to build things. In this task no one was given the solution at the beginning of the experiment. For the first time the parents had no advantage over the boy—a most uncomfortable position for many parents, particularly the fathers. This stress situation was created deliberately to maximize the possibility of the problem generating affect, as was often the case, with some hostility being directed at the observers. After seven minutes the parents were given the solution to the problem. The purposes of this experiment were: (a) to see how self-reliant the parents expected their son to be. After receiving the solution what kind of clues would the parents give the boy? How hard would they expect him to work on his own? (b) To obtain measures of the affect created in an unusually frustrating situation. How would the parents handle their frustration? Would they turn it against the boy? . . .

Independence Training, Sanctions, and Achievement Motivation

Earlier we distinguished between achievement training and independence training; the latter was broken down into two components: self-reliance training and the granting of relative autonomy in decision making. Associated with *both* independence and achievement training are sanctions—rewards and punishments—administered by the parents to reinforce appropriate behavior in the child. The data to index these variables were obtained by examining the interaction between parents and child as they engaged in the experimental tasks, and by observing the decision-making process in those instances where the subjects were asked to make a group estimate or choice of what the boy should do.

The scoring of parent-child interaction produced a voluminous amount of data: hundreds of acts were scored during the average three-hour experimental session. . . .

SELF-RELIANCE TRAINING

Directional statements (S and N) were used as measures of self-reliance training; a large number of N type acts in which the child is *not told exactly* what to do, but merely given a clue would indicate independence training, while a high incidence of specific directions (S) would be a sign of a little such training. We had predicted that the parents of high need Achievement boys would generate more "N" acts and fewer "S" acts than the parents of boys with low achievement motivation. The data show that the fathers and mothers of high *n* Achievement boys give out *proportionately* more "N" acts and fewer "S" acts, but the differences are not significant. For total number of acts, the fathers of high *n* Achievement boys score higher on "N" acts and lower on "S" acts; the mothers of high *n* Achievement boys also score lower on "S" acts, but unlike the fathers they also score lower on "N" type acts. Although in all but one case—the lower N score for mothers of high *n* Achievement boys—the differences are in the direction predicted, in none of these cases are the differences statistically significant.

Pushing statements (+P and −P) are acts aimed at motivating the boy to work harder. An argument can be made for considering this type of act as reflecting either independence *or* achievement training, but in the context in which we observed this type of behavior it seemed to us to be primarily an index of independence training. We believe that a large number of pushing statements indicates *low* self-reliance training, for such statements often came from parents who appeared unable to sit back and let their boy work at his own speed but felt impelled to make him do well by urging or shouting him on. This type of parent seemed to assume that the boy had little internal need to excel, and that without external pressure he would soon run out of gas. As had been predicted, the fathers of high *n* Achievement boys gave fewer pushing statements than the fathers of boys with low achievement motivation. However, the reverse was true for the mothers: in this case it was the mothers of high n Achievement boys who had the higher score for pushing type statements. In none of these cases, however, are the differences statistically significant.

AUTONOMY

An index of the autonomy permitted the boy in decision making, another aspect of independence training, was derived by observing the family decision-making process in three tasks: Block Stacking (third trial), Patterns, and Ring Toss. The observers scored three types of behavior in this process: (1) the number of acts each subject contributed to the decision making; (2) the number of times each subject initiated the decision process by being the first to present a choice for consideration; (3) the number of times an individual made the decision for the group or stated the final judgment. In all these decision-conflict situations somebody must state the final resolution, whether authoritatively or only as the summation of consensus. This final summation or statement was scored as "deciding." Intercorrelations between these three types of acts were computed; all correlations were sufficiently high to permit their being combined into a single score labeled "autonomy." The transformation of raw scores into standard scores was not necessary. It should be remembered that in this experiment the lower the parental autonomy score, the greater the autonomy permitted the boy.

We expected that the parents of high need Achievement boys would give their son more autonomy in the decision-making process than would be granted boys with low n Achievement. The data are in the direction predicted with respect to the fathers, but quite the reverse is true in the case of the mothers: the mothers of low n Achievement boys tend to grant greater autonomy to their sons. Unfortunately, none of these differences is statistically significant.

SANCTIONS

Typically, positive and negative reinforcements are associated with any learning situation—rewards for success and punishment for failure. We had predicted that the parents of boys with high achievement motivation would score higher on Warmth (positive affect) and lower on Rejection (negative affect) than the parents of low n Achievement boys. *The data show that the mothers of high* n *Achievement boys score significantly higher on Warmth than the* mothers of low n *Achievement boys* $(F = 8.87, P < .01)$. The differences between fathers, although in the predicted direction, are not significant $(F = 4.13, P < .10)$.

Fathers of boys with high *n* Achievement tend to score lower on Rejection. The reverse is true for the mothers: *the Rejection scores are higher for mothers of high Achievement motivation boys than for the mothers of low n Achievement boys*. None of these differences in Rejection, however, are statistically significant.

PARENTAL PROFILES AND MOTIVATION

In the analysis of data so far the relationship of each variable to achievement motivation was examined separately. The Split Plot type of analysis of variance was next employed to permit the examination of all variables simultaneously for each parent.... [For example,] Figure 22-1 shows that the fathers of high *n* Achievement boys when compared with the fathers of low *n* Achievement boys tend to give higher estimates and choices for the Block Stacking and Patterns tasks, place their sons farther away from the peg in the Ring Toss experiment, are more warm, less rejecting, give their boy more autonomy, are less pushing, and give more nonspecific directions and fewer specific ones. The two groups of mothers when compared with one another present a somewhat different picture. The mothers of high *n* Achievement boys also tend to give higher estimates and choices for the Block Stacking and Patterns tasks, place their sons farther away from the peg in the Ring Toss experiment, give fewer specific directions, and are more warm. However, they are more rejecting, give the boy less autonomy, are more pushing, and give fewer nonspecific directions....

SOCIAL CLASS AND CHILD-TRAINING PRACTICES

The research design made it improbable that the class differences in training practices would be great, for the sample was selected in such a way as to make both classes equal with respect to the dependent variable. That is, the *n* Achievement scores of lower-class boys were on the average equal to the scores of middle-class boys—a situation known not to be true for the more general universe of middle- and lower-class boys.... [The] data, though sometimes in the direction predicted, indicate that the training practices of middle-class parents are not on the whole markedly different from those of lower-class parents....

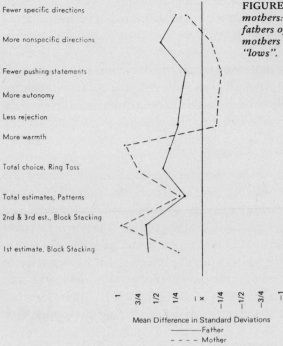

Fewer specific directions

More nonspecific directions

Fewer pushing statements

More autonomy

Less rejection

More warmth

Total choice, Ring Toss

Total estimates, Patterns

2nd & 3rd est., Block Stacking

1st estimate, Block Stacking

FIGURE 22-1. *Profiles for fathers and mothers: mean difference between fathers of "highs" and fathers of "lows"; mothers of "highs" and mothers of "lows".*

1 3/4 1/2 1/4 | × −1/4 −1/2 −3/4 −1

Mean Difference in Standard Deviations
———— Father
– – – – Mother

Discussion and Summary

The question of how achievement training, independence training, and sanctions are related to achievement motivation may be rephrased by asking, How does the behavior of parents of boys with high n Achievement differ from the behavior of parents whose sons have low n Achievement?

To begin with, the observers' subjective impressions are that the parents of high n Achievement boys tend to be more competitive, show more involvement, and seem to take more pleasure in the problem-solving experiments. They appear to be more interested and concerned with their son's performance; they tend to give him more things to manipulate rather than fewer; on the average they put out more affective acts. More objective data show that the parents of a boy with high n Achievement tend to have higher aspirations for him to do well at any given task, and they seem to have a higher regard for his competence at problem solving. They set up standards of excellence for the boy even when none is given, or if a standard is given will expect him to do "better than average." As he progresses they tend to react to his performance with warmth and approval, or, in the case of the mothers especially, with disapproval if he performs poorly.

It seems clear that achievement training contributes more to the development of n Achievement than does independence training. Indeed, the role of independence training in generating achievement motivation can only be understood in the context of what appears to be a division of labor between the fathers and mothers of high n Achievement boys.

Fathers and mothers both provide achievement training and independence training, but the fathers seem to contribute much more to the latter than do the mothers. Fathers tend to let their sons develop some self-reliance by giving hints rather than always telling "how to do it." They are less likely to push and more likely to give the boy a greater degree of autonomy in making his own decisions. Fathers of high n Achievement boys often appear to be competent men who are willing to take a back seat while their sons are performing. They tend to beckon from ahead rather than push from behind.

The mothers of boys with high achievement motivation tend to stress achievement training rather than independence training. In fact, they are likely to be more dominant and to expect less self-reliance than the mothers of boys with low n Achievement. But their aspirations for their sons are higher and their concern over success greater. Thus, they expect the boys to build higher towers and place them farther away from the peg in the Ring Toss experiment. As a boy works his mother tends to become emotionally involved. Not only is she more likely to reward him with approval (Warmth) but also to punish him with hostility (Rejection). *In a way, it is this factor of involvement that most clearly sets the mothers of high* n *Achievement boys apart from the mothers of low* n *Achievement boys:* the former score higher on every variable, except specific directions. And although these mothers are likely to give their sons more option as to exactly (fewer Specifics) what to do, they give them less option about doing something and doing it well. Observers report that the mothers of high n Achievement boys tend to be striving, competent persons. Apparently they expect their sons to be the same.

The different emphasis which the fathers and mothers of high n

Achievement boys place upon achievement and independence training suggests that the training practices of father and mother affect the boy in different ways. Apparently, the boy can take and perhaps needs achievement training from both parents, but the effects of independence training and sanctions, in particular Autonomy and Rejection, are different depending upon whether they come from the father or mother. In order for high n Achievement to develop, the boy appears to need more autonomy from his father than from his mother. The father who gives the boy a relatively high degree of autonomy provides him with an opportunity to compete on his own ground, to test his skill, and to gain a sense of confidence in his own competence. The dominating father may crush his son (and in so doing destroys the boy's achievement motive), perhaps because he views the boy as a competitor and is viewed as such by his son. On the other hand, the mother who dominates the decision-making process does not seem to have the same effect on the boy, possibly because she is perceived as *imposing her standards* on the boy, while a dominating father is perceived as *imposing himself* on the son. It may be that the mother-son relations are typically more secure than those between father and son, so that the boy is better able to accept higher levels of dominance and rejection from his mother than his father without adverse affect on his need to achieve. Relatively rejecting, dominating fathers, particularly those with less than average warmth—as tended to be the case with the fathers of low n Achievement boys—seem to be a threat to the boy and a deterent to the development of n Achievement. On the other hand, above-average dominance and rejection, coupled with above-average warmth, as tends to be the case with mothers of high n Achievement boys, appear to be a spur to achievement motivation. It will be remembered that the fathers of high n Achievement boys are on the average less Rejecting, less Pushing, and less Dominant—all of which points to their general hands-off policy.

It is unlikely that these variables operate separately, but the way in which they interact in the development of achievement motivation is not clear. Possibly the variables interact in a manner which produces cyclical effects roughly approximating the interaction that characterized the experimental task situations of this study. The cycle begins with the parents imposing standards of excellence upon a task and setting a high goal for the boy to achieve (e.g., Ring Toss, estimates and choices in Block Stacking and Patterns). As the boy engages in the task, they reinforce acceptable behavior by expressions of warmth (both parents) or by evidences of disapproval (primarily mother). The boy's performance improves, in part because of previous experience and in part because of the greater concern shown by his parents and expressed through affective reaction to his performance and greater attention to his training. With improved performance, the parents grant the boy greater autonomy and interfere less with his performance (primarily father). Goals are then reset at a higher level and the cycle continues.

23

VATTEL ELBERT DANIEL

RITUAL AND STRATIFICATION IN CHICAGO NEGRO CHURCHES

It is our hypothesis that religious ritual performs different functions for different classes within an urban American Negro population, while at the same time performing a function common to the entire class and one that is also common to all members of the particular denomination or sect with which the individual church is identified. In attempting to determine the relation of ritual and general church behavior in urban Negro churches to the part of the society in which these churches function, we have been concerned primarily with the church's function in the social adjustment of groups of persons. Hence, we have used the sermons, prayers, songs, and behavior, in studying ceremonials and beliefs of types of communicants representing class and economic differences in urban Negro life. The types of ritual have been studied as indexes of the degree of adaptation to the social pressures that cause persons and groups to try to conform to the types of religious behavior characteristic of middle class and upper class white urban society.

We chose 40 churches in that part of Chicago which has the densest Negro population, the selection being made so as to give the necessary distribution as to location, size, denomination, type of ritual, and social class of communicant. Personally instructed research assistants with observation guides obtained written reports of the services of these churches. As far as possible, four reports were received for each church, although not all of them were made by the same field worker. After studying these documents, the investigator

Reprinted in part with permission from *American Sociological Review* 7 (June 1942): 352-361.

made several trips to each church and prepared verbatim reports of the services. Particular attention was paid to anything in the sermons, prayers, hymns, and behavior that indicated the social pressures that were affecting the pastor or his people. When possible, special projects were assigned the assistants, and one of them made a case study of her own church.

After the observation documents were prepared, they were used to classify the churches as to ritual and ceremonial. This classification was based upon an anlaysis of the observation documents into ceremonial, emotional, and ideational elements. Then these types were compared with each other to determine the significance of the differences.

The investigation then interviewed the pastors to find out what they were attempting to do for the worshippers in the church services which they conducted, what were the problems of adjustment to urban life as they saw them, how they thought their type of ritual compared with other types, and what members should be interviewed to find out how successful the pastors were in obtaining their objectives. Particular note was made of statements referring to the class of people attending the churches and the reasons why certain classes of persons attended certain churches. . . . The general life of each class was then related to its life in the type of church which is frequented. An attempt has been made to show that type of ritual is a function of type of life in the part of the society in which one finds oneself.

Classification and Comparison of Ritual Types

The use of ritual as a key concept in the study of Negro church life has several advantages. Among them are the following: ritual can be objectively recorded; these records, instead of merely listing barren details, give portraits of an ideal-forming institution in action, featuring four types of worshippers, (1) the crowd that dances, (2) the group which indulges in demonstrative assent, (3) the congregation which prefers sermon-centered services, and (4) the church with formal liturgy. We have named these types of worshippers: (1) ecstatic sects or cults; (2) semidemonstrative groups; (3) deliberative churches; and (4) liturgical denominations.

In our classification of churches according to ritual and cere-monial, we have used the following criteria: emotional demonstra-tiveness; thought content of sermons; prayers; hymns; and the use of liturgy. We have kept in mind, however, that emotional demonstra-tiveness is not always crowd behavior in the extreme sense. When it is prescribed, expected action, it is a part of a type of ritual. In applying it as a criterion, we rated the actions of the worshippers in terms of the characteristics of the act. These characteristics of emotional demonstrativeness are frequency, intensity and speed, length or duration, and the number of persons participating. Thought content of ritual elements was studied or analyzed as to other-worldliness as opposed to emphasis upon current problems; conflict with established denominations as contrasted with a positive state-ment and application of doctrine; and reference to rural background and homely illustrations, rather than to facts of history and of general literature. The liturgy test was used to determine the opportunity for spontaneous action or the lack of such opportunity, because of the obligation of following a prescribed order of service adopted by the denomination. It soon became evident that there would be marginal cases that would have to be decided on the predominance of some particular type of behavior that would cause them to be placed in certain categories. In these cases, the opportunity for the exercise of emotional demonstrativeness, the use of this opportunity, and the frequency, intensity, duration, and universality of the demonstrations, were the deciding factors.

The Interpretation of Observation Documents

After classifying the churches as liturgical, deliberative, semidemon-strative, and ecstatic on the bases mentioned above, the observation documents were analyzed into ceremonial, emotional, and ideational elements, and a synthesis was made of those that were characteristic of each church type. The items listed in the analysis include equipment in relation to atmosphere for worship; the order of service, including the use of liturgy; sacerdotalism; types and themes of music and prayer; the message of the minister; formal invitations to join the church; the offering; and the presence and degree of emotional demonstrativeness. . . .

The synthesis of common elements in the ceremonials of liturgical churches is given in Table 23-1.

TABLE 23-1.
Ritual Elements of Five Liturgical Services

CLASSIFICATION	ELEMENTS
Equipment	Altars, candelabra with lighted candles, vestments, organs, hymn boards, prayer books, special hymnals; in some cases, shrines and stations of the cross; stained glass windows and statues add to the effect of the setting upon the worship; comfortable pulpit seats and pews.
Liturgy and Sacerdotalism	A rigidly prescribed ritual; activity of the priest predominates.
Hymn Themes	Adoration; better life; comfort; resurrection; absolution; communion.
Prayer Themes	Confession, absolution, consecration, oblation, implication, humble access, Thanksgiving; a prayer for the whole state of Christ's Church (*Kyrie Eleison*); prayer of Simeon (*Nune Dimittis*).
Sermon Topics	"The Church and Fiery Trials"; "The Great Supper"; "The Holy Catholic Church"; "The Prayer of Consecration"; "Easter Day"; etc.

... The greatest departure from the liturgical and deliberative church services is noted in Table 23-2 which classifies elements of worship of the ecstatic sects.

TABLE 23-2.
Elements of Worship in Nine Ecstatic Cults

CLASSIFICATION	ELEMENTS
Equipment	Varies from stained glass windows of edifices to painted or curtained show windows of stores; most of these have mottoes on the walls; some have vestments for choirs and ushers' blue armbands with gilt lettering; usually there is a vase of flowers and a piano together with other instruments of percussion, such as drums, tamborines, triangles, and sometimes a wind instrument, usually a trumpet; comfortable pulpit seats with pews varying from the standardized type to both straight-back and folding chairs; collection plates or baskets.
Liturgy and Sacerdotalism (or their opposites)	A high degree of informality; even when a special ritual is followed, it is highly theatrical and it is recognized by rapid and rhythmic movement; at times, in some of the cults, the ecstasy becomes so great that pandemonium reigns.

TABLE 23-2. (con'd.)

CLASSIFICATION	ELEMENTS
Hymn Themes	Comfort; ecstasy and holiness; Heaven; salvation; adoration; loyalty; steadfastness.
Prayer Ritual and Themes	Two sects use the Lord's Prayer only. In one of these, all stand with raised hands and little fingers interlocked, repeating the Prayer in unison. In a third cult, the entire congregation, standing with hands raised, pray rapidly, loudly, and differently. Some of the prayers are conventional in type, and include the following: Invocation; Divine Aid; Adoration; Confession; Absolution; Consecration.
Sermon Patterns and Topics	Some conventional sermons and themes, but usually the sermons are simply pastoral expositions of scripture passages read by members of the congregation, a verse at a time. The principal emphases are sexual sins and their consequences; healing by fasting and prayer; God helps the poor.
Emotional Lay Participation	Varies from verbal assents to a state of ecstasy in which each member "receives the Holy Ghost." The saint-making ritual is sometimes used for making believers "saints." In most cases, the frenzy includes yelling, tapping, stamping, shouting, and, in some instances, running and jumping, including the type which resembles the movements of a jumping jack. Loud praying while standing with hands uplifted, and speaking in tongues while in a similar position constitute the climax of the ecstatic behavior, although this was not so prevalent as were the rhythmic hand-clapping and foot-patting.
Special Aspects of Cult Rituals	The hand-raising ceremony, in which the right hand is raised, sometimes both hands, as devotees pray loudly; speaking in tongues, in which the believers repeat rapidly and loudly unintelligible symbols; footwashing, which is the final ceremony in admitting members received into the cult; healing ritual, in which the sick are anointed with oil and surrounded by a praying, singing, and dancing group; saint-making ritual, in which believers are supposed to receive the Holy Ghost, after white-robed saints kneel with them and pray loudly, accompanied by rapidly repeated rhythmical assent, while the pianist plays a revival hymn; baptizing of sacred objects—at the end of a regular baptismal service, members bring sacred objects which are also baptized and blessed.
Testimony Stereotypes	Many believers of the church find stereotyped expression in lay testimony. Conceptions include those of praising the Lord because He is risen; of thanking Him for providing for every need; of the old-time religion as the religion of exhilaration; of faith-healing; and of the second advent, or of "soon" coming of Jesus.

Ritual, Belief, and Social Situation

... Since one of the important functions of these churches is to minister to various [social] classes within the racial group through differentiation in ritual, it was necessary for the investigator to study these classes of persons representing different types of social participation based upon economic life, family background, education, and other factors. In doing this, he found that the function of religious ritual in the life of the urban Negro varies according to the class with which the worshipper is identified. ...

Summary

... In this study, we have ... found through an analysis of the type of life lived outside the church, that the type of ritual engaged in reflects the life of the society of which the worshipper is a member. The social nature of the bizarre behavior of the ecstatic sects prevents that type of isolation that accentuates inferiority and takes the devotee into a world where temporarily he can live above the handicaps of everyday life. The congenial informality of the semidemonstrative church groups affords fellowship, personal recognition, and tension release, so consoling to the former ruralite in the urban situation. The members of the deliberative and of the liturgical churches seem already to have adjusted themselves to city life and their church services stress meeting squarely the issues of life rather than seeking escape through emotional release. ...

24

JAMES F. SHORT, JR., RAY A. TENNYSON,
AND KENNETH I. HOWARD

BEHAVIOR DIMENSIONS
OF GANG DELINQUENCY

Apparently the gang of today is not the gang of yesterday. The rich "natural histories" compiled by the "old Chicago school" . . . give accounts of gang behavior that differ in important respects from delinquency as it is hypothesized to exist today. For example, *specialization* of delinquency pattern has received considerable emphasis in current literature as compared with the past. Weapons and the intent of gang conflict are more lethal, and "kicks" more addicting. Theoretically, delinquency is seen as rooted less in community tradition and "fun," and more in frustration and protest or in the serious business of preparing for manhood, whether in the female-based households of an autonomous lower class or in the mysterious and powerful underworld of organized crime.

Resolution of theoretical differences, between the past and the present and among currently competing theories, requires greater precision, theoretically and empirically, in the delineation of the dependent variables. We shall group these under the term "gang delinquency," avoiding for the moment the knotty problem of specifying the nature of "subcultural delinquency" or the even greater problem of defining delinquent subcultures. We will limit our discussion largely to the measurement of individual *behavior*, rather than individual or group norms, values or self-concepts. . . .

Reprinted in part with permission from *American Sociological Review* 28 (June 1963): 411-428.

The Research Setting

Data were collected from 598 members of 16 "delinquent gangs" assigned detached workers by the Program for Detached Workers of the YMCA of Metropolitan Chicago. The gangs ranged in size from 16 to 68 members, on the basis of workers' judgments concerning who should and who should not be considered members. . . .

The unknown and ever-changing characteristics of the gang population, and the difficulty of gaining research *entrée* to a gang without some "service" legitimation, made conventional sampling techniques inappropriate for our purposes. Our gangs were deliberately chosen from the *delinquent* end of a delinquent-nondelinquent continuum, the primary effort being directed toward locating carriers of conflict, criminal, and retreatist subcultures.

The search for gangs concentrated on the "criminal" and "drug use" types, principally because conflict-oriented gangs, particularly among Negroes, were abundant. . . . *Finding* gangs whose primary activities and norms were oriented around drug use or rational, systematic, economically motivated criminal activity, proved to be a major problem. . . . It took more than a year of extensive inquiries among police and local community adults, coupled with field investigations by detached workers and our own research personnel, to locate a drug-oriented group. Although much criminal activity was found in nearly all groups, criminally oriented gangs such as those hypothesized by Cloward and Ohlin were equally difficult to locate. The failure to locate a criminal group, or more than one drug-using group, despite our highly motivated effort to do so, is a "finding" of some importance, for it casts doubt on the generality of these phenomena, if not on their existence. Our subsequent search for gangs to fit a research design based upon the typology of conflict, criminal, and retreatist gangs, and the analysis which follows must be viewed against this background. We were led to seek groups not primarily oriented around fighting, but with extensive involvement in the pursuit of "kicks" or various forms of theft. We hoped that systematic study of these groups would permit more precise identification of the nature of delinquent subcultures, either on the basis of between- or within-group behavioral differentiation.

The Data

. . . Consideration of alternative methods of generating data on the behavior of the gang boys under observation led to the rejection of most of the usual methods; instead, a system of ratings by the detached workers seemed the most feasible and reliable method of obtaining the needed data. . . .

The availability of detached workers as intimate observers of the boys, particularly in the gang setting, offered a rare opportunity to gain more complete and objective insights into the behavior of these boys than could be provided by any other method. Weekly interviews with the workers convinced us that they shared intimately in the on-going life of the gang. Such behavioral information as was not known by direct contact with a boy could usually be inferred from conversations among the boys or directly with the worker in the endless "bull sessions" on the street corner. The nature of these contacts seemed particularly conducive to objective reporting of the type of behavior we were interested in measuring, i.e., street corner behavior. This behavior could be described in concrete terms and it did not require abstract conceptualization by our informants.

What we needed was a "baseline" of information on the behavior of our population, information which could be statistically manipulated and related to other variables we were studying. Toward this end a list of 69 behavioral categories was drawn up. Because we were interested more in incidence of behaviors and their relative frequency, rather than absolute frequencies, and because workers' observations could not extend to actual counts of behavior, we asked only that each boy be rated in terms of whether he had *engaged* in a particular type of behavior only a few times or many times. Workers were asked to report only after they had been in contact with a group for at least six months, to restrict their reporting to boys whom they and the group recognized as group members, and to limit their reports to information in which they were confident. An item-by-item review of their reports was undertaken by the research staff to insure the most accurate reporting possible. Most gang members were rated by only one rater, though two gangs had more than one worker over the rating period, and members of these were rated by each worker having at least six months contact. A high degree of consensus was noted in these ratings. Comparison of worker reports with police records reveals no marked tendency for workers to "under report" or "over report." Length of contact with the gang, beyond the six-month minimum requirement, is unrelated to behavior ratings so far as "reliability" is concerned. Our assumption is that obtained differences between gangs were due to differences in behavior rather than differences in later characteristics.

There are great differences in the incidence of these [69] behaviors among our gang boys, and apparantly some of these are related to racial composition of the population. In this form, however, the data are not interpretable as behavior patterns. We turn next, therefore, to the reduction of these data.

The Dimensionality of Delinquent Behavior

Empirically, our problem was to determine the nature of behavioral patterns characterizing the boys and gangs studied. . . . Unfortunately, the theories are not very helpful in this matter, for they lack specificity in describing the patterns of behavior they purport to explain. Hence the problem: the theories regard delinquency as multidimensional, but they do not tell us precisely the nature of these dimensions. . . . We therefore chose a model which would tell us how the behavior of these boys "hangs together"—whether in demonstrable packages which could be interpreted in the light of subcultural theory, or in a more or less undifferentiated way. . . .

[A factor analysis was carried out and] five factors were extracted and rotated using Varimax. The first unrotated factor accounted for much more of the common variance than did any succeeding factor, again pointing to the existence of a general delinquency trait; but there was ample evidence from the factor analysis that somewhat specialized adaptations also existed among our subjects. . . .

Factor I is essentially a *conflict* factor, its highest loading items being individual fighting (.79), group fighting (.76), carrying concealed weapons (.67), and assault (.67). . . .

Factor II has highest loadings of individual sports (.71), team sports (.68), social activities (.60), and gambling (.48). Other loadings higher than .40 are obtained for joy riding, truancy, and hanging. The latter behaviors have similarly high loadings on other factors, however. This factor may be characterized as a configuration of *stable corner activities.* . . .

Factor III is difficult to characterize. It has as its highest loading items sexual intercourse (.77), statutory rape (.68), petting (.67), signifying (.53), hanging on the corner (.44), and the use, buying and selling of alcohol (.39). It also has the only moderately high loading of any factor for work experience (.36), accounting for nearly all of this item's common variance. We have chosen to call this a *stable sex* pattern and to regard the loading of work experience as a further indication of a type of relatively adaptive behavior which is represented by the factor.

Factor IV is characterized by high loadings for quite different sex behaviors, namely homosexuality (.53), fathering an illegitimate child (.50), and common law marriage (.48). Additionally, it has as its highest loading the use, buying, and selling of narcotics (.56) and of marijuana (.55). This factor accounts for virtually all of the low communalities of suicide and pimping, with loadings of .36 and .27, respectively. In contrast with Factor III, work experience has a loading of only .06, sex intercourse .17, statutory rape .18, petting .01, hanging .00, and signifying .00 on Factor IV. The combination of narcotics involvement, the "deviant" sex behaviors, and attempted suicide, leads us to identify this factor as *retreatist.*

Factor V includes the highest loadings of auto theft (.69), driving without a license (.65), public nuisance (.58), theft (.53), use, buying, and selling of alcohol (.48), and running away from home (.44). In addition, this factor includes moderately high loadings for joy riding (.41) and truancy (.39). The versatility of this combination of offenses within a variety of institutional contexts . . . leads us to characterize this factor as an *auto-theft authority-protest* pattern. . . .

We note that no clearly "criminal subculture" factor was extracted by our procedures. The variance of criminal behaviors is spread over all of the factors to a greater extent than either conflict or retreatist behaviors. . . . Thus, the criminal behaviors studied are associated with different configurations of offenses rather than as a factor themselves. No rationally directed effort to acquire money emerges in isolation from other factors. Instead, criminal activity is associated with conflict, retreatism, and general rebellious activity, and to some extent also with stable corner boy activity. Only the stable sex factor fails to share at least 10 percent of the variance of at least one of these "criminal" behaviors. . . .

Behavior Factor Profiles of 16 Gangs

We turn now to an examination of the mean factor scores of our 16 gangs. . . . In this section we limit ourselves to the relation of race to group mean factor scores. Following Cloward and Ohlin, we expected that Negro gangs would have higher conflict factor scores than would white gangs. That is, both legitimate and illegitimate economic opportunities seem objectively more limited for Negroes than for whites—hence, the expectation of greater conflict orientation among Negro than among white gangs. . . .

Several findings emerge:

1. The most conflict-oriented gangs are Negro. All six gangs with mean scores above the total population mean are Negro. The *mean rank* of Negro gangs on Factor I is 7.7 (out of 16) as compared with 10.2 for white gangs. (There is much variation in conflict orientation among Negro gangs, however. Three of the four least conflict-oriented gangs also are Negro.) . . .

2. Negro gangs are, on the average, higher on Factors II and III, with mean ranks of 7.5 and 7.8, respectively, compared with mean ranks of 10.8 and 10.0 for white gangs.

3. Only on Factor V do white gangs clearly rank higher than Negro gangs. Four of the five white gangs have positive group means for this factor, and three of the four highest ranking groups are white. Mean rank for white gangs is 5.6, compared to 9.8 for Negro gangs.

. . . We believe that the data are useful in introducing greater precision in the measurement of the behavior of individuals and groups studied and that further analyses of data from the several phases of our research program will permit more complete documentation and modification of hypotheses concerning the subcultural nature of gang delinquency.

Conclusion

The full implications of our findings for subcultural theories of juvenile delinquency cannot be assessed until the data are viewed in combination with observational data from detached workers and our own staff, and in terms of analyses of their relation to etiological variables specified by the theories. The former add the richness and detail of situational and group-process determinants which the ratings employed in the factor analysis miss entirely. At the same time, without the more systematic and "objective" ratings, one can never be certain as to the representativeness of his observations or his own objectivity in recall and choice of behavior reported. Our tentative conclusion is that delinquent subcultures exist, but that they are not as "pure" as they have been pictured, and they become articulated in ways much more complex than existing theories specify. . . .

PART VI

Sampling

INTRODUCTION

Major limitations of observation, apart from providing limited access to what people think and feel [see Introduction, pp. 5-9], include the difficulties of sampling the groups or behaviors to be observed. In practice, many a sociological observer restricts his attention to a single, fairly small group, perhaps has even chosen it primarily to suit his convenience, and studies it over a comparatively brief period of time. Yet such a restricted sampling procedure is patently not inherent in observation; it may be offset or overcome through various modifications and extensions of the method.

At least three possible variations and extensions are abundantly clear from the foregoing studies. First, the observer often studies *more than just a single group* or behavioral event—as Whyte [Part I] tests his emerging model on several corner gangs or Bales [Part I] uses a succession of task groups in the search for "uniformities of interaction" (see also the discussion of "comparison groups" by Glaser and Strauss, 1965, pp. 5-12). Second, the observer often finds means of *transcending the usual restrictions on size* of the group or society studied: he may use microphones (as in the study by Drabek and Haas [Part II]) or multiple observers (as in Lang and Lang's study of a parade [Part III]); he may combine observation with other sources of data in order to investigate large bureaucracies or entire communities (cf. Dalton [Part III] or Gans [Part I]); or he may develop or test macrocosmic theories through direct observation of selected segments of societies (as, e.g., in the examination of the dynamics of Mexican politics by Anderson and Cockroft, 1966; Cockroft, 1972).

Third, the observer typically selects his cases according to an important principle that will appear haphazard only to the purist in representational sampling: the principle of *sampling as a means of facilitating the analysis* (cf. M. W. Riley, 1963, pp. 282-283, 295-304). He may choose a sample of one, partly

257

in search of the insightful experience; but partly also as the negative case that would be sufficient to disprove a universal hypothesis,[1] as Whyte [Part I] studies the proverbially "disorganized area" to establish the point that organization actually exists there. Or the observer may use a sample of cases to control a key analytical variable that cannot be experimentally manipulated, as Strodtbeck [Part IV] samples to reflect categories in the "cultural phrasing of power." Or as an experimenter, the observer uses experimental and control samples to manipulate the independent variable [Part IV].

The studies in Part VI point to two other means of enhancing the utility of sampling in observational studies: (1) cross-sectional sampling; and (2) samples that extend the temporal scope. In regard to the first, Stouffer (1954, p. v) dramatizes *cross-sectional sampling* as one aspect of the "technological revolution" in survey research, extolling the "class of inventions [that involve] the applications of mathematical principles to the selection of a sample which can reproduce the responses of a population, with a small calculable error." Why not apply these principles to what people do as well as to what they say? As if in answer to this question, Reiss (1968, pp. 351-367) maintains that the distinctions typically drawn between observation and survey research are due more to "trained incapacity" than to inherent differences. The study by *Stanton, Back, and Litwak*, demonstrating the feasibility of role playing by specially trained interviewers, specifies one device for combining some of the advantages of observation and of cross-section surveys. In a related example, *Black* combines representational sampling with observation of the situational conditions under which policemen write official crime reports—thus explicitly treating the source of the traditionally accepted "statistics" as a problematic phenomenological feature of everyday life (for further reports of this research see Black and Reiss, 1970; Reiss, 1971). Here the sample (consisting of some 5700 police-citizen encounters) was systematically selected by days of the week, hours of the day, and officers' beats, a procedure that draws attention to the importance of sampling time and events as well as populations. (See commentaries by M. W. Riley, 1964, pp. 990-991; Reiss, 1968, pp. 357-358; Webb et al., 1966, pp. 133-137.)

The classic work in experimental genetics by Fisher and in statistics by Yule and Kendall had made clear as early as 1950 that, as Rosenthal puts it (1966, p. 2), "man may simply be unable to select random sets of events to be observed without such external aids as tables of random numbers."[2] Even when the researcher strives for representativeness, inevitable selective biases operate in samples based on judgment. The danger of inadvertent distortions in findings is stressed by Merton's (1947) demonstration that self-selected informants, e.g., as widely used in participant observation, are atypical both in their positions in the

258

community structure and in their readiness to supply qualitative detail. Hence the incipient applications to observation of representational sampling (ideally based on probability principles), as in the studies by Stanton, Back, and Litwak, and by Black, hold great promise. They set the stage for powerful generalization from the concrete cases under study to some larger universe of theoretical concern.[3]

However representative the sample for a particular era, much observation suffers limitations of *temporal scope*—the second aspect of sampling that demands attention. Studies that draw their data from that limited time frame, the present, cannot fully exploit the dynamic potential of observation [Part I]; they do not trace social processes over extended time periods or record long-term change (See Riley and Nelson, 1971). Possible clues to surmounting this difficulty are implicit in the two remaining studies in this part. *Le Play*, whose early work reminds us that the clear definition of a sampling unit (the family) is by no means a twentieth-century invention, extended his studies over many decades by devoting a lifetime to them and by stimulating a school of followers to carry on after his death (Sorokin, 1928, pp. 68-69; Pitts, 1968, pp. 87-88; Lazarsfeld, 1961; Goldfrank, 1972). *Freeman and Winch*, in their attempt to measure societal complexity, also avoid some of the restrictions of time. Their method is not to make direct observations of their own, but to rely instead upon secondary analysis of reports by other ethnographers.[4] Both studies, though not directly concerned with representativeness, suggest how sampling can be used for cross-temporal comparison and for wider testing of general propositions. Without successive cohorts of individuals dedicating their lives to direct observation, however, such accomplishment depends upon recourse to secondary analysis of available data.

Some Methodological Implications

In summary, two possibilities for improving observational research seem clearly indicated. As a first avenue of improvement, observation can achieve greater scientific rigor, without sacrificing its unique ability to discern the nature and meaning of social behavior, through adaptation and application of representative sampling. Cross-section sampling—not only of single societies, but also of many societies—can reach to macroscopic levels. It can, moreover, reduce that portion of bias resulting from the observer's unwitting selection of cases according to his own cultural and personal predilections and those of the people observed. To be sure, such adapatations will undoubtedly require development of new techniques and new applications of probability principles, parallel to (though perhaps more complex than) those already in use for survey design. These adaptations will, of course, also require new methods of training and organizing field staffs of competent observers (cf. Reiss, 1968).

If rigorous sampling can be assumed for the future, how—as a second avenue of improvement—can the temporal scope of observation also be extended? The need for such extension is underscored by Thernstrom's demonstration (1965) of the "perils of historical naiveté" in Lloyd Warner's study of Newburyport. Apart from the clues implicit in the studies by Le Play and by Freeman and Winch, what other means might be developed? Since the observer cannot himself revisit the past, this question raises once again [as in the Introduction, pp. 6, 8] the issue of where to set the boundary line around the method of direct observation. Videotapes are often used at the scene of action. Do these tapes then constitute "observations" for another analyst? If so, how do they differ from letters which *are* the interaction among distant members of a group? And, when the researcher has recourse to letters, consider the new resources available to him! He can reach into the past, as Thomas and Znaniecki (1918) did with the correspondence of Polish peasants in examining the impact of industrial change on family life. What of other possible grist for the mill of "observation"—legislation, contract agreements, and other documentary reports of interaction, as used, e.g., by Smelser (1968, pp. 76-91) in historical studies of British working-class families, or by Davies (1962) in historical analysis of revolutions? In the future, we expect not only that each means of assembling data will increasingly be supplemented by the others, but also that the line between observation and the "traces" surviving from past behavior (Webb et al., 1966) will become blurred.[5]

In such ways, the method of observation may be on the threshold of a revolution in sampling. Such a revolution could overcome many traditional restrictions on representativeness, on size and number of groups, and on the temporal compass of social process and change, without losing the potentiality of observation for arriving at penetrating insights.

NOTES

1. Frequently cited in respect to observation is Florian Znaniecki's method of "analytic induction," as discussed, e.g., by Robinson (1951); Turner (1953).

2. Systematic sampling, not immune from the usual sampling biases from refusals and incomplete coverage, also allows for more ready analysis of the "control effects" incurred by observation [Part III]. Reiss (1968: 358-366)

reports, e.g., that race of observer in police encounters makes a difference for some kinds of observations but not for others.

3. There are instances, of course, in which no sampling frame can be constructed to correspond to the conceptual universe.

4. Such reports can also be used, of course, for cross-cultural as well as cross-temporal comparison; see, e.g., Murdock (1949); Zelditch (1955). Among the numerous discussions of the comparative method, see, e.g., Porter (1967); Leach (1968).

5. Similarly, the use of documents and other products of interaction can extend the *geographic* scope of observation, when multiple observers cannot feasibly work simultaneously in many parts of the world. Thus the researcher can "observe" the relations among nations, as Inoguchi (1972) uses exchanges of formal letters to investigate friendship and hostility among heads of state; or the records of space scientists can be "observed" by sociologists in analyzing demographic and ecological phenomena around the globe.

25
HOWARD STANTON, KURT W. BACK, AND EUGENE LITWAK

ROLE PLAYING IN
SURVEY RESEARCH

Sociologists at times feel troubled by the extent to which their discipline, which presumes to study groups, depends on verbal or written reports of individuals seen separately. Yet systematic observation of group life, whether in a natural or laboratory setting, may be for many problems either inappropriate or unduly expensive. A possible alternative in the dilemma may be role playing in the interview, a technique which can provide samples of group behavior in relevant sequences of situations without sacrificing the advantages of survey technique.

For instance, instead of asking, "Do you get angry when a salesperson puts pressure on you?" the interviewer plays the salesperson who puts pressure on the respondent. Instead of asking, "What do you think of doctors?" the interviewer proposes that the respondent play the role of doctor while he himself acts as a variety of patients. Instead of asking, "How strongly do you feel about racial equality?" the interviewer sets up a scene and stages an appropriate impromptu drama from which he may infer the respondent's attitudes.

Role playing, because of its history as a clinical and therapeutic technique, might be considered too esoteric to be made a standardized procedure in large surveys. Several questions would have to be answered: What about refusal rates? Do the interviewers need elaborate training? How analyze and code the complex role playing responses? How reliable are the data? Do the respondents actually

Reprinted in part with permission from *American Journal of Sociology* 62 (September 1956): 172-176.

behave as they would in real life? This paper presents some answers based on the successful use of role playing during the last three years in three surveys conducted by the authors with widely different populations.

a) In 21 households (54 interviews) of foster-parents in Chicago, parent-child relations were studied. Rapport had been established through the child-placing agency, but the role playing was proposed unannounced. Three scenes were used to measure the respondent's autonomy under personal stress, two to measure the respondent's empathy, and three to measure the couple's creativity as a team.

b) In 83 households (116 interviews) of upper-middle-class United States families a study was made of marital adjustment. Rapport established in interviews 20 years ago made it easy to get consent for reinterviewing, but the role-playing scenes were set up unannounced as part of a regular interview. Two scenes were used to measure the creativity of couples together.

c) In 244 households (412 interviews) with residents of slums and housing projects in Puerto Rico, a study was conducted of social-psychological factors in housing. The interview included role playing, given in true survey fashion; the interviewer had to secure his own entry. Three scenes were used to measure respondent's flexibility, two to determine the limits of the respondent's positive and negative feelings about public housing, and one to reveal the respondent's perception of the housing administration's role.

In the first use of role playing, survey fashion, during the spring of 1953 we exaggerated the differences between it and the conventional procedures. The couple was interviewed by appointment at home by three interviewers using two tape recorders. By the spring of 1956 we had become somewhat more assured and used an ordinary interviewing staff armed with nothing more than a few copies of the schedule.

Many people have difficulty visualizing how the interviewer gets the respondent in and out of scenes. The following is a translated excerpt from a tape-recorded interview staged during the housing study in Puerto Rico:

INT.: . . . We're going to do something like a little game. You're going to be one person, and I'm going to be another. For example, we'll be neighbors. I live there in the house next door. I am *comadre* of yours, and right now, well, I've got company and I don't have. . . .

RES.: Listen, this is like the radio stories, right?

I.: . . . Yes. You may even come out of this a movie star. Well, . . . I have some visitors at my house, some relatives, and I find that I don't have enough rice to make an *asopao de pollo.* . . . I've come to see if I can borrow a little from you, right? We're going to do it just as if it were happening, right? . . . [*The interviewer gets up, walks out the front door, turns, knocks, and says:*] Hola, *comay* Juana, how are things going? How are you?

R.: Well, all right, as God wills.

I.: Well, *chica,* you don't know that my family has come from Ponce, and I find that I don't have enough rice for an *asopao.* . . . You don't have a little that you could lend me?

R.: Ay, Petrita, but I don't think I've got any either.

[*The subject finds she has no rice, but she has a few pennies which she lends to her friend. The scene ends with the interviewer saying:*]

I.: Well, if I have a little plate of *asopao* left over, I'll send it over to you.

R.: Good, very good, because I don't cook that way.

I.: Well, I'm going because I left the people alone in the house.

R.: I'll expect the little plate!

I.: Um-huh.

R.: Goodbye.

I.: You see? *Ave Maria!* you are really an artist! It's a wonder that you're not acting on the radio or tel. . . .

R.: You think so? *Ave Maria!* don't make fun of me, *señorita.*

I.: What a thing to say! You can see that you did it wonderfully! Well, now we're going to do something else. We're going to pretend that I'm your grandfather. . . .

Those unfamiliar with role playing, or familiar with it in other settings, might expect a high rate of refusals to act the scenes suggested. In fact, however, out of 2939 scenes in the three studies, only 12 were not carried out. In each case refusal appeared caused by the content of the scene rather than by the idea of role playing itself; in most cases it meant "I don't know what to do" more than "I won't do it." Different scenes—like different questions—produce different rates of refusals, but generally the drama stimulates the interest of the subjects.

The ease in training interviewers depended upon the type of role to be played. Some scenes required no active participation of the interviewer, while others required him constantly to stimulate his respondents. The latter, of course, required more training, but in either case the interviewers were trained in a relatively short time during the regular training session. In none of the studies has training time exceeded six hours, although more training might have been desirable.

No general instructions were given on constructing appropriate scenes. Basically, good scene construction is no different from good question construction; both call for a well-defined problem, an ingenious solution, and thorough pretesting.

There are several areas in which the use of role playing is especially pertinent. Sometimes it is necessary to know how people act under emotional stress, as in studies of marriage and family life. If it is difficult for an individual to recall and discuss these topics calmly with an interviewer, it may be more profitable and valid actually to *see* his behavior. Role playing permits observation, at the same time preserving rapport, since both interviewer and interviewee can dissociate themselves from the role as soon as it is finished.

The study of parent-child relations posed just this problem. To select a good foster-home, the child-placing agency needed to know how the parents would react to the inevitable, almost daily, stresses. Would they become unduly tense, rejecting, punitive, submissive, or neglectful, or would they on the whole play the "good" parent? Verbal assertion in the course of a friendly interview is a doubtful index. The solution was the staging of scenes in which the respondent was put under stress by the interviewer. In one scene, for example, the interviewer played a parent; the respondent, a married son (or daughter). The interviewer began by treating the respondent in a patronizing way, as if he still considered him a child; later he began to criticize the son's (or daughter's) spouse severely; finally, he twisted the scene around so that the respondent was made to appear unfair and unkind to his parent.

To know how the respondent will act, it is not enough to know his intention. . . . It is necessary to know also the intensity and saliency of the responses. Moreover, it is necessary to know how other people involved with the respondent are going to act. Thus, the respondent's vote will be more accurately predicted if one knows how his family is going to vote. Another problem is the limits of attitudes; for instance, whether a person who is generally in favor of an issue has any negative feelings.

In the Puerto Rican study we were interviewing families who lived in public housing or in slums designated for redevelopment. To discover the limits of their positive and negative feelings about housing projects, we used two projective scenes. In one the respondent was to play the part of a social worker trying to convince a slum dweller (the interviewer) to move. In the second he was asked to play the role of a tenant being asked by a member of a tenant committee (the interviewer) for complaints to be taken up in a coming meeting. In both scenes the respondent was stimulated until no further new points were brought out. The saliency, intensity, and personal context of the positive and negative responses were made evident in the course of the drama. In addition, the sheer volume of feelings tapped in this way made their interrelations more evident.

It if often important in a study to know how the respondent perceives significant others. Thus, the interviewer may seek to find out how an employer views union leaders, how a voter perceives certain political leaders, what students think of their teachers, and how members of a community perceive criminals. But it may be difficult for the respondent to express himself verbally. In addition, feelings of hostility or propriety may lead to one-sided answers. Yet the respondent may be able to act out the other's role in a consistent, elaborate, and revealing manner.

In the housing study, to discover how respondents conceived of the housing project administration, the interviewer played a tenant, while the respondent played an administrator who had dropped in to "see how things were going." Given such neutral instructions and a relatively neutral role-playing partner, the respondent betrayed not only his picture of the administration but also his attitude toward it. . . .

One alleged objection to the use of role playing as a survey procedure is that it is difficult to analyze. In the three studies four different types of role playing were used, involving sixteen scenes. For some types the interviewer scored the answer during the drama or during the interview just as she would any regular question. A checklist can be used or response noted according to a predetermined code or graphing done on a more or less complex diagram without, apparently, affecting the involvement of the respondent in the scene. In just one kind of scene was it necessary for the interviewer to score the scene after the interview, but this took no more than two minutes. We have also used interviewer-observer teams, but this is seldom necessary.

The reliability of role-playing responses varies in the same way as the reliability of any other technique. In the parent-child study [for example] interrater reliability was checked by scoring from eleven tape-recorded stress scenes. Rank correlations between the four raters ranged from .81 to .97, averaging .90. . . .

Perhaps the most important question about any survey technique is: Are the results valid? Do these fragmentary samples of prompted interaction accurately reveal whatever it is the researcher wants to learn about the respondents? Of course, role playing is not uniformly valid or invalid, any more than is any other technique, but our studies indicate that the results may reach high levels of validity.

[For example] validity was tested . . . by association with another measure of the same variable. For 35 subjects in the course of the parent-child study we secured descriptions of their usual behavior from observers who knew them well. These outside reports were made on the same scoring sheet as was used to score role-playing responses. The simple sum of scores (representing "ability to maintain ideal behavior under stress") from these outside observers was compared with the same sum taken from behavior rated during role playing. The rank correlation between the two sets of scores was .82. . . .

These studies demonstrate that role playing can be used as a tool of survey research, as a portable method for observing social behavior. Like traditional questions, its utility is based on the ingenuity of the investigator who must devise scenes tailored to the purposes of the study. However, since it gets data in a way slightly different, it provides the investigator some powerful insights. . . .

PRODUCTION OF
CRIME RATES

Sociological approaches to official crime rates generally fail to make problematic the production of the rates themselves. Theory has not directed inquiry to the principles and mechanisms by which some technically illegal acts are recorded in the official ledger of crime while others are not. Instead crime rates ordinarily are put to use as data in the service of broader investigations of deviance and control. Yet at the same time it has long been taken for granted that official statistics are not an accurate measure of all legally defined crime in the community.

The major uses of official crime statistics have taken two forms; each involves a different social epistemology, a different way of structuring knowledge about crime. One employs official statistics as an index of the "actual" or "real" volume and morphology of criminal deviance in the population. Those who follow this approach typically consider the lack of fit between official and actual rates of crime to be a methodological misfortune. Historically, measurement of crime has been the dominant function of crime rates in social science. A second major use of official statistics abandons the search for "actual" deviance. This is managed either by defining deviance with the official reactions themselves—a labeling approach—or by incorporating the official rates not as an index of deviant behavior but as an index of social control operations. In effect this second range of work investigates "actual" social control rather than "actual" deviance. Hence it encounters methodological problems of

Reprinted in part with permission from *American Sociological Review* 35 (August 1970): 773-748.

its own, since, without question, social control agencies do not record all of their official attempts to counteract or contain what they and others regard as deviant conduct. A striking feature of police work, for instance, is the degree to which officers operate with informal tactics, such as harrassment and manipulative human-relations techniques, when they confront law-violative behavior. In sum, when official statistics are used an a *means* of measurement and analysis, they usually function imperfectly. This is not to deny that such methods can be highly rewarding in some contexts.

This paper follows an alternative strategy that arises from an alternative conceptual starting point. It makes official records of crime an end rather than a means of study. It treats the crime rate as itself a social fact, an empirical phenomenon with its own existential integrity. A crime rate is not an epiphenomenon. It is part of the natural world. From this standpoint crime statistics are not evaluated as inaccurate or unreliable. They are an aspect of social organization and cannot, sociologically, be wrong. From the present perspective it nevertheless remains interesting that social control systems process more than they report in official statistics and that there is a good deal more rule-violative behavior than that which is processed. These patterns are themselves analytically relevant aspects of crime rates. . . .

Crime rates . . . are rates of deviance socially recognized by official agencies of criminal-law enforcement. They are official rates of *detection* ("crimes known to the police") and of *sanctioning* (arrest rates and conviction rates). Enforcement agencies handle many technically illegal acts that they omit from their official records. This paper explores some of the conditions under which the police produce official rates of crime detection in field encounters with citizens.

Social Organization of Crime Detection

Detection of deviance involves: (1) the discovery of deviant *acts* or behavior and (2) the linking of *persons* or groups to those acts. Types of deviance vary widely according to the extent to which either or both of these aspects of detection are probable. . . . These differential detection probabilities stem in part from the empirical patterns by which various forms of violative behavior occur in time and social space. In part they stem as well from the uneven climate of social control.

The organization of police control lodges the primary responsibility for crime detection in the citizenry rather than in the police. The uniformed patrol division, the major line unit of modern police departments, is geared to respond to citizen calls for help via a centralized radio-communications system. Apart from traffic violations, patrol officers detect comparatively little crime through their own initiative. This is all the more true of legally serious crime. . . .

Nevertheless, rates of known crimes do not perfectly reflect the volume of citizen complaints. A complaint must be given official status in a formal written report before it can enter police statistics, and the report by no means automatically follows receipt of the complaint by the police. In the present investigation patrol officers wrote official reports in only 64 percent of the 554 crime situations where a complainant, but no suspect, was present in the field setting. The decision to give official status to a crime ordinarily is an outcome of face-to-face interaction between the police and the complainant rather than a programmed police response to a bureaucratic or legal formula. The content and contours of this interaction differentially condition the probability that an official report will be written, much as they condition, in situations where a suspect is present, the probability that an arrest will be made.

Whether or not an official report is written affects not only the profile of official crime rates; it also determines whether subsequent police investigation of the crime will be undertaken at a later date. Subsequent investigation can occur only when an official report is forwarded to the detective division for further processing, which includes the possibility of an arrest of the suspect. Hence the rate of detection and sanctioning of deviant *persons* is in part contingent upon whether the detection of deviant *acts* is made official. In this respect justice demands formality in the processing of crimes. This paper considers the following conditions as they relate to the probability of an official crime report in police-complainant encounters: the legal seriousness of the alleged crime, the preference of the complainant, the relational distance between the complainant and the absentee suspect, the degree of deference the complainant extends to the police, and the race and social-class status of the complainant.

Field Method

Systematic observation of police-citizen transactions was conducted in Boston, Chicago, and Washington, D.C., during the summer of 1966. Thirty-six observers—persons with law, social science, and police administration backgrounds—recorded observations of routine encounters between uniformed patrolmen and citizens. Observers accompanied patrolmen on all work-shifts on all days of the week for seven weeks in each city. However, the times when police activity is comparatively high (evening shifts, particularly weekend evenings) were given added weight in the sample.

Police precincts were chosen as observation sites in each city. The precincts were selected so as to maximize observation in lower socio-economic, high crime rate, racially homogeneous residential areas. This was accomplished through the selection of two precincts in Boston and Chicago and four precincts in Washington, D.C.

The data were recorded in "incident booklets," forms structurally similar to interview schedules. One booklet was used for each incident that the police were requested to handle or that they themselves noticed while on patrol. These booklets were not filled out in the presence of policemen. In fact, the officers were told that our research was not concerned with police behavior but only with citizen behavior toward the police and the kinds of problems citizens make for the police. Thus the study partially utilized systematic deception.

A total of 5713 incidents were observed and recorded. In what follows, however, the statistical base is only 554 cases, roughly one-in-ten of the total sample. These cases comprise nearly all of the police encounters with complainants in crime situations where no suspect was present in the field situation. They are drawn from the cases that originated with a citizen telephone call to the police, 76 percent of the total, [and constitute] the *majority of crime situations* that the police handle in response to citizen telephone calls for service. There is no suspect available in 77 percent of the felonies and in 51 percent of the misdemeanors that the police handle on account of a complaint by telephone. There is only a complainant. These proportions alone justify a study of police encounters with complainants. In routine police work the handling of crime is in large part the handling of complainants. Policemen see more victims than criminals.

Legal Seriousness of the Crime

Police encounters with complainants where no suspect is present involve a disproportionately large number of felonies, the legally serious category of crime. This was true of 53 percent of the cases in the sample of 554. . . . In other words, the police arrive at the scene too late to apprehend a suspect more often in serious crime situations than in those of a relatively minor nature. . . .

When the offender has left the scene in either felony or misdemeanor situations, however, detection and sanctioning of the offender is precluded unless an official report is written by the police. Not surprisingly, the police are more likely to write these reports in felony than in misdemeanor situations. Reports were written in 72 percent of the 312 felonies, but in only 53 percent of the 242 misdemeanors. It is clear that official recognition of crimes becomes more likely as the legally defined seriousness of the crime increases. Even so, it remains noteworthy that the police officially disregard one-fourth of the felonies they handle in encounters with complainants. These are not referred to the detective division for investigation; offenders in these cases thus unknowingly receive a pardon of sorts. . . .

The Complainant's Preference

Upon arriving at a field setting, the police typically have very little information about what they are going to find. At best they have the crude label assigned to the incident by a dispatcher at the communications center. Over the police radio they hear such descriptions as "a B and E" (breaking and/or entering), "family trouble," "somebody screaming," "a theft report," "a man down" (person lying in a public place, cause unknown), "outside ringer" (burglar-alarm ringing), "the boys" (trouble with juveniles), and suchlike. Not infrequently these labels prove to be inaccurate. In any case policemen find themselves highly dependent upon citizens to assist them in structuring situational reality. Complainants, biased though they may be, serve the police as primary agents of situational intelligence.

What is more, complainants not infrequently go beyond the role of providing information by seeking to influence the direction of police action. When a suspect is present the complainant may pressure the police to make an arrest or to be lenient. When there is no available suspect, it becomes a matter of whether the complainant prefers that the crime be handled as an official matter or whether he wants it handled informally. Of course many complainants are quite passive and remain behaviorally neutral. During the observation period the complainant's preference was unclear in 40 percent of the encounters involving a "cold" felony or misdemeanor. There were 184 felony situations in which the complainant expressed a clear preference; 78 percent lobbied for official action. Of the 145 misdemeanor situations where the complainant expressed a clear preference, the proportion favoring official action was 75 percent, roughly the same proportion as that in felony situations. It seems that complainants are, behaviorally, insensitive to the legal serious-ness of crimes when they seek to direct police action.

Police action displays a striking pattern of conformity with the preferences of complainants. Indeed, in not one case did the police write an official crime report when the complainant manifested a preference for informal action. This pattern seen in legal perspective is particularly interesting given that felony complainants prefer informal action nearly as frequently as misdemeanor complainants. Police conformity with those complainants who do prefer official action, however, is not so symmetrical. In felony situations the police comply by writing an official report in 84 percent of the cases, whereas when the complaint involves a misdemeanor their rate of compliance drops to 64 percent. Thus the police follow the wishes of officially oriented complainants in the majority of encounters, but the majority is somewhat heavier when the occasion is a legally more serious matter. In the field setting proper the citizen complainant has much to say about the official recognition of crimes, though the law seemingly screens his influence. . . .

Relational Distance

Like any other kind of behavior, criminal behavior is located within networks of social organization. One aspect of that social organiza-tion consists in the relationship existing between the criminal offender and the complainant prior to a criminal event. . . . Citizen adversaries may be classified according to three levels of relational distance: (1) fellow family members; (2) friends, neighbors, or acquaintances; and (3) strangers. The vast majority of the cases fall into the "stranger" category. . . .

Table 26-1 shows that when a complainant expresses a preference for official action the police comply most readily when the adversaries are strangers to one another. They are less likely to comply by writing an official crime report when the adversaries are friends, neighbors, or acquaintances, and they are least likely to give official recognition to the crime when the complainant and suspect are members of the same family. . . .

Overview

The foregoing analysis [including further analyses by the complainant's deference to police and the complainant's race and occupation] yields a number of empirical generalizations about the production of crime rates. For the sake of convenience they may be listed as follows:

1. The police officially recognize proportionately more legally serious crimes than legally minor crimes.
2. The complainant's manifest preference for police action has a significant effect upon official crime reporting.
3. The greater the relational distance between the complainant and the suspect, the greater is the likelihood of official recognition.
4. The more deferential the complainant toward the police, the greater is the likelihood of official recognition of the complaint.
5. There is no evidence of racial discrimination in crime reporting.
6. There is some evidence that the police discriminate in favor of white-colar complainants, but this is true only in the official recognition of legally serious crime situations.

On the surface these findings have direct methodological relevance for those who would put official statistics to use as empirical data, whether to index actual crime in the population or to index actual police practices. Crime rates, as data, systematically underrepresent much crime and much police work. To learn some of the patterns by which this selection process occurs is to acquire a means of improving the utility of crime rates as data.

TABLE 26-1.

Percent of Police Encounters with Complainants According to Type of Crime and Relational Tie between Citizen Adversaries, by Situational Outcome: Complainant Prefers Official Action

	Type of Crime and Relational Tie between Citizen Adversaries								
	Felony			Misdemeanor			All Crimes		
Situational Outcome	Family Members	Friends, Neighbors, Acquaintances	Strangers	Family Members	Friends, Neighbors, Acquaintances	Strangers	Family Members	Friends, Neighbors, Acquaintances	Strangers
Official Report	(4)	62	91	(3)	43	74	41	51	84
No Official Report	(5)	38	9	(5)	57	26	59	49	16
Total Percent	–	100	100	–	100	100	100	100	100
Total Number	(9)	(16)	(92)	(8)	(23)	(62)	(17)	(39)	(154)

It should again be emphasized that these patterns of police behavior have consequences not only for official rates of detection as such; they also result in differential investigation of crimes and hence differential probabilities of arrest and conviction of criminal offenders. Thus the life chances of a criminal violator may depend upon who his victim is and how his victim presents his claim to the police. The complainant's role is appreciable in the criminal process. Surely the complainant has a central place in other legal and nonlegal control contexts as well, though there is as yet little research on the topic. Complainants are the consumers of justice. They are the prime movers of every known legal system, the human mechanisms by which legal services are routed into situations where there is a felt need for law. Complainants are the most invisible and they may be the most important social force binding the law to other aspects of social organization.

THE EUROPEAN WORKERS

Societies, Social Science, and Methodology

In 1827, when I was leaving École Polytechnique, I saw the beginning of those social ills which today have become so dangerous; and like my eminent confères, I at first dreamed of a means to remedy these. Since then, discouraged by various influences, my friends abandoned these projects. . . . I alone presisted . . . and, after a half-century of strenuous work, I am presenting my conclusions. The contrast between our results cannot be attributed to any superiority which I possess—rather it is explained by the differences in the methods which we have applied in our work. . . . My friends were convinced that the ills mentioned above could not be cured other than by the invention of a new social system. . . . I agreed that a reliable scientific procedure was necessary in order to cure those ills whose seriousness we all recognized, but I inferred that this science—like our natural sciences—must be founded not upon concepts established *a priori*, but upon facts systematically observed and upon inferences derived from rigorous reasoning. . . .

To understand social science thoroughly, we are not obliged to decipher manuscripts and resort to the historians. In our field trips we can collect various data, and then fit them together with the help of our own reasoning powers. . . .

Reprinted in part from Frédéric Le Play, *Les Ouvriers Européens*, I (1897), trans. Pearl J. Lieff and Paul W. Massing, in *Sociological Research. I. A Case Approach*, Matilda White Riley (New York: Harcourt Brace Jovanovich, 1963), pp. 80-98.

How by Observing Some Families the Criterion of
Good and Bad Social Orders May Be Developed

In 1828, through my interest in social problems, I started on the path toward the solution—which I have pointed out in this work. . . . I was encouraged by my colleagues, who unselfishly were ready to share in my tiring endeavors. . . . At last after several years of sustained effort, my original conception of the observational method, which had been inspired only by reason and analogy, began to prove itself by the results. Although I had not yet reached any definite conclusions, it dawned on me that populations thought and acted differently in several important respects depending on whether they were satisfied or dissatisfied with their lot and that consequently, sooner or later, the method, would yield to me the secret of well-being in a society. This is just what happened. The revolution of 1848 influenced me to make a new effort to draw, from 20 years of observations, the conclusions which my shocked colleagues rejected. . . . The following truths appeared to me indisputable.

Everywhere happiness consists in the satisfaction of two principal needs which are absolutely imposed by the very nature of man. . . . The first is the practice of moral law. . . . The second is the enjoyment of one's daily bread. . . .

The method of writing monographs gives us . . . the means to understand how these two needs are taken care of within the moral and material life of each family. It shows us the lasting qualities of the two fundamental elements of the basic system among flourishing peoples. . . . For a half-century, many of the observers mentioned in Volumes II to VI of *The European Workers,* and in Volumes I to V of *Workers of Two Worlds* frequently used this method in all regions of Europe and in many other countries of the world. They found in this work enough enlightenment to escape the yoke of contemporary innovations and return to an understanding of the great traditions of humanity. . . . The simplicity and usefulness of the method is attested to by the consistency and universality of findings obtained by a small number of monographs. . . .

Peoples are made up of families, not of individuals: the observation technique, which would be vague, indefinite, and inconclusive, if it were to extend in any given locality to individuals of different age and sex, becomes precise, definite, and conclusive as soon as it deals with families. It is in this obvious fact, based upon the social nature of man, that the practical effectiveness of family monographs rests.

How To Do Monographs

. . .The numerous details which are listed in the following chapters and which form the body of all the monographs, could only be acquired by long and painstaking investigation. . . . The observer must delve into every corner of the home; list furniture, dishes, linen, clothing; evaluate the real estate, available sums of money, domestic animals . . . in general all the property of the family; estimate the food reserves, meals; follow in detail the work of the members outside as well as inside the home. The study of the domestic chores may present the observer with unending complications. . . . Still more delicate are those investigations which address themselves to the intellectual and moral life, religion, education, recreation, feelings about kinship and friendship, relationships with proprietors, associates, domestics and apprentices, and lastly to details of family history. Actually this last task is easier to accomplish than one would at first believe: because in general workers like to talk about memories of their childhood. . . .

The observer must ask innumerable questions of the family he is studying, therefore causing them loss of time. . . . It may be presumed that a mass of questions may cause mental fatigue among people not accustomed to reflective thought and little able to coordinate their ideas.

Long experience has proven that these anticipated fears are groundless; at least the very nature of the work has always furnished the means to dispel them. Since the time of my first field trip, I have worked on 300 monographs, and have never failed to finish them to my complete satisfaction and to that of the family under observation. It has even often happened that my departure has been a cause for regret, sometimes even a sort of grief for all the members of the family. . . . Every intelligent observer understands the necessity of utilizing the following means to gain the good will of the family. Never ask a question brusquely or one which may appear to be insolent. Try to shorten . . . the preliminaries by getting the recommendation of some wisely chosen authority. Assure yourself of the confidence and the sympathy of the family by making them understand the goal of public service and the dedication which inspire the observer. Hold the attention of the subjects by telling them things which might interest them. Compensate them by allowances of money for the loss of their time which the questioning causes them. Discreetly praise the wisdom of the men, the charm of the women, the politeness of the children, and give well-chosen little gifts to all.

But all these elements of success are worthless or become even detrimental if they are not graced by the master virtue of the observer: respect for scientific endeavor. . . . In social science matters, observation applied to lasting facts offers guarantees of accuracy which do not exist in pure reasoning applied to the changeable conditions of private life or of politics. . . .

Guarantees of Accuracy Given by the Monographs

In this type of work as in all other scientific work, nothing can replace devotion to the truth which establishes the integrity of the scholar. . . . Guarantees of accuracy must be inherent in the method itself as much as possible. The family monogrpahs fulfill this condition. For an outside observer the surest means of understanding the material and moral life of man is very similar to the techniques which chemists employ to disclose the secret nature of minerals . . . . Quantitative verification of the same kind is always at the disposal of the scholar who analyzes, systematically, the family as a social unit. . . .

Families, that is to say, those distinct social units which make up the whole of humanity, number in the millions. Each consists of several individuals. Each individual has his own life . . . each is endlessly altered by the stimuli with which the social institutions affect him. . . .

Indeed, as can be confirmed by studying the monographs published in *The European Workers*, all the acts which constitute the life of a family of workers result, more or less immediately, in income or expenditures. For it is in the nature of things that the money income of a family . . . be exactly equal to the sum of expenses and savings. Consequently, an observer can obtain complete knowledge of a family, when, having analyzed all the items contained in the two parts of the domestic budget, he finds exact agreement between the two totals.

This methodical principle seems on first sight to reduce social science to a study of the material elements of human life. In reality, it leads by the most direct route to the opposite result. Analysis of household budgets often produces startling evidence of this fact. Often in this respect a single figure tells more than a lengthy discourse. Thus, for example, it is not possible to doubt the degradation of a stevedore in the outskirts of Paris . . . who expends annually 185 fr. or 12 percent of his income for drink but does not give a cent for the moral education of his five children between four and fourteen years of age.

The Two Research Guidelines on the Principal Conditions of Well-Being or Misfortune

. . .The material, intellectual, and moral life of the simplest family consists of innumerable details. In his research the observer should include as many as possible; but in the description he should neglect those details which do not serve the special purpose of the method, the work of social reform. . . . To reach safely the conclusions of his study he has two infallible guidelines, if he observes in all details the family situation concerning its understanding of the moral law, and enjoyment of its daily bread. He is always in a position to show that the family fares ill or flourishes according to whether these two main prerequisites for well-being or misfortune are present or not. These details appear very precisely in the figures which make up the gist of the monograph, that is to say, the household budget. . . .

The Three Parts of the Monographic Model

In some respects the monographs give to the reader an understanding of the populations better than if he actually visited the places described. . . . This kind of usefulness increases with time; and in the future, our collections will offer to the reader a type of retrospective travel which the historians of our era will not supply.

This however is not the only purpose of these monographs; they should be consulted more often than read. . . . They are files of numerous facts in which scholars may seek information. . . . To aid in the comparison of places and individuals, I have reduced each monograph to an average of about 50 pages, keeping only the indispensable data. I have been able to attain this conciseness without deviating from my main goals. For this purpose I have always grouped the data into three parts:

1. The main subsection of the monograph, or the distinctive characteristics of the workman described;

2. The monograph proper, or the description of the family summarized in terms of the household budget;

3. . . . Two supplements which explain the household budget simply and fully. . . .

SOCIETAL COMPLEXITY: AN EMPIRICAL TEST OF A TYPOLOGY OF SOCIETIES

Among pairs of polar ideal types, one of the early and best known is Tönnies' *Gemeinschaft* and *Gesellshaft*, terms by which he characterized two types of social organization. Dukheim made a similar distinction in contrasting *solidarité mécanique* with *solidarité organique*. Contrasts have been drawn between sacred and secular societies—Robert E. Park, in his lectures in the twenties, contrasted sacred and secular societies—culture and civilization, kinship and territory, and more recently stated in the folk-urban continuum and in the dichotomy, tradition-directed and other-directed types of character. These, a few of many similar distinctions, are polar ideal constructs, differing only in the emphasis which each places on some specific aspect of social patterning. They make the same basic distinction and consequently will be considered in the present analysis as concepts referring to societal complexity.

Some writers have argued that these concepts imply empirical relationships; others that they are distortions, albeit voluntary, of them. The latter writers would hold that, if these concepts have any utility whatsoever, it would be merely to sensitize observers. It is the judgment of the present authors that there is a measure of truth on both sides and that this seemingly irreconcilable argument can be resolved through examining the nature of ideal typologies. . . .

The aim of the present study is to select a set of societal variables regarded as registering societal complexity, to determine whether or

Reprinted in part from *American Journal of Sociology* 62 (March 1957): 461-466.

not they constitute a single dimension, and hence to ascertain whether there is empirical evidence of a unitary attribute, societal complexity. The Guttman technique of scale analysis, which was employed, permits three possible outcomes: a single scale or quasi scale; two or more scales; or no systematic interrelationships at all. Only the first possibility would lend support to the hypothesis.

Developed for the study of attitudes, the Guttman technique involves the systematic ordering of complex qualitative data. It is reasonable to suppose that the scaling model may be as helpful in cross-cultural research as in the investigation of attitudes.

Selection of variables for this study raised some special problems. Some of the criteria for classifying societies as to complexity are ambiguous. It would be difficult to rank societies, for example, according to their degree of in-group feeling. Many of the terms employed in the ethnographic reports which are the only source of data are vague, making it difficult or impossible to compare their data. Therefore, variables were sought which the ethnographers would report with the minimum of interpretation. Eight such variables have been used. They have been dichotomized, and one category (designated *b* in Table 28-1) is construed as representing less complexity, while the other (designated *a*) represents greater complexity (see Table 28-1). . . .

In order to insure independence and increase applicability, the sample was chosen to make the most of cultural variability. The 48 societies were selected by the procedure reported by George Peter Murdock, *Outline of World Cultures* (New Haven: Human Relations Area Files, 1954). The societies suggested by Murdock represent most major culture areas of the world, and their geographic and historical heterogeneity should certainly assure variability. . . .

Data were obtained from the Cross-cultural Survey and the Human Relations Area Files. Since an effort had been made to employ only relatively unambiguous variables and to require only dichotomous judgments and since, therefore, there was little room for the exercise of discretion, the reliability of ratings was not estimated. A schedule consisting of eight simple dichotomies was devised; so the investigator was required only to look under the appropriate classification and ascertain the facts, as, for example, whether the Koreans had a written language or not or whether the Aranda used a symbolic medium of exchange.

TABLE 28-1.

Characteristics of Social Complexity in the Scalogram Analysis

CHARACTERISTIC	CLASSIFICATION OF COMPLEXITY	
1. Exogamy	a,	Incest taboos extended only to include secondary relatives
	b,	Further extension of taboos
2. Punishment	a,	Crimes against person or property punished through government action
	b,	Crimes avenged by the person wronged, his kin group, or the gods
3. Government	a,	Full-time bureaucrats unrelated to government head present
	b,	Part-time bureaucrats, bureaucrats related to government head, or none
4. Education	a,	Formal, with full-time specialized teacher
	b,	Informal, without full-time specialized teacher
5. Religion	a,	Full-time specialized real priest — not diviner or healer — present
	b,	No full-time specialized priest present
6. Economy	a,	Symbolic medium of exchange — real money — present
	b,	Barter and exchange the sole economic mechanisms
7. Mate selection	a,	Beauty stressed in desirability of a mate either alone or along with skill and fertility
	b,	Skill and fertility demanded to the exclusion of beauty
8. Written language	a,	Written language present
	b,	Written language absent

Application of Guttman's scaling model to the data did not yield a perfect scale. Two items—exogamy and mate selection—varied independently of the other six. The Israel Alpha Technique was employed to test for the presence of a quasi scale. Results were negative, and the two offending items were dropped, whereupon the remaining six formed a nearly perfect arrangement. . . . While reproducibility was not perfect for the six items, there were only nine scale errors, and the resulting array closely approximated the model. . . . The data . . . clearly demonstrate a scale among six of the eight tested items: punishment, government, education, religion, economy, and written language vary together to form a unidimensional array.

In conclusion, the demonstration of unidimensionality among six characteristics is evidence that the items constitute a scale. Since these qualities are all subsumable under folk urbanism, *Gemeinschaft Gesellschaft,* and the other polar constructs of that order, the conclusion is that Redfield, Tönnies, *et al.* have indeed been describing a unidimensional phenomenon—societal complexity. Furthermore, this analysis has established a series of scale types or positions of societal complexity. . .which may be used to describe and arrange societies, as well as merely to sensitize observers, as some have claimed. The types characterize each culture as to the given variables; moreover, they allow comparison of the complexity of one culture with another. The result not only indicates the generalizability of cultural phenomena but provides suggestive material for constructing further theories of cultural form and process. . . .

WORKS CITED

Anderson, Bo and Cockroft, James D. (1966), 1972. "Control and co-optation in Mexican politics." In *Dependence and Underdevelopment*, ed. James D. Cockroft, André Gunder Frank, and Dale L. Johnson, pp. 219-224. New York: Anchor Books.

Angell, Robert C., and Freedman, Ronald. 1953. "The use of documents, records, census materials, and indices." In *Research Methods in the Behavioral Sciences*, ed. Leon Festinger and Daniel Katz, pp. 300-326. New York: The Dryden Press.

Asch, Solomon E. 1952. *Social Psychology*. Englewood Cliffs, N.J.: Prentice Hall.

————. 1956. "Studies of independence and conformity. I. A minority of one against a unanimous majority." *Psychological Monographs: General and Applied*. 70 (9): whole no. 416.

Bales, Robert Freed. 1970. *Personality and Interpersonal Behavior*. New York: Holt, Rinehart, and Winston.

Ball, Donald W. 1967. "An abortion clinic ethnography." *Social Problems* 14 (Winter): 293-301.

Bandura, Albert, et al. 1963. "A comparative test of the status envy, social power, and secondary reinforcement theories of identificatory learning." *Journal of Abnormal and Social Psychoology* 67: 527-534.

Bauer, Raymond A. 1966. *Social Indicators*. Cambridge, Mass.: The MIT Press.

Bavelas, Alex 1951. "Communication patterns in task-oriented groups." In *The Policy Sciences*, ed. D. Lerner and H. D. Lasswell, pp. 193-202. Stanford: Stanford University Press.

Becker, Howard S. 1958. "Problems of inference and proof in participant observation." *American Sociological Review* 23(December): 652-660.

————. 1970. "Field work evidence." In Howard S. Becker, *Sociological Work: Method and Substance*, pp. 39-62. Chicago: Aldine Publishing Company.

Berger, Joseph, et al. 1972. *Sociological Theories in Progress*, vol. 2. New York: Houghton Mifflin Co.

Black, Donald J., and Reiss, Albert J., Jr. 1970. "Police control of juveniles." *American Sociological Review* 35 (February): 63-77.

Blau, Peter M. 1954. "Co-operation and competition in a bureaucracy." *American Journal of Sociology* 59 (May): 530-535.

Blumer, Herbert G. 1969. *Symbolic Interactionism*. Englewood Cliffs, N.J.: Prentice-Hall.

Brown, Julia S., and Gilmartin, Brian G. 1969. "Sociology Today: lacunae, emphases, and surfeits." *The American Sociologist* 4(4):283-291.

Bruyn, Severyn. 1963. "The methodology of participant observation." *Human Organization* 22 (Fall): 224-235.

Campbell, Donald T. 1957. "Factors relevant to the validity of experiments in social settings." *Psychological Bulletin*, 54:297-312.

————. 1969. "Reforms as experiments." *American Psychologist* 24 (April): 409-429.

————, and Stanley, Julian C. 1963. *Experimental and Quasi-experimental Designs for Research*. Chicago: Rand McNally.

Caudill, William. 1958. *The Psychiatric Hospital as a Small Society*. Cambridge, Mass.: Harvard University Press.

Cicourel, Aaron V. 1964. *Method and Measurement in Sociology*. New York: The Free Press.

Cockroft, James D. 1972. "Coercion and ideology in Mexican politics," In *Dependence and Underdevelopment*, ed. James D. Cockroft, André Gunder Frank, and Dale L. Johnson, pp. 245-267. New York: Anchor Books.

Cohen, Morris R., and Nagel, Ernest. 1934. *An Introduction to Logic and Scientific Method*. New York: Harcourt, Brace & Javanovich.

Coleman, James S. 1964. *Models of Change and Response Uncertainty*. Englewood Cliffs, N.J.: Prentice-Hall.

Conklin, Harold C. 1968. "Ethnography." In *International Encyclopedia of the Social Sciences*, ed. David L. Sills, 5:172-178. New York: The Macmillan Company and The Free Press.

Coser, Lewis A. 1959. "A question of professional ethics." *American Sociological Review* 24 (June):397-398.

Dalton, Melville. 1959. *Men Who Manage*. New York: John Wiley & Sons.

Davies, James C. 1962. "Toward a theory of revolution." *American Sociological Review* 27 (February):5-19.

Deutsch, M. 1949. "An experimental study of the effects of cooperation and competition upon group process." *Human Relations* 2:199-231.

Erikson, Kai T. 1967. "A comment on disguised observation in sociology." *Social Problems* 14 (Spring) :366-373.

————. 1970. "Sociology and the historical perspective." *The American Sociologist* 5 (November):331-338.

Franzen, R. 1950. "Scaling responses to graded opportunities." *Public Opinion Quarterly* 14 (Fall):484-490.

Friedrichs, Robert W. 1970. *A Sociology of Sociology*. New York: The Free Press.

Glaser, Barney, and Strauss, Anselm. 1965. "The discovery of substantive theory: a basic strategy underlying qualitative research." *The American Behavioral Scientist* 8 (February):5-12.

————. 1967. *The Discovery of Grounded Theory*. Chicago: Aldine Publishing Company.

Gold, Raymond L. 1958. "Roles in sociological field observations." *Social Forces* 36 (March):217-223.

Goldfrank, Walter I. 1972. "Reappraising Le Play." In *The Establishment of Empirical Sociology*, ed. Anthony Oberschall, pp. 130-151. New York: Harper & Row.

Greer, Scott. 1969. *The Logic of Social Inquiry.* Chicago: Aldine Publishing Company.

Hempel, Carl G. 1952. "Fundamentals of concept formation in empirical science." In *International Encyclopedia of Unified Science,* ed. Otto Neurath, Rudolf Carnap, and Charles Morris, vol. 2, no. 7. Chicago: University of Chicago Press.

Homans, George C. 1946. "The small warship." *American Sociological Review* 11 (June):294-300.

Huesler, Corrine. 1970. "The gilded asylum." In *The Participant Observer,* ed. Glenn Jacobs, pp. 92-121. New York: George Braziller.

Hughes, Everett C. 1943. *French Canada in Transition.* Chicago: University of Chicago Press.

Hyman, Herbert H., et al. 1954. *Interviewing in Social Research.* Chicago: University of Chicago Press.

Inoguchi, Takashi. 1972. "Measuring friendship and hostility among Communist powers: some unobtrusive measures of esoteric communication." *Social Science Research* 1 (April):79-105.

Kluckhohn, Florence R. 1940. "The participant-observer technique in small communities." *American Journal of Sociology* 46 (November):331-343.

Korsch, Barbara M., and Negrete, Vida Francis. 1972. "Doctor-patient communication." *Scientific American* 227 (August):66-75.

LaPiere, Richard T. 1934. "Attitudes vs. actions." *Social Forces* 13 (December):230-237.

Lazarsfeld, Paul F. 1961. "Notes on the history of quantification in sociology— trends, sources and problems." In *Quantification: A History of the Meaning of Measurement in the Natural and Social Sciences,* ed. Harry Woolf, pp. 147-203. Indianapolis: The Bobbs-Merrill Company.

————. 1968. Foreword to Morris Rosenberg, *The Logic of Survey Analysis,* pp. vii-x. New York: Basic Books.

Leach, Edmund R. 1968. "The comparative method in anthropology." In *International Encyclopedia of the Social Sciences,* ed. David L. Sills, 1:339-345. New York: The Macmillan Company and The Free Press.

Lécuyer, Bernard, and Oberschall, Anthony R. 1968. "The early history of social research." In *International Encyclopedia of the Social Sciences,* ed. David L. Sills, 15:36-53. New York: The Macmillan Company and The Free Press.

Leik, Robert K. 1965. "'Irrelevant' aspects of stooge behavior: implications for leadership studies and experimental methodology." *Sociometry* 28 (September): 259-271.

Lynd, Robert S., and Lynd, Helen M. 1929. *Middletown.* New York: Harcourt, Brace & Javanovich.

————. 1937. *Middletown in Transition: A Study in Cultural Conflicts.* New York: Harcourt, Brace & Jovanovich.

Medley, Donald M., and Mitzel, Harold E. 1963. "Measuring classroom behavior by systematic observation." In *Handbook of Research on Teaching,* ed. N. L. Gage, pp. 247-328. Chicago: Rand McNally.

Merei, Ferenc. 1949. "Group leadership and institutionalization." *Human Relations* 2:23-39.

Merton, Robert K. 1947. "Selected problems of field work in the planned community." *American Sociological Review* 12 (June): 304-312.

————. 1972. "Insiders and outsiders: a chapter in the sociology of knowledge." *American Journal of Sociology* 77 (July):9-47.

Merton, Robert K., Reader, George G., and Kendall, Patricia L., eds. 1957. *The Student Physician.* Cambridge, Mass.: Harvard University Press.

Milgram, Stanley. 1965a. "Some conditions of obedience and disobedience to authority." *Human Relations* 18: 57-75.

————. 1965b. "Liberating effects of group pressures." *Journal of Personality and Social Psychology* 1:127-134.

————, Mann, Leon, and Harter, Susan. 1965. "The lost-letter technique: a tool of social research." *Public Opinion Quarterly* 29: 437-438.

Miner, Horace. 1956. "Body ritual among the Nacirema." *American Anthropologist* 58:503-507.

Moore, Mary E. 1955. "Comment on an article by Vidich and Shapiro, 'A comparison of participant observation and survey data.'" *American Sociological Review* 20 (February):576-577.

Murdock, George P. 1949. *Social Structure.* New York: The Macmillan Company.

Orne, Martin T. 1962. "On the social psychology of the psychological experiments." *American Psychologist* 17 (November):762-783.

Palson, Charles, and Palson, Rebecca. 1972. "Swinging in wedlock." *Society* 9 (February):28-37.

Parsons, Talcott. 1949. *Essays in Sociological Theory, Pure and Applied.* New York: The Free Press.

Phillips, Derek L. 1972. *Knowledge From What? Theories and Methods in Social Research.* Chicago: Rand McNally.

Pitts, Jesse R. 1968. "Frédéric Le Play." In *International Encyclopedia of the Social Sciences,* ed. David L. Sills, 9:84-91. New York: The Macmillan Company and The Free Press.

Porter, John. 1967. "Some observations on comparative studies." *International Institute for Labour Studies: Bulletin* 3:(November):82-104.

Powers, Edwin. 1949. "An experiment in prevention of delinquency." *The Annals of the American Academy of Political and Social Science* 261 (January):77-88.

Reiss, Albert J., Jr. 1968. "Stuff and nonsense about social surveys and observations." In *Institutions and the Person,* ed Howard S. Becker et al., pp. 351-367. Chicago: Aldine Publishing Company.

————. 1971. *The Police and the Public.* New Haven: Yale University Press.

Riesman, David, and Watson, Jeanne. 1964. "The sociability project." In *Sociologists at Work,* ed. Phillip E. Hammond, pp. 235-321. New York: Basic Books.

Riley, John W., Jr. 1962. "Reflections on data sources in opinion research." *Public Opinion Quarterly* 26: 313-322.

Riley, Matilda White. 1963. *Sociological Research. I. A Case Approach.* New York: Harcourt, Brace & Jovanovich.

————. 1964. "Sources and types of sociological data." In *Handbook of Modern Sociology,* ed. Robert E. L. Faris, pp. 978-1026. Chicago: Rand McNally.

————, Cohn, Richard, Toby, Jackson, and Riley, John W., Jr. 1954. "Interpersonal orientations in small groups: a consideration of the questionnaire approach." *American Sociological Review* 19 (December): 715-724.

————, and Nelson, Edward E. 1971. "Research on stability and change in social systems." In *Stability and Change in Social Systems: A Volume in Honor of Talcott Parsons,* ed. Bernard Barber and Alex Inkeles, pp. 407-449. Boston: Little, Brown.

Works Cited

Robinson, W. S. 1951. "The logical structure of analytic induction." *American Sociological Review* 16 (December): 812-818.

Roethlisberger, Fritz J., and Dickson, William J. (1939) 1961. *Management and the Worker: An Account of a Research Program Conducted by the Western Electric Company, Hawthorne Works, Chicago.* Cambridge, Mass.: Harvard University Press.

Rosenhan, D. L. 1973. "On being sane in insane places." *Science* 179 (January 19):250-258.

Rosenthal, Robert. 1966. *Experimenter Effects in Behavioral Research.* New York: Appleton-Century-Crofts.

Roth, Julius A. 1962. "Comments on 'secret observation.'" *Social Problems* 9 (Winter):283-284.

Ruebhausen, Oscar M., and Brim, Orville G., Jr. 1965. "Privacy and behavioral research." *Columbia Law Review* 65:1184-1211.

Sheldon, Eleanor Bernert, and Moore, Wilbert E. 1968. *Indicators of Social Change.* New York: Russell Sage Foundation.

Sherif, Muzafer. 1951. "A preliminary experimental study of intergroup relations." In *Social Psychology at the Crossroads,* ed. John H. Rohrer and Muzafer Sherif, pp. 397-421. New York: Harper & Row.

Sieber, Sam D. 1973. "The integration of fieldwork and survey methods." *American Journal of Sociology* 78 (May):1335-1359.

Smelser, Neil J. 1968. *Essays in Sociological Explanation.* Englewood Cliffs, N.J.: Prentice-Hall.

Sommer, Robert. 1961. "Leadership and group geography." *Sociometry* 24 (March):99-110.

————. 1965. "Further studies of small group ecology." *Sociometry* 28 (December):337-348.

Sorokin, Pitirim A. 1928. *Contemporary Sociological Theories.* New York: Harper & Row.

Stouffer, Samuel A. 1954. Foreword. pp. v-vi in Herbert H. Hyman et al., *Interviewing in Social Research.* Chicago: University of Chicago Press.

Sudnow, David. 1972. "Temporal parameters of interpersonal observation." In *Studies in Social Interaction,* ed. pp. 259-279. New York: The Free Press.

Swanson, G. E. 1951. "Some problems of laboratory experiments with small populations." *American Sociological Review* 16 (June):349-358.

Thernstrom, Stephan. 1965. "'Yankee City' revisited: the perils of historical naiveté." *American Sociological Review* 30 (April):234-242.

Thomas, D. et al. 1929. "Some new techniques for studying social behavior." *Child Development Monographs,* 1.

Thomas, William I., and Znaniecki, Florian. 1918. *The Polish Peasant in Europe and America,* vol. 1. Chicago: University of Chicago Press.

Toby, Jackson. 1955. "Undermining the student's faith in the validity of personal experience." *American Sociological Review* 20 (December):717-718.

Turner, Ralph H. 1947. "The navy disbursing officer as a bureaucrat." *American Sociological Review* 12 (June): 342-348.

————. 1953. "The quest for universals in sociological research." *American Sociological Review* 18 (December):604-611.

Vidich, Arthur J., and Shapiro, Gilbert. 1955. "A comparison of participant observation and survey data." *American Sociological Review* 20 (Feburary):28-33.

Vidich, Arthur J., Bensman, Joseph, and Stein, Maurice R. 1964. *Reflections on Community Studies.* New York: John Wiley & Sons.

Von Hoffman, Nicholas. 1970. "Sociological snoopers and. . . ." *Trans-Action* 7 (May):4,6.

Warner, W. Lloyd, and Lunt, Paul S. 1941. *The Social Life of a Modern Community.* New Haven: Yale University Press.

Wax, Murray L. 1972. "Tenting with Malinowski." *American Sociological Review* 37 (February):1-13.

Webb, Eugene J., et al. 1966. *Unobstrusive Measures.* Chicago: Rand McNally.

Weber, Max. [1922]1947. *The Theory of Social and Economic Organization,* trans. A. M. Henderson and Talcott Parsons. New York: The Free Press.

Weick, Karl E. 1968. "Systematic observational methods." In *The Handbook of Social Psychology*, 2nd ed., ed. Gardner Lindzey and Elliot Aronson, pp. 357-451. Reading Mass.: Addison-Wesley.

Weiss, Robert S. 1968. "Issues in holistic research." In *Institutions and the Person,* ed. Howard S. Becker et al., pp. 342-350. Chicago: Aldine Publishing Company.

Whyte, William Foote. 1955. *Street Corner Society.* Chicago: University of Chicago Press.

Zelditch, Morris, Jr. 1955. "Role differentiation in the nuclear family: a comparative study." In *Family, Socialization and Interaction Process,* Talcott Parsons and Robert F. Bales, pp. 307-351. New York: The Free Press.

————. 1962. "Some methodological problems of field studies." *American Journal of Sociology* 67 (March):566-76.

INDEX